Technology
Leadership for
School Improvement

Technology Leadership for School Improvement

Rosemary Papa
Northern Arizona University
Editor

Los Angeles | London | New Delhi
Singapore | Washington DC

For information:

SAGE Publications, Inc.
2455 Teller Road
Thousand Oaks, California 91320
E-mail: order@sagepub.com

SAGE Publications India Pvt. Ltd.
B 1/I 1 Mohan Cooperative Industrial Area
Mathura Road, New Delhi 110 044
India

SAGE Publications Ltd.
1 Oliver's Yard
55 City Road
London EC1Y 1SP
United Kingdom

SAGE Publications Asia-Pacific Pte. Ltd.
33 Pekin Street #02-01
Far East Square
Singapore 048763

Printed in the United States of America

Library of Congress Cataloging-in-Publication Data

Technology leadership for school improvement/edited by Rosemary Papa.
    p. cm.
Includes bibliographical references and index.
ISBN 978-1-4129-7210-9 (pbk. : alk. paper)
    1. Educational technology—Study and teaching. 2. Information technology—Study and teaching.
3. Teachers—Training of. 4. Teachers—In-service training. I. Papa, Rosemary.

LB1028.3.T4275 2011
371.33068—dc22   2009032717

This book is printed on acid-free paper.

10   11   12   13   14   10 9 8 7 6 5 4 3 2 1

Acquiring Editor:	Diane McDaniel
Editorial Assistant:	Ashley Conlon
Production Editor:	Sarah K. Quesenberry
Copy Editor:	Melinda Masson
Typesetter:	C&M Digitals (P) Ltd.
Proofreader:	Christina West
Indexer:	Wendy Allex
Cover Designer:	Candice Harman
Marketing Manager:	Carmel Schrire

BRIEF CONTENTS

Preface   xv

Part I. Leadership Policy and Innovative Practice   1

Chapter 1.   **Entrepreneurial Leadership for Technology: An Opposable Mind**   3
Theodore Creighton

Chapter 2.   **Technology Leadership Standards: The Next Generation**   21
Rosemary Papa

Chapter 3.   **Administration of Technology: Teaching, Learning, and Resource Management**   45
Ric Brown

Chapter 4.   **Designing and Using Academic Information Systems: Providing Decision Support Systems for Educational Leaders**   61
Stephen Lawton

Part II. Leadership Teaching and Learning   89

Chapter 5.   **Leading Adult Learners: Preparing Future Leaders and Professional Development of Those They Lead**   91
Rosemary Papa and Jessica Papa

Chapter 6.   **Planning, Designing, Implementing, and Evaluating Technology**   109
Shadow W. J. Armfield

Chapter 7. Web 2.0 Learning Environments in
Distance Learning   129
Chih-Hsiung Tu and J. Michael Blocher

Chapter 8. Design of Creative Online Learning Spaces   147
Mary I. Dereshiwsky

Part III. Leadership: Social, Cultural, and Legal   165

Chapter 9. School, Technology, and Society:
Home-School Communications and Access   167
Laura Sujo-Montes and Lawrence Gallagher

Chapter 10. Security, Internet Safety, Copyright, and Plagiarism   189
Janet Tareilo and Theodore Creighton

Part IV. Leadership Digital Assessments and Evaluation   209

Chapter 11. Online Evaluation   211
Mary I. Dereshiwsky

Chapter 12. Using Technology for Assessing and Evaluating
Student Learning and Instructional Practices   231
Cynthia Conn

Chapter 13. Program Evaluation and Technology Integration
Strategies   253
Rosemary Papa

Glossary   277

Index   283

About the Editor   293

About the Contributors   295

DETAILED CONTENTS

Preface   xv

Part I. Leadership Policy and Innovative Practice   1

Chapter 1. Entrepreneurial Leadership for Technology: An Opposable Mind   3

So, What's the Problem?   4
Entrepreneurial Leadership for Technology Defined   5
Framing Leadership for Technology in a Historical Context   6
    Behavioral Leadership   7
    Situational Leadership   7
    Contingency Leadership   8
    Path-Goal Leadership   9
    Transformational Leadership   9
A Conceptual Framework for Entrepreneurial Leadership
    in Technology   10
    The Opposable Mind   10
An Opposable Mind: Karen Symms Gallagher, USC Rossier
    School of Education   12
An Opposable Mind: Rich Baraniuk and the Rice University
    Connexions Project   13
Conclusions   15
Key Principles for Leaders to Know   16
Case Study 1.1 Strategic Technology Planning for Reading   16
Case Study 1.2 Paradoxes of Technology Leadership   16
Web Resources   17
References   18

Chapter 2. Technology Leadership Standards: The Next Generation   21

From Codes to Standards   22
    AASA Code of Ethics   22

ISLLC 2008 Policy Standards   23
Research About Standards   26
Transforming Education With Tools   28
ISTE Standards   28
The Leader's Tool Kit   36
Conclusions   38
Key Principles for Leaders to Know   39
Case Study 2.1 Strategies to Meet Technology Standards
With Limited Funding   39
Case Study 2.2 Efficacy of Online Education   39
Web Resources   40
References   42

**Chapter 3. Administration of Technology: Teaching,
Learning, and Resource Management**   **45**

What Kind of Educational Technology Leader Are You?   46
Salient Factors to Consider in Managing Educational Technology   49
Curricular Outcomes and Needs   49
Administrative Outcomes and Needs   52
Evaluating Your Educational Technology Decisions   54
Conclusions   55
Key Principles for Leaders to Know   56
Case Study 3.1 Assessing Software   56
Case Study 3.2 Personnel Issues in Hiring a Technologist   57
Web Resources   57
References   58

**Chapter 4. Designing and Using Academic Information Systems:
Providing Decision Support Systems for Educational Leaders**   **61**

System Design   63
Who or What Is Being Measured?   64
What Characteristics Are Being Measured?   66
How Are Characteristics Defined and Measured?   67
Why Measure a Characteristic?   68
What Are the Relationships Among Characteristics?   69
How Can Standards Be Set to Assess Data?   70
Applying the Principles   71
Existing Information Systems   72
State Level   72
District Level   73
Classroom Level   77
Selection of an Academic Information System   79
Conclusions   81

Key Principles for Leaders to Know   82
Case Study 4.1 Developing Student Information Systems   83
Case Study 4.2 Academic Information Systems and Data
    Usage Issues   84
Web Resources   84
References   85

Part II. Leadership Teaching and Learning   89

Chapter 5. Leading Adult Learners: Preparing Future Leaders and Professional Development of Those They Lead   91

Learners of All Ages   92
Adult Learning Theories   93
    Behaviorism   95
    Cognitive Constructivism   95
    Social Constructivism   96
    Humanism   96
    Motivation   96
    Intelligence   97
    Adult Learning and Pedagogy   97
Engaging Adult Learners   98
    Mentoring Adult Learners   99
    Teaching and Leading Adult Learners   101
Conclusions   102
Key Principles for Leaders to Know   103
Case Study 5.1 Applying Adult Learning Theories   103
Case Study 5.2 Self-Reflection and Professional Development   104
Web Resources   105
References   106

Chapter 6. Planning, Designing, Implementing, and Evaluating Technology   109

Transforming the School   110
    Communities of Practice   111
    Technology Integration   112
    Challenges   113
Professional Development: Building the Community   114
    Planning   117
    Learning the Technologies   118
    Designing   120
    Implementing and Evaluating   121
    The Second Cycle   122
    Evaluating Technologies   123

Key Principles for Leaders to Know   124
Case Study 6.1 Technology Resistance Among Teachers   125
Case Study 6.2 Technology Integration With Limited Funds   125
Web Resources   126
References   126

Chapter 7. Web 2.0 Learning Environments in Distance Learning   129

Mistaken Perceptions   130
The Net Generation   131
    Current Use of Course Management System Software
      for Distance Learning   132
    Web 2.0 Disrupts Distance Learning   132
Constructs for Web 2.0 Learning Environments   133
    Cognitive Dimension   133
    Social Dimension   134
    Networking Dimension   134
    Integration Dimension   135
    Collaboration   135
    Community   136
District Structure and Processes   136
    Architecture of Learning   137
    Authority Destructions   137
    Personal Learning Space   137
The Strengths of Web 2.0 Tools   138
    Planning Personal Learning Space   139
Professional Development   140
Critical Issues   140
Conclusions   141
Key Principles for Leaders to Know   141
Case Study 7.1 Web 2.0 Learning Environments   142
Case Study 7.2 Personal Learning Environment in Web 2.0   143
Web Resources   143
References   144

Chapter 8. Design of Creative Online Learning Spaces   147

It's All in the Delivery: How to Effectively Package
  Instructional Content   148
    Putting It to the Test: Adding Assessments to
      Your Online Classes   151
    Let's Chat: Creating Discussion Posting Areas   153
    Tell Me About It: Creating an Announcement Posting
      Area in Your Online Course   153
    Inquiring Minds Want to Know: Creating a
      Question-and-Answer Discussion Forum   154

Adding Those Creative Personal Touches   155
The Rules of the Road: Your Online Course   156
So How Do I Make This Happen? Converting Class Notes and Other
   Learning Activities Into Online Instructional Materials   157
Conclusions   158
Key Principles for Leaders to Know   158
Case Study 8.1 Transitioning Courses to Full Online Classes   159
Case Study 8.2 Student Issues and Online Learning   159
Web Resources   160
References   163

Part III. Leadership: Social, Cultural, and Legal   165

Chapter 9. School, Technology, and Society: Home-School Communications and Access   167

21st-Century Skills   168
Digital Divide   169
The Administrator of Today   171
Professional Development in Schools   173
Technology for Management   173
   Student Data Management Systems   174
   Personal Digital Assistants   174
   Project Management Software   174
   Web 2.0 and Social Networking Tools   174
Technologies for a Diverse Student Population   174
   The Role of Culture in the Use of Technology   175
   Technology in Schools With High Ethnic
      Minority Enrollment   176
   Technology for Students With Disabilities   177
Conclusions   182
Key Principles for Leaders to Know   183
Case Study 9.1 How Would You Use Technology?   185
Web Resources   185
References   186

Chapter 10. Security, Internet Safety, Copyright, and Plagiarism   189

Impact of Technology   190
Providing Safety for All   191
   Acceptable Use Policies   192
   Government Involvement   192
   The Principal and Internet Safety   194
   Strategies for Campus Leaders   194
Security Issues   197
   Preparedness and Protection   197

Securing the School   199
Copyright and Open Educational Resources   200
    Open Educational Resources   200
    The Open Creative Commons Copyright   202
Cyberplagiarism   202
Conclusions   203
Key Principles for Leaders to Know   203
Case Study 10.1 Acceptable Use Policy   204
Case Study 10.2 Planning to Safeguard Student Access   205
Web Resources   205
References   206

Part IV. Leadership Digital Assessments and Evaluation   209

Chapter 11. Online Evaluation   211

Curtain Up: Getting the Online Course Set Up and Ready to Go   212
Getting Students Started on the Right Foot: What to
    Look for in Your Classroom Visits   216
        Responding to Students' Initial Postings   217
        Updating the Announcement Posting Area as Needed   218
        Being Responsive to Posted Questions and Answers   219
As the Semester Progresses: What to Look for in
    Your Classroom Visits   219
        Adding to Announcements: The Weekly
            Wrap-up and Preview   220
        Questions and Answers: Keep It Covered   221
        Can We Talk? Engagement in Discussions   221
        Testing, Testing, 1-2-3: Quizzes, Assignments, and Tests   222
Winding Down the Course   223
Cyberbullying: What Teachers Should Be Doing   224
Conclusions   225
Key Principles for Leaders to Know   226
Case Study 11.1 Teacher Responsibilities for Online Learning   226
Web Resources   227
References   229

Chapter 12. Using Technology for Assessing and Evaluating
Student Learning and Instructional Practices   231

Authentic Assessment of Student Learning Outcomes   233
Developing a District- or School-Level Assessment System   234
    Curriculum Mapping   234
    Developing an Assessment System   236

       Scoring Guides (Rubrics)   238
       Standards-Based Scoring Guides   244
    Tools for Implementing Authentic Assessments   244
       Electronic Portfolios   245
       Quiz or Survey Tools   247
       Spreadsheets   248
   Conclusions   248
   Key Principles for Leaders to Know   248
   Case Study 12.1 Student Learning Outcomes in Technology   249
   Case Study 12.2 Student Learning Using Electronic Portfolios   250
   Web Resources   250
   References   251

Chapter 13. Program Evaluation and Technology Integration Strategies   **253**

   Program Evaluation   254
       Mission and Goals   254
       Objectives to Implement Goals   254
       Activities to Complete Objectives   255
       Methods to Access Effectiveness of the Objectives   256
       Decision Making Based on Data   256
       Looping Back Through Revision and Reflection,
          Research, and Craft Knowledge   256
   Integration Strategies   257
       Part I: Leadership Policy and Innovative Practice   258
       Part II: Leadership Teaching and Learning   261
       Part III: Leadership: Social, Cultural, and Legal   264
       Part IV: Leadership Digital Assessments and Evaluation   270
   Final Word on Codes, Standards, and Adult Learning   272
   Conclusions   273
   Key Principles for Leaders to Know   274
   Case Study 13.1 Technology Planning for Program Evaluation   274
   Web Resource   274
   References   274

Glossary   **277**

Index   **283**

About the Editor   **293**

About the Contributors   **295**

PREFACE

Global education and technology have altered the landscape of what learners know and how they learn, and it is critical for K–12 leaders to understand the new educational terrain. The big picture presented by *Technology Leadership for School Improvement* is for school leaders to envision and facilitate use of technology in the digital world that is ubiquitous to our students.

First, and in the broadest sense, this book gives attention to technology standards, data-driven decision making, and visionary, courageous, and creative leadership in this digital environment. Second, this book intends that technology leaders should learn as they expect their classroom teachers to teach. Finally, the multiple voices of authors add strength to the rich content that is addressed. While a single author text has been the literary standard for depth and breadth of content and ease of student use, it is not the approach we considered sound given the nature of this ever-changing digital environment. As Surowiecki (2005) clearly describes, large groups of people are smarter than an elite few. *Technology Leadership for School Improvement* brings together the wisdom of researchers, practitioners, and writers to provide chapters that are clearly written and concise and that present the most contemporary thinking in the field. Contributing authors Shadow W. J. Armfield, J. Michael Blocher, Ric Brown, Cynthia Conn, Theodore Creighton, Mary I. Dereshiwsky, Lawrence Gallagher, Stephen Lawton, Jessica Papa, Rosemary Papa, Laura Sujo-Montes, Janet Tareilo, and Chih-Hsiung Tu guarantee the reader the most comprehensible and readable text in the field.

This book is intended to serve as a theoretical as well as hands-on textbook for educational leadership students at the graduate level for managing and administering technology use in their school setting. As well, it can serve as a practical guide for practicing school administrators as they navigate the administration of the ever-changing landscape of education technology.

Pedagogical Features

Numerous pedagogical features have been included in the book to assist professors in course development and delivery, assist graduate students in grasping the concepts, and assist current administrators new to technology.

- Each chapter starts with **critical questions** that provide the **chapter objectives** for the reader.

- The writing is done by researchers and practitioners to **ensure usable and research-based information**.

- Each chapter provides both **theoretical background and applied examples** for the reader.

- **Case studies** in each chapter provide the reader with applied situations to analyze. Each case study provides specific **discussion questions and activities** to guide complete understanding of the information presented.

- **Key words** are highlighted with definitions provided the initial time they are presented.

- **Key principles for leaders to know** cogently summarize each chapter at its conclusion.

- **Web resources** at the end of each chapter guide readers to seek additional information and knowledge.

Ancillaries

Technology Leadership for School Improvement is accompanied by an open-access companion site, tailored to match the content of the book.

This site features PowerPoint slides for each chapter, e-flashcards, and a variety of useful Web resources. Case studies from the book, as well as additional case studies provided by the author, are featured in easily printable Word documents. Visit the companion site at **www.sagepub.com/papa**.

Reference

Surowiecki, J. (2005). *The wisdom of crowds.* New York: Anchor Books.

Acknowledgments

To my mentors Dr. Charles M. Achilles and Dr. Fenwick English. And, to those who inspire me: Ric, Jessica and Kyle, Giselle, Sophia, Josephine Rosemary, Jim and Anna Mae, Carol and Dick, and Ralph and Josephine.

The publisher and reviewers provided insightful comments that certainly improved the quality of the text. The reviewers listed here added immensely to the text's readability.

David Barnett, Morehead State University

Kathleen Bowes, Widener University

Sherah Carr, Mercer University

Susan Eichenholtz, Adelphi University

Scott Fredrickson, University of Nebraska, Kearney

Stephanie Pamela Huffman, University of Central Arkansas

Kathleen King, North Central College

John K. Rugutt, Illinois State University

Leigh Zeitz, University of Northern Iowa

PART I

Leadership Policy and Innovative Practice

Part I sets the stage for this book by providing the requisite background in leadership policy and practice for school improvement. **Chapter 1: Entrepreneurial Leadership for Technology** presents models to engage the reader in ideas for technology leadership. **Chapter 2: Technology Leadership Standards** provides the standards for technology that will guide schools and administrators for the foreseeable future. **Chapter 3: Administration of Technology** asks the readers to reflect on their leadership and management style in order to effectively face the challenges of technology in the school setting. Finally, **Chapter 4: Designing and Using Academic Information Systems** assists the emerging leader to make decisions supported by data.

Chapter 1

ENTREPRENEURIAL LEADERSHIP FOR TECHNOLOGY

An Opposable Mind[1]

Theodore Creighton

Before we proceed in this chapter, we must decide if a specific leadership behavior is needed to effectively lead technology in our schools. More important, should we suggest that there is something about leadership in the broad sense that is uniquely different from leadership for such a specialized teaching and learning component as technology?

There is an abundance of empirical evidence that relates the leadership of the principal to a school's effectiveness (Fullan, 2001; Fullan & Stiegelbaurer, 1991; Hallinger & Heck, 1996, 1998; Leithwood & Riehl, 2003; Louis, 1994). The most recent and most exhaustive literature review and empirical study related to school technology leadership is the seminal work of Anderson and Dexter (2005), who conclude all the literature on leadership and technology "acknowledges either explicitly or implicitly that school leaders should provide administrative oversight for educational technology" (p. 51). They admit, however, that most of the literature tends to be narrow in identifying specifically what the knowledge and skill sets are that define technology leadership. The obvious skills mentioned include (a) principals should learn how to operate technology and use it, (b) principals should ensure that other staff in the building receive learning opportunities, (c) principals should have a vision for the role of educational technology in school, and (d) principals should assess and evaluate the role of academic and administrative uses of technology and make decisions from those data.

The International Society for Technology in Education (ISTE, 2002) standards include perhaps the most recent set of suggestions in the literature about what school principals should do as leaders of technology in schools. The National Educational Technology Standards for Administrators (ISTE, 2009) are integrated into the ISTE standards and are grouped into five specific areas:

1. Visionary Leadership

2. Digital Age Learning Culture

3. Excellence in Professional Practice

4. Systemic Improvement

5. Digital Citizenship

The following questions are addressed in this chapter:

- What are the key aspects of a technology plan leaders need to know to optimize high-quality student outcomes?

- How can leaders tie technology plans to institutional mission and priorities?

- What can leaders do to avoid excessive detail and technical jargon?

- Once change in the curriculum and instructional strategies are implemented, how can technology plans be realigned?

So, What's the Problem?

Some (including this author) might argue that perhaps technology leadership as practiced by today's principal is outdated unless it helps faculty and students address the great challenges presented by technology in our schools. Much of what we see happening in schools (along with the literature just presented) focuses on the management of technology. Our principal preparation programs, mine included, cover technology leadership lightly if at all and rarely extend beyond the most basic skills (i.e., word processing, spreadsheets, and database use). A theme of this chapter is that effective technology leadership has more to do with teaching pedagogy and human relations and much less to do with technology itself.

A principal's mission must now include designing and implementing new strategies to help teachers and students recognize, understand, and integrate technology with teaching and learning in the classroom. The mere presence of hardware and software in the classroom does not ensure meaningful learning for students. We are beyond the point of deciding whether or not we will accept technology in our schools. The crucial task at hand is to decide how to implement this technology effectively into instruction.

As early as 2000, Avolio discussed the relationship between leadership and technology and suggested that leaders must play a more proactive role in implementing technology and, more specifically, interface the human and information technology components. Many point to the problem of overemphasis of the technological aspect at the exclusion of the human resource function. Avolio warned of the creation of "information junkyards" (p. 4). The essence of technology leadership is to produce a change in attitudes, feelings, thinking, behavior, and performance with individuals.

To carry out this improvement in technology leadership, principals must be willing to alter existing leadership **practice**, or professional activity, evidenced in most schools, and they must also be open to the probability of participating in a transformation of traditional leadership skills, knowledge, and habits of mind.

Today's rapidly changing environment requires the technology leader to become involved in discovering, evaluating, installing, and operating new technologies of all kinds, while keeping teaching and student learning as the guide and driving force behind it all. Vaill (1998) issued an accompanying caution: "The technologies the organization employs entail learning time to exploit their productive and economic potential" (p. 45). If schools are constantly "upgrading" their technologies, they may never reach a productive flow of instruction, a flow on which effective teaching and learning are based.

Many schools have state-of-the-art hardware, computer labs, and other technology peripherals but are using them in ways that will do little to enhance student learning in rigorous and challenging ways. Technology leadership means much more than simply purchasing and implementing programs "stuffed" with fancy hardware and software. To really influence reform in schools, principals as technology leaders must stay focused on the individual needs of teachers and students, rather than race to adopt the "flavor of the month" program. Clearly, schools do not have a very good track record of sustaining significant change. The school technology leader is in the position to make sound instructional decisions regarding technology and program implementation. It is my hope this chapter will help answer the "how" associated with such a daunting task.

Entrepreneurial Leadership for Technology Defined

The term **entrepreneurial leadership** originated in the business world and can be simply defined as "translating ideas into actions." More specifically, Gunther McGrath and McMillian (2000) help us focus in on the concept.

Entrepreneurial leaders pursue only the best opportunities and avoid exhausting themselves and their organizations by chasing after every option. They passionately seek new opportunities, always looking for the chance to profit from change and disruption. (p. 3)

This new breed of leader seems to always seek original ways of doing things with little concern for how difficult they may be or whether the resources are available. Such leaders are willing to "disrupt the status quo" (Grogan & Donaldson, 2007, p. 22) and have the ability to hold several opposing thoughts in their minds at once and then reach a synthesis that contains elements of each but improves on each (Martin, 2007).

Framing Leadership for Technology in a Historical Context

In the past 50 years, there have been as many as 65 different classifications developed to define the dimensions of leadership (Northouse, 2004). Within those classifications, there are several specific theoretical forms of leadership—**situational leadership**, which is the idea that there is a different form of leadership for each different situation; **transformational leadership**, in which attention is paid to the needs and desires of an organization's members to achieve their highest potential; moral leadership; and others. I agree that leaders of technology have something to learn from the study of leadership, but I am reminded of a quote from a world-renowned statistician related to the many theories and models:

All models are wrong—but some are useful.

—George E. P. Box, Professor Emeritus,
University of Wisconsin

As I hope to demonstrate in this chapter, all of the traditional forms of leadership are not especially useful and applicable in today's turbulent and fast-paced world, especially in the area of technology leadership in our schools. Progressing through this brief historical context, I suggest we have a very current model before us (Martin, 2007) that is conceptual and viable and can help us frame entrepreneurial leadership for technology.

In the early 1800s, leadership characteristics or "traits" were studied to determine what made certain people great leaders. For example, if we could identify the traits possessed by Abraham Lincoln, we could perhaps duplicate them in others. The "trait approach" was based on the belief that leaders were born with certain characteristics that made them great leaders and that they were different from others who were more passive followers. These traits included intelligence, self-confidence, self-determination, integrity, and sociability.

In the middle of the 20th century, many researchers (e.g., Stogdill, 1948) argued that no identifiable set of traits separated effective leaders from ineffective leaders. Leadership began to emerge as a relationship between people and situations. This was actually the conceptual beginning of the theory we now call situational leadership.

Behavioral Leadership

Researchers, after realizing that trying to identify leadership traits or characteristics was not dependable, began to study **behavioral leadership**, or behaviors based on structure and consideration. In other words, they wanted to observe individuals as they were actually leading an organization or a group of people.

During the 1960s and early 1970s, two major research studies looked at the behavior of leaders: the Ohio State study and the University of Michigan study. The first study focused on asking employees to report the number of times their leaders displayed certain kinds of behavior. Two specific types of leadership behavior surfaced: (a) behavior centered on structure and (b) behavior based on consideration. In other words, leaders provide *structure* for employees and *consider* and *care about* the people under them. The University of Michigan study revealed similar results, identifying two specific types of leadership behavior: (a) production oriented and (b) employee oriented. *Production orientation* involved completion of tasks, paralleling the structure behavior found in the Ohio study. *Employee orientation* involved the consideration behavior of the Ohio study.

In essence, these two studies indicated that effective leaders had to concern themselves with both task orientation and relationship orientation. The studies also found that some organizations might need leaders more focused on tasks while others might benefit from leadership with strong human-relations skills.

Situational Leadership

Hersey and Blanchard (1993) are credited with the development of the theory of situational leadership. In essence, *situational leadership theory* involves a different form of leadership for each different situation. The contention is that an effective leader must adapt his or her style to the requirements of different situations. The two components of situational leadership (directive and supportive behavior) again parallel the structure and consideration constructs of the Ohio study and the production orientation and employee orientation of the Michigan study. Figure 1.1 shows such an alignment.

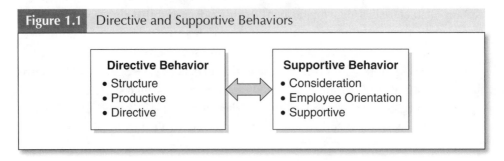

Figure 1.1   Directive and Supportive Behaviors

As popular as the Hersey and Blanchard (1993) theory is, little research has been completed giving evidence that applying the theory really does improve performance. Critics argue that the model does not adequately address "developmental levels" of subordinates. In addition, situational leadership theory does not fully address one-to-one versus group leadership in an organizational setting (Northouse, 2004, pp. 62–63).

Contingency Leadership

About a decade after Hersey and Blanchard (1993) presented the situational leadership theory, *contingency leadership theory* surfaced. This theory is also related to what the literature refers to as "leader-match theory" (Fiedler & Chemers, 1984, p. 23), where leaders are matched to different situations. So, when we discuss **contingency leadership** we are basically talking about a match between a leader's style and various situations.

Fiedler and Chemers (1984) suggest that a leader's style is either task motivated or relationship motivated. Task-motivated leaders deal mostly with goal setting and accomplishment, while relationship-motivated leaders concentrate more on closer interpersonal relationships with employees. These styles fit nicely into Figure 1.2 and are geared toward management and leadership behaviors.

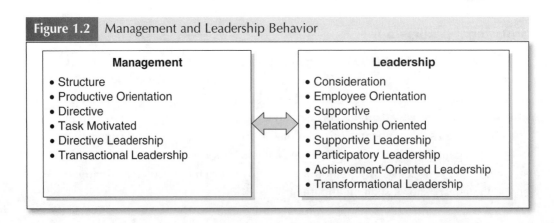

Figure 1.2   Management and Leadership Behavior

Fiedler and Chemers (1984) were the first to specifically categorize situational variables: (a) leader-member relationships, (b) task structure, and (c) position power. Leader-member relations involve workers' confidence in and loyalty to their leader. Leaders with appropriate task structure are very clear and specific when relating goals and objectives to members of the organization. Position power is simply the amount of authority a leader has in making decisions.

Path-Goal Leadership

In the early 1970s, House and Dressler (House, 1971; House & Dressler, 1974) popularized the *path-goal theory.* **Path-goal leadership** focuses on what motivates members of the organization to perform well and whether or not they feel appropriately rewarded for their work. So the challenge for the leader is to implement a leadership style that best meets the motivational needs of the worker.

House and Dressler (House, 1971; House & Dressler, 1974) suggest that effective leadership requires making the "path to the goal" clear to all in the organization and involves (a) appropriate coaching, (b) removal of the obstacles that make reaching the goal difficult, and (c) making work satisfying to all. Within the path-goal theory are four distinct styles of leadership: (a) directive leadership, (b) supportive leadership, (c) participatory leadership, and (d) achievement-oriented leadership. We could easily add the components of the path-goal theory to our Figure 1.2.

Transformational Leadership

Transformational leadership theory surfaced quite recently and is credited to the work of James MacGregor Burns (1978). Burns presents two types of leadership: *transactional* and *transformational.* He perceives most of the models presented so far in this chapter to be transactional, in that they focus on what happens between leaders and their followers. Principals and superintendents who offer bonuses to teachers who successfully raise student test scores exhibit transactional leadership. Teachers who routinely give students a grade for work completed are practicing transactional leadership. In both of these examples, the "exchange" between the leader and follower is quite simple: You do this, and I will give you that.

Leaders who practice transformational leadership, on the other hand, pay special attention to the needs and desires of the followers and try to help members achieve their highest potential. Basically, the theme is to give more attention to the follower's needs than the leader's needs. Transformational leaders often exhibit strong values and ideals and can motivate people to act in ways that support the organization above their own interests (Kuhnert, 1994).

A Conceptual Framework for Entrepreneurial Leadership in Technology

The technology leaders we will discuss in this chapter do not fit into any of the formal leadership theories just presented. One of the purposes in presenting the historical look at leadership over the last half century is to demonstrate that *technology leadership* is not so much a theory in itself but rather is a product of the progression of leadership theory. School leaders can certainly benefit from the work of Fiedler and Chemers (1984), Hersey and Blanchard (1993), House (1971), House and Dressler (1974), MacGregor Burns (1978), and Stogdill (1948). But the quiet, less visible, noncharismatic education leaders in technology presented in the last section of this chapter really spend more time and effort in an area not discussed by the authors and researchers above.

The Opposable Mind[2]

The progression of leadership theory has led us to the seminal work of Roger Martin (2007) who has spent the last 15 years, first as a management consultant and then as a dean of a business school, studying leaders who have striking and exemplary success records, trying to discern a shared theme running through their successes. The leaders he has interviewed and studied share a common trait, aside from their talent and innovation, that he calls the **opposable mind**: "They have the predisposition and the capacity to hold two diametrically opposing ideas in their heads" (p. 6). And then with patience and without panic or settling for one alternative or the other, they are able to produce a solution that is superior to either opposing idea. Martin calls this skill and ability **integrative thinking**, or the predisposition and capacity to consider diametrically opposing ideas and then produce a solution superior to either of them.

A little more background of Martin's (2007) work is necessary to lead into the conceptual framework for entrepreneurial leadership for education technology. As Martin worked on his idea of integrative thinking, he searched for a metaphor that would give us deeper insight and meaning to the opposable mind. "Human beings," he reasoned, "are distinguished from nearly every other creature by a physical feature known as the opposable thumb" (p. 6). Because of the tension we can create by opposing the thumb and fingers, we do amazing things that no other creature can do—write, thread a needle, carve a diamond, paint a picture, throw a 90-mile-per-hour baseball, and guide a catheter up through an artery to unblock it. All these actions would be impossible without the crucial tension between the thumb and fingers.

Martin (2007) further reasons:

Similarly, we are born with an *opposable mind* we can use to hold two conflicting ideas in constructive tension. We can use that tension to think our way
through to a new and superior idea. Were we able to hold only one thought or
idea in our heads at a time, we wouldn't have access to the insights that the
opposable mind can produce. And just as we can develop and refine the skill
with which we employ our opposable thumbs to perform tasks that once seemed
impossible, I'm convinced we can also, with patient practice, develop the ability to use our opposable minds to unlock solutions to problems that seem to
resist every effort to solve them. Using our opposable minds to past unappetiz-
ing alternatives, we can find solutions that once appeared beyond the reach of
our imaginations. (p. 7)

Before investigating a conceptual framework for entrepreneurial leadership
for technology in education, it may be helpful to look at Martin's (2007) working definition of *integrative thinking,* followed by some specific examples of
integrative thinkers who have demonstrated entrepreneurial leadership for
technology:

The ability to face constructively the tension of opposing ideas and, instead of
choosing one at the expense of the other, generate a creative resolution of the
tension in the form of a new idea that contains elements of the opposing ideas
but is superior to each. (p. 15)

In leading technology for our schools, we are often faced with problems that
appear to have two especially unsatisfactory solutions. If there is a relationship
between Martin's (2007) integrative thinking and entrepreneurial leadership for
technology, and I suggest there is, then we might investigate how technology
leaders actually think about problems and solutions. How do technology leaders determine the many options before them in a way that leads to an intelligent
and practical solution? What is it that causes them to perhaps consider both
solutions A and B but then select a new option C, which might have components of A and B but is much more innovative and stretches from the status quo
of A and B?

To get at some answers to the questions posed, we need to look at Martin's
(2007) framework for the process of thinking and deciding. Figure 1.3 combines
what we already know about leadership (i.e., Figures 1.1 and 1.2) with Martin's
process and steps in decision making: *salience, causality, architecture,* and
resolution.

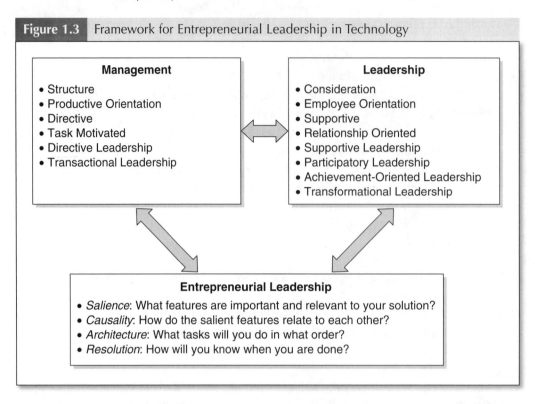

Figure 1.3   Framework for Entrepreneurial Leadership in Technology

Management
- Structure
- Productive Orientation
- Directive
- Task Motivated
- Directive Leadership
- Transactional Leadership

Leadership
- Consideration
- Employee Orientation
- Supportive
- Relationship Oriented
- Supportive Leadership
- Participatory Leadership
- Achievement-Oriented Leadership
- Transformational Leadership

Entrepreneurial Leadership
- *Salience*: What features are important and relevant to your solution?
- *Causality*: How do the salient features relate to each other?
- *Architecture*: What tasks will you do in what order?
- *Resolution*: How will you know when you are done?

Martin (2007) captures the flow of the process:

> Whatever we decide, we'll arrive at our choice by considering a set of features we deem *salient;* creating a mental model of the *causal relationships* among those features; arranging those causal relationships into an *architecture* intended to produce a specific outcome; thereby reaching a *resolution* of the problem at hand. With different salience, causality, and architecture, we would almost certainly arrive at a different outcome. (p. 29)

Using what we know about leadership and now Martin's (2007) work with integrative thinking, let's look at a couple of education leaders and follow their process of thinking and decision making.

AN OPPOSABLE MIND   Karen Symms Gallagher, USC Rossier School of Education

Karen Symms Gallagher is the dean of the University of Southern California (USC) Rossier School of Education. Her recent accomplishments include facilitation of the redesigned and transformed doctorate in education at USC. Currently, she is studying the potential learning implications of students' personal cell phones. The following is taken from her presentation to emeritus faculty at the USC Rossier School on February 15, 2007, titled "Education Schools in a Flat World: Sorting Through the Choices We Face."

Karen has decided on and is investigating two salient questions about technology and learning: (a) Does the use of devices that students have for their own personal information gathering or communication need translate into more interaction with curriculum content? (b) Are we being seduced by the use of popular technology or being savvy about matching student learning with information technology capability?

As cellular capacity as a technology continues to expand and as ownership of cell phones becomes ubiquitous, Karen asks how college professors can ignore the potential for cellular phones to replace laptops as a teaching tool. In community colleges, for example, where students attend part-time and often have less access to more costly information technology, the availability of cable television service delivered right to students' cell phones should be an exciting expansion of the formal classroom to the individual student level.

Right now, such cell phone service is available in many cities in the United States. This means that professors don't have to individualize lessons for students. Rather, students have the means to facilitate their own learning. Students who are going to school in remote locations, students who are English language learners and need additional practice, or students who may need special accommodations because of disabilities can use their cell phones to access instructional materials. Because the ownership of cell phones is so widespread among college students at all levels, issues of equity may be less relevant than they have been when ownership of laptops is required.

Karen Symms Gallagher has certainly progressed through Martin's (2007) first two components of thinking and deciding. She has decided on what she feels is important or salient, and she is addressing causality in thinking about ways we can make sense of the technology before us. Likely, she will now expand her integrative thinking to look at architecture and decide and determine what and in what order tasks will be needed to produce certain outcomes. Rather than choosing one of the current dominant models and accepting the limitations of it (e.g., laptop use in the classroom), Symms Gallagher is using her opposable mind to hold several models in her mind at once, consider their strengths and weaknesses, and then design a creative resolution of the tension between them.

AN OPPOSABLE MIND   Rich Baraniuk and the Rice University Connexions Project

The state of technology today yields itself to more efficient means of sharing, storing, and organizing information through use of the Internet. The Connexions project, developed in 1999 by C. Sidney Burrus and Richard Baraniuk of Rice University, is one such innovative forum for collecting, organizing, and sharing educational data. The use of textbooks has

(Continued)

(Continued)

become an inefficient, outdated means of distributing information due to the long process of publication combined with the constant state of evolution of human knowledge. Though articles and books remain valuable as learning tools, the additional benefit of electronics, computer technology, and the Internet allows for a continual process of updating information.

The idea for the Connexions project was born when Richard Baraniuk approached fellow professor C. Sidney Burrus to vent frustration over the distinct separation of mathematical ideas, design methods, applications, legal and ethical implications, and business possibilities related to mechanical engineering (Burrus, 2007). Baraniuk expressed frustration about the disconnect resulting from these different courses taught by different professors and originally proposed writing a new book that would connect all of these engineering ideas. In his response, Burrus challenged Baraniuk to "design a completely new teaching tool using modern computer and informational technology" (p. 20). The result of this discussion yielded the basic ideas needed to create what is now called "Connexions."

The Connexions philosophy involves the creation of a collaborative, educational environment by developing, sharing, and rapidly publishing scholarly content on the Internet. Furthermore, Connexions is a place to view, collect, and disseminate educational material in the format of small knowledge chunks called "modules," making learning a dynamic process (Creighton, 2008). These educational materials (modules and courses) are housed on the servers at Rice University and funded by the Hewlett Foundation, Rice University, and private donors. The Connexions project is an open source and available at http://cnx.org.

Baraniuk reasons that content should be modular and nonlinear and posits that most textbooks are a mass of information in linear format: One topic follows after another. However, our brains are not linear—we learn by making connections between new concepts and things we already know. Connexions mimics this by breaking down content into smaller chunks, called modules, that can be linked together and arranged in different ways. This lets students see the relationships both within and between topics and helps demonstrate that knowledge is naturally interconnected, not isolated into separate classes or books.

Baraniuk and Burrus use their *opposable minds* and *integrative thinking* to face constructively the tension of opposing ideas and, instead of choosing one at the expense of the other, generate a creative resolution of the tension in the form of a new idea that contains elements of the opposing ideas but is superior to both.

Today, Connexions is one of the most used open-education resources on the Web, employed in traditional college and K–12 settings, in distance learning, and by lifelong learners around the globe. Demand is surging; currently the Connexions servers handle over 16 million hits per month representing over 600,000 visitors from 196 countries.

Volunteers are translating modules and courses into a variety of different languages, including Spanish, Portuguese, Japanese, Chinese, Vietnamese, and Thai; many of these are our most popular. Connexions content development is grassroots organized and interinstitutional. Its most active content development areas at present include education leadership, music, engineering, physics, chemistry, bioinformatics, and history.

Conclusions

In this chapter, I have suggested that because of the infusion of technology in our schools, leadership as we presently know it will experience further transformation. The gap between autocratic and participatory leadership must grow even wider if we are to successfully use technology for maximizing teaching and learning. Even in our common participatory technology leadership in schools, one often sees *in-groups* and *out-groups* regarding technology use and implementation. Leaders who create (either intentionally or unintentionally) an in-group and out-group "may see the best technology system blocked from effectively creating collaboration resulting in low levels of trust within the organization" (Avolio, 2000, p. 13).

In-groups are usually composed of technology consultants and coordinators partnered with teachers possessing adequate to exemplary skills and interest in using technology. On the other hand, those who lack either technical expertise or interest make up the out-group and are not so visible, involved, or committed.

Philip Schlechty (1997), in his book titled *Inventing Better Schools,* specifically addresses a redefined leadership for implementing technology in our schools and suggests that a new way of thinking is needed:

Supporting technological change requires much more than instituting workshops; it requires as well the creation of opportunities to practice and observe, and opportunities to be coached and coach others. When the effort to install technological changes fail[s], it is likely that leaders have simply not appreciated and provided the quality of support and training that is needed. Or the effort may fail because of the fact that in schools, as in other organizations, technological changes often require structural changes, too.

Systemic change calls upon leaders to do all things they must do to lead procedural and technological change—and more. It also calls on them to think, to conceptualize, to see relationships between and among events that might escape others, to help others see these relationships and overcome fear, and to assure, cajole, coach, and inspire hope. Most of all, systemic change calls upon leaders to be wise and sometimes demanding but always to be supportive of and reassuring to teachers and students. (pp. 207–208)

Key Principles for Leaders to Know

- Make certain any technology plan is focused on high-quality student outcomes.
- Tie technology plans to institutional mission and priorities.
- Avoid excessive detail and technical jargon.
- If change in curriculum and instructional strategies is implemented, realign technology plans.

CASE STUDY 1.1 | Strategic Technology Planning for Reading

One of the ESEA/NCLB (The Elementary and Secondary Education Act and No Child Left Behind) important goals is that "by 2012–2014, all students will be proficient in reading by the end of third grade"(U.S. Department of Education, 2002). You have been charged by your superintendent with monitoring and addressing this goal with and through the use of technology. You are to prepare a strategic plan on how to accomplish this goal by 2010 or sooner. As part of your plan, you want to implement more innovative and effective uses of technology.

Discussion: What are the *salient* features or components of a curriculum plan? Explain how innovative technology might help in realizing the desired outcomes.

Activity: Draw a figure or framework for your entire plan, including Martin's (2007) four steps: *salience, causality, architecture,* and *resolution.*

CASE STUDY 1.2 | Paradoxes of Technology Leadership

The potential for technology presents both the greatest opportunity and the greatest threat to schools and their leaders. Successful principals as entrepreneurial leaders of technology will be those who decide to think and focus on how best to intersect technology with teaching and learning. Here are three paradoxes we face as technology leaders:

1. Technology can improve the interaction and dialogue between teachers and students, resulting in improved student learning, *BUT* it can also isolate, marginalize, and reduce effectiveness in the classroom.

2. Technology can offer its power to all students, *BUT* it can also segregate and deny that power.

3. Technology can assist with engaging students in meaningful learning and promote higher-level thinking, *BUT* it can also mirror traditional instructional pedagogy.

Discussion: Reflecting on these three paradoxes, discuss the following three questions:

1. Where do you want to go?

2. Why do you want to go there?

3. How will you know when you have arrived?

Activity: Using your opposable mind, give examples *you have observed* in schools for each of these three paradoxes.

Web Resources

The **International Journal of Educational Leadership Preparation** (http://ijelp .expressacademic.org/) is the official publication of the National Council of Professors of Educational Administration and is peer reviewed for quality and scholarly contribution to the field of educational administration. Many resources exist in this publication focused on the effective leadership of technology education.

ISTE's **National Educational Technology Standards** (http://www.iste.org/AM/Template .cfm?Section=NETS) have served as a road map since 1998 for improved teaching and learning by educators. ISTE standards for students, teachers, and administrators help measure proficiency and set goals for the knowledge, skills, and attitudes needed to succeed in today's Digital Age.

Rice University Connexions Project (http://cnx.org). Content should be modular and nonlinear. Most textbooks are a mass of information in linear format: One topic follows after another. However, our brains are not linear—we learn by making connections between new concepts and things we already know. Connexions mimics this by breaking down content into smaller chunks, called modules, that can be linked together and arranged in different ways. This lets students see the relationships both within and between topics and helps demonstrate that knowledge is naturally interconnected, not isolated into separate classes or books.

References

Anderson, R., & Dexter, S. (2005). School technology leadership: An empirical investigation of prevalence and effect. *Educational Administration Quarterly, 41*(1), 49–80.

Avolio, B. (2000). *Full leadership development: Building the vita forces in organizations.* London: Sage.

Burrus, C. S. (2007). Connexions: An open educational resource for the 21st century. *Educational Technology, 47*(6), 19–22.

Creighton, T. (2008, August). *The NCPEA Connexions project: Beta 1.2.* Paper presented at The National Council of Professors of Educational Administration Annual Conference, San Diego, CA.

Fiedler, F., & Chemers, M. (1984). *Improving leadership effectiveness: The leader match concept* (2nd ed.). New York: Wiley.

Fullan, M. (2001). *Leading in a culture of change.* San Francisco: Jossey-Bass.

Fullan, M., & Stiegelbaurer, S. (1991). *The new meaning of educational change.* New York: Teachers College Press.

Gallagher, K. (2007, February). *Education schools in a flat world: Sorting through the choices we face.* Paper presented at the USC Rossier School of Education, Los Angeles.

Grogan, M., & Donaldson, J. (2007). *Disrupting the status quo: The action research dissertation as a transformative strategy.* Retrieved August 14, 2009, from http://cnx.org/content/m14529/latest

Gunther McGrath, R., & McMillian, I. C. (2000). *The entrepreneurial mindset: Strategies for continuously creating opportunities in an age of uncertainty.* Boston: Harvard Business Press.

Hallinger, P., & Heck, R. (1996). Reassessing the principal's role in school effectiveness: A review of the empirical research. *Educational Administration Quarterly, 32,* 5–34.

Hallinger, P., & Heck, R. (1998). Exploring the principal's contribution to school effectiveness. *School Effectiveness and School Improvement, 92,* 157–191.

Hersey, P., & Blanchard, K. (1993). *Management of organizational behavior: Utilizing human resources* (5th ed.). Englewood Cliffs, NJ: Doubleday.

House, R. (1971). A path-goal theory of leader effectiveness. *Administration Science Quarterly, 16,* 321–368.

House, R., & Dressler, G. (1974). The path-goal theory of leadership. *Journal of Contemporary Business, 3,* 81–97.

International Society for Technology in Education (ISTE). (2002). *National Educational Technology Standards for Administrators 2002.* Retrieved August 14, 2009, from http://www.iste.org/Content/NavigationMenu/NETS/ForAdministrators/2002Standards/NETS_for_Administrators_2002_Standards.htm

International Society for Technology in Education (ISTE). (2009). *National Educational Technology Standards for Administrators 2009.* Retrieved August 14, 2009, from http://www.iste.org/Content/NavigationMenu/NETS/ForAdministrators/NETS_for_Administrators.htm

Kuhnert, K. (1994). Transforming leadership: Developing people through delegation. In B. Bass & B. Avolio (eds.), *Improving organizational effectiveness through transformational leadership* (pp.10–25). Thousand Oaks, CA: Sage.

Leithwood, K., & Riehl, C. (2003). *What we know about successful school leadership.* Philadelphia: Laboratory of Student Success, Temple University.

Louis, K. (1994). Beyond managed change: Rethinking how schools improve. *School Effectiveness and School Improvement, 5,* 2–24.

MacGregor Burns, J. (1978). *Leadership.* New York: Harper & Row.

Martin, R. (2007). *The opposable mind: How successful leaders win through integrative thinking.* Boston: Harvard Business School Press.

Northouse, P. (2004). *Leadership: Theory and practice* (3rd ed.). London: Sage.

Schlechty, P. (1997). *Inventing better schools: An action plan for educational reform.* San Francisco: Jossey-Bass.

Stogdill, R. (1948). Personal factors associated with leadership: Issues and debates. *Journal of Psychology, 25,* 35–71.

U.S. Department of Education. (2002). *No Child Left Behind Act of 2002.* Retrieved August 14, 2009, from http://www.ed.gov/nclb/landing.jhtml

Vaill, P. (1998). *Spirited leading and learning.* San Francisco: Jossey-Bass.

Notes

1. In *The Opposable Mind,* Roger Martin (2007) goes beyond the question of what great leaders think to the more important and more interesting question of how they think.

2. Roger Martin is the author of *The Opposable Mind: How Successful Leaders Win Through Integrative Thinking,* published by Harvard Business School Press (2007).

Chapter 2

TECHNOLOGY LEADERSHIP STANDARDS

The Next Generation

Rosemary Papa

> *Standards: The knowledge and skills that should be mastered in order to achieve a level of proficiency in a particular area. Standards are also a means of setting criteria for accomplishing or judging a particular activity or event.*
>
> —Council of Chief State School Officers, 2008

The move from good leader to great leader can be a quantum leap. Technology can play a significant role in becoming a great leader as technological literacy is critical to the 21st-century understanding of student engagement. Educational leaders lead in the hopes of being inspiring. How we build a learning ecosystem for both students and teachers defines us: Are you a good educational leader or a great educational leader?

This chapter focuses on the next generation of professional codes and standards that emphasize the role of the educational leader. The support for this comes from the following codes and standards addressed in this chapter: the Code of Ethics for Educational Leaders (American Association of School Administrators [AASA], 2007); the Educational Leadership Policy Standards—ISLLC (Interstate School Leaders Licensure Consortium, 2008); (Council of Chief State School Officers [CCSSO], 2008); and the ISTE (International Society for Technology in Education) NETS (National Educational Technology Standards) for technology facilitators

(2001a), for technology leaders (2001b), for students (2007), for teachers (2008), and for administrators (2009).

The following questions are addressed in this chapter:

- What are the codes/standards leaders need to know in optimally managing and especially in using technology for teachers and students?

- What have been the recent reaffirmations made to codes/standards?

- What influence do standards have on the changing technology practices of the learner?

- How do leaders use the technology standards in the improvement of their leadership skills?

- What are the roles of technology standards in leader accountability and/or evaluation?

From Codes to Standards

AASA Code of Ethics

While debate surrounds the genesis of measurement-based standards, there is little controversy that ethics and the development of ethical guidelines for school leaders began over 50 years ago. The AASA recently readopted the **Code of Ethics for Educational Leaders** (see Table 2.1). AASA (2007) describes the educational leader's professional conduct as one that

> must conform to an ethical code of behavior, and the code must set high standards for all educational leaders. The educational leader provides professional leadership across the district and also across the community. This responsibility requires the leader to maintain standards of exemplary professional conduct while recognizing that his or her actions will be viewed and appraised by the community, professional associates, and students. The educational leader acknowledges that he or she serves the schools and community by providing equal educational opportunities to each and every child. The work of the leader must emphasize accountability and results, increased student achievement, and high expectations for each and every student. To these ends, the educational leader subscribes to the following statements of standards. (p. 1)

Leaders within educational organizations are held to higher standards within society. This we understand. Our ability to role model is critical to everyone we interact with. This illuminates the need for leaders taking responsibility for their own personal use and understanding of technology.

Table 2.1	AASA (2007) Code of Ethics for Educational Leaders

The Educational Leader:

1. Makes the education and well-being of students the fundamental value of all decision making.

2. Fulfills all professional duties with honesty and integrity and always acts in a trustworthy and responsible manner.

3. Supports the principle of due process and protects the civil and human rights of all individuals.

4. Implements local, state, and national laws.

5. Advises the school board and implements the board's policies and administrative rules and regulations.

6. Pursues appropriate measures to correct those laws, policies, and regulations that are not consistent with sound educational goals or that are not in the best interest of children.

7. Avoids using his or her position for personal gain through political, social, religious, economic, or other influences.

8. Accepts academic degrees or professional certification only from accredited institutions.

9. Maintains the standards and seeks to improve the effectiveness of the profession through research and continuing professional development.

10. Honors all contracts until fulfillment, release, or dissolution is mutually agreed upon by all parties.

11. Accepts responsibility and accountability for one's own actions and behaviors.

12. Commits to serving others above self.

Source: Copyright © AASA. Reprinted with permission.

ISLLC 2008 Policy Standards

Recent revised policy standards have emerged for educational leaders that are anchored in both empirical research and craft knowledge. These standards, known as **ISLLC 2008**, are not intended to be stuck in cement—not meant to be the "end all, be all."

In 2007, the recommendations from the research panel to the National Policy Board for Educational Administration (NPBEA, 2006–2007) were:

1. Ensure that the ISLLC policy standards form the foundation for further work on creating practice standards (both program and school based).

2. Create structures and procedures to ensure that the ISLLC standards are regularly updated to reflect changes in the knowledge base.

3. Support research efforts to study the implementation and effects of the ISLLC policy standards and subsequent program and practice standards throughout the profession.

4. Revise the title of ISLLC to "Educational Leadership Policy Standards: ISLLC 2008." See Table 2.2.

Table 2.2	Educational Leadership Policy Standards: ISLLC 2008

Standard 1: An education leader promotes the success of every student by facilitating the development, articulation, implementation, and stewardship of a vision of learning that is shared and supported by all stakeholders.

Functions:

a. Collaboratively develop and implement a shared vision and mission

b. Collect and use data to identify goals, assess organizational effectiveness, and promote organizational learning

c. Create and implement plans to achieve goals

d. Promote continuous and sustainable improvement

e. Monitor and evaluate progress and revise plans

Standard 2: An education leader promotes the success of every student by advocating, nurturing, and sustaining a school culture and instructional program conducive to student learning and staff professional growth.

Functions:

a. Nurture and sustain a culture of collaboration, trust, learning, and high expectations

b. Create a comprehensive, rigorous, and coherent curricular program

c. Create a personalized and motivating learning environment for students

d. Supervise instruction

e. Develop assessment and accountability systems to monitor student progress

f. Develop the instructional and leadership capacity of staff

g. Maximize time spent on quality instruction

h. Promote the use of the most effective and appropriate technologies to support teaching and learning

i. Monitor and evaluate the impact of the instructional program

Standard 3: An education leader promotes the success of every student by ensuring management of the organization, operation, and resources for a safe, efficient, and effective learning environment.

Functions:

    a. Monitor and evaluate the management and operational systems

    b. Obtain, allocate, align, and efficiently utilize human, fiscal, and technological resources

    c. Promote and protect the welfare and safety of students and staff

    d. Develop the capacity for distributed leadership

    e. Ensure teacher and organizational time is focused to support quality instruction and student learning

Standard 4: An education leader promotes the success of every student by collaborating with faculty and community members, responding to diverse community interests and needs, and mobilizing community resources.

Functions:

    a. Collect and analyze data and information pertinent to the educational environment

    b. Promote understanding, appreciation, and use of the community's diverse cultural, social, and intellectual resources

    c. Build and sustain positive relationships with families and caregivers

    d. Build and sustain productive relationships with community partners

Standard 5: An education leader promotes the success of every student by acting with integrity, with fairness, and in an ethical manner.

Functions:

    a. Ensure a system of accountability for every student's academic and social success

    b. Model principles of self-awareness, reflective practice, transparency, and ethical behavior

    c. Safeguard the values of democracy, equity, and diversity

    d. Consider and evaluate the potential moral and legal consequences of decision making

    e. Promote social justice and ensure that individual student needs inform all aspects of schooling

Standard 6: An education leader promotes the success of every student by understanding, responding to, and influencing the political, social, economic, legal, and cultural context.

Functions:

    a. Advocate for children, families, and caregivers

    b. Act to influence local, district, state, and national decisions affecting student learning

    c. Assess, analyze, and anticipate emerging trends and initiatives in order to adapt leadership strategies

Source: Adopted by the National Policy Board for Educational Administration (NPBEA), December 12, 2007.

The most important characteristic of the work of the research panel (cochaired by R. Papa and J. Murphy) was that the standards would be *regularly* updated to reflect changes in the knowledge base and that the standards of 2008 would be research based, not just craft knowledge based. Empirical research ($n = 83$ studies) was defined as evidence gathered through quantitative, qualitative, or mixed-method research. Craft knowledge ($n = 47$ sources) was defined as abilities, awareness, information, and other accumulated knowledge based on field and classroom experience (CCSSO, 2008). Using the conceptual framework of the original ISLLC standards from 1996, changes were expanded to include dynamics of the changing field of educational leadership, including the increasing role technology plays.

These standards identified research and categorized it through two lenses: empirical research and craft knowledge practices. These set the stage for the needed revisions of the programmatic (guide curriculum development) and practice (measurable) standards/dispositions that are used for National Council for Accreditation of Teacher Education (NCATE) accreditation. As noted by Creighton and Young (2003), Fenwick English, the renowned father of curriculum mapping and auditing, stated, "We must have absolute confidence that the regulatory process is untainted by personal biases or conflicts of interest not be present. This is not the case now" (p. 36).

Research About Standards

Criticism of the NCATE standards is well known. The standards in educational leadership first introduced and adopted by various professional agencies in 1996 were practice based with the sole foundation coming from craft knowledge. According to Fenwick English,

> standardized leaders can be produced with a standardized curriculum. This is what I mean by efficiency centered. Another word for "standardization" is uniformity. That is where the ELCC [Educational Leadership Constituent Council] standards take us. To have standards without standardization one thinks of law and medicine. One wants competent lawyers and doctors without reducing the complexity of the challenges facing those professions. The nature of the knowledge bases of those applied fields has a much longer history than education administration and they have established a tradition of change within their knowledge bases that is different from ours. Much of the "progress" in medicine, for example, has occurred "out of the knowledge base" of the time. In law there is always the possibility of a *Brown v. Board of Education* type decision which overturns everything that came before it and leads to a whole new data base of case

law. There is no such recognition of the ELCC or NCATE about this with education leadership. (Creighton & Young, 2003, pp. 33–34)

Given this backdrop, our task as school leaders is to recognize the limitation of standards and understand that competence is in many respects a moving trajectory. The opportunities that standards raise for the profession have to do with understanding the artful side of leadership. The assessment and/or evaluation of standards sets boundaries to what we do, both in implementation and in the evidence of implementation that must be addressed through informed leadership practices.

Since the turn of the century, working conditions, promising and best practices, benchmarks, and research have rapidly changed primarily due to technology tools and practices that are increasingly ubiquitous to how we learn.

Within the ISLLC 2008 standards is a greater focus on technology. Embedded within three of the standards are three functions explicitly tied to the important role of technology and its relationship to educational leadership (see Table 2.3).

For example, a recent study was done with New Jersey chief school administrators (Babo, 2009) on how the new ISLLC 2008 standards impact principal summative evaluation practices. Fifty-two principals (11%) participated in a survey. The results showed that some of the standards and their respective functions were

Table 2.3 ISLLC 2008 Technology to Support Success of Every Student
Standard 2: An education leader promotes the success of every student by advocating, nurturing, and sustaining a school culture and instructional program conducive to student learning and staff professional growth.
Function h: *Promote the use of the most effective and appropriate technologies to support teaching and learning*
Standard 3: An education leader promotes the success of every student by ensuring management of the organization, operation, and resources for a safe, efficient, and effective learning environment.
Function b: *Obtain, allocate, align, and efficiently utilize human, fiscal, and technological resources*
Standard 6: An education leader promotes the success of every student by understanding, responding to, and influencing the political, social, economic, legal, and cultural context.
Function c: *Assess, analyze, and anticipate emerging trends and initiatives in order to adapt leadership strategies*

Source: Council of Chief State School Officers. (2008). *Educational Leadership Policy Standards: ISLLC 2008.* Washington, DC: Author. http://www.ccsso.org/Publications/Download.cfm?Filename=ISLLC2008final.pdf.

deemed to be of greater importance than others. Concerning the ISLLC Standard 2 that emphasizes technology and its impact on student learning, this study found that "only 31% of the respondents thought it essential that principals promote the use of the most effective and appropriate technologies to support teaching" (p. 7).

Thirty-one percent is not an acceptable number for today and tomorrow's educational leader. As Table 2.3 shows, ISLLC 2008 strongly recommends that school leaders actively participate in both understanding and use of technology tools to foster the highest level of effective teaching and learning practices.

The reality for many leaders is that they are being held accountable in their evaluations for how standards are met. Without a focused understanding of standards and the skills to implement curriculum changes coupled with strong professional development for one's staff, the impact of technology may be limited by the leader's ability to understand its importance.

Transforming Education With Tools

ISLLC 2008 is published by the Council of Chief State School Officers, a non-partisan, nationwide, nonprofit organization of the public officials who head departments of elementary and secondary education. These standards (See Tables 2.2 and 2.3) are high-level policy standards intended to provide guidance to state policymakers and other professional organizations that set standards for the pre-K–12 curriculum. CCSSO (2008) described ISLLC 2008:

> Education leadership is more important than ever. States recognize that schools and districts will not meet demanding requirements for improving achievement without effective leaders. The recently released education leadership standards, known to most of you as the "ISLLC Standards," represent the latest set of high-level policy standards for education leadership. The standards provide guidance to state policymakers as they work to improve education leadership preparation, licensure, evaluation, and professional development. (p. 1)

ISTE Standards

What is the relationship among the AASA Code of Ethics, the ISLLC 2008 policy standards, and the ISTE NETS for students, teachers, and administrators? Principals and superintendents play a pivotal role in determining how well technology is understood and used in schools. The NETS enable us to better define what students, teachers, and administrators need to know and are able to do. According to ISTE Chief Executive Officer Don Knezek, integrating technology throughout a school system is, in itself, significant systemic reform. We have a wealth of evidence attesting to the importance of leadership in implementing and sustaining systemic reform in schools. It is critical, therefore, that we attend seriously to leadership for technology in schools. (ISTE, 2009)

Several years ago, the **ISTE** embarked on an effort to refresh the National Educational Technology Standards. These efforts have resulted in the new **NETS-S** (NETS for Students; see Table 2.4), **NETS-T** (NETS for Teachers; see Table 2.5), and **NETS-A** (NETS for Administrators; see Table 2.6) that help guide what students, teachers, and administrators should know and be able to do to learn effectively and live productively in an increasingly digital world.

NETS-S

Table 2.4   NETS for Students 2007
1. Creativity and Innovation Students demonstrate creative thinking, construct knowledge, and develop innovative products and processes using technology. Students: a. apply existing knowledge to generate new ideas, products, or processes b. create original works as a means of personal or group expression c. use models and simulations to explore complex systems and issues d. identify trends and forecast possibilities 2. Communication and Collaboration Students use digital media and environments to communicate and work collaboratively, including at a distance, to support individual learning and contribute to the learning of others. Students: a. interact, collaborate, and publish with peers, experts, or others employing a variety of digital environments and media b. communicate information and ideas effectively to multiple audiences using a variety of media and formats c. develop cultural understanding and global awareness by engaging with learners of other cultures d. contribute to project teams to produce original works or solve problems

(Continued)

Table 2.4	(Continued)

3. Research and Information Fluency

   Students apply digital tools to gather, evaluate, and use information. Students:

   a. plan strategies to guide inquiry

   b. locate, organize, analyze, evaluate, synthesize, and ethically use information from a variety of sources and media

   c. evaluate and select information sources and digital tools based on the appropriateness to specific tasks

   d. process data and report results

4. Critical Thinking, Problem Solving, and Decision Making

   Students use critical thinking skills to plan and conduct research, manage projects, solve problems, and make informed decisions using appropriate digital tools and resources. Students:

   a. identify and define authentic problems and significant questions for investigation

   b. plan and manage activities to develop a solution or complete a project

   c. collect and analyze data to identify solutions and/or make informed decisions

   d. use multiple processes and diverse perspectives to explore alternative solutions

5. Digital Citizenship

   Students understand human, cultural, and societal issues related to technology and practice legal and ethical behavior. Students:

   a. advocate and practice safe, legal, and responsible use of information and technology

   b. exhibit a positive attitude toward using technology that supports collaboration, learning, and productivity

   c. demonstrate personal responsibility for lifelong learning

   d. exhibit leadership for digital citizenship

6. Technology Operations and Concepts

   Students demonstrate a sound understanding of technology concepts, systems, and operations. Students:

   a. understand and use technology systems

   b. select and use applications effectively and productively

   c. troubleshoot systems and applications

   d. transfer current knowledge to learning of new technologies

Source: National Educational Technology Standards for Students, Second Edition, © 2007, ISTE® (International Society for Technology in Education), www.iste.org. All rights reserved.

NETS-T

Table 2.5	NETS for Teachers 2008

Effective teachers model and apply the National Educational Technology Standards for Students (NETS-S) as they design, implement, and assess learning experiences to engage students and improve learning; enrich professional practice; and provide positive models for students, colleagues, and the community. All teachers should meet the following standards and performance indicators. Teachers:

1. Facilitate and Inspire Student Learning and Creativity

   Teachers use their knowledge of subject matter, teaching and learning, and technology to facilitate experiences that advance student learning, creativity, and innovation in both face-to-face and virtual environments. Teachers:

   a. promote, support, and model creative and innovative thinking and inventiveness

   b. engage students in exploring real-world issues and solving authentic problems using digital tools and resources

   c. promote student reflection using collaborative tools to reveal and clarify students' conceptual understanding and thinking, planning, and creative processes

   d. model collaborative knowledge construction by engaging in learning with students, colleagues, and others in face-to-face and virtual environments

2. Design and Develop Digital-Age Learning Experiences and Assessments

   Teachers design, develop, and evaluate authentic learning experiences and assessments incorporating contemporary tools and resources to maximize content learning in context and to develop the knowledge, skills, and attitudes identified in the NETS-S. Teachers:

   a. design or adapt relevant learning experiences that incorporate digital tools and resources to promote student learning and creativity

   b. develop technology-enriched learning environments that enable all students to pursue their individual curiosities and become active participants in setting their own educational goals, managing their own learning, and assessing their own progress

   c. customize and personalize learning activities to address students' diverse learning styles, working strategies, and abilities using digital tools and resources

   d. provide students with multiple and varied formative and summative assessments aligned with content and technology standards and use resulting data to inform learning and teaching

3. Model Digital-Age Work and Learning

   Teachers exhibit knowledge, skills, and work processes representative of an innovative professional in a global and digital society. Teachers:

   a. demonstrate fluency in technology systems and the transfer of current knowledge to new technologies and situations

(Continued)

Table 2.5	(Continued)

b. collaborate with students, peers, parents, and community members using digital tools and resources to support student success and innovation

c. communicate relevant information and ideas effectively to students, parents, and peers using a variety of digital-age media and formats

d. model and facilitate effective use of current and emerging digital tools to locate, analyze, evaluate, and use information resources to support research and learning

4. Promote and Model Digital Citizenship and Responsibility

Teachers understand local and global societal issues and responsibilities in an evolving digital culture and exhibit legal and ethical behavior in their professional practices. Teachers:

a. advocate, model, and teach safe, legal, and ethical use of digital information and technology, including respect for copyright, intellectual property, and the appropriate documentation of sources

b. address the diverse needs of all learners by using learner-centered strategies and providing equitable access to appropriate digital tools and resources

c. promote and model digital etiquette and responsible social interactions related to the use of technology and information

d. develop and model cultural understanding and global awareness by engaging with colleagues and students of other cultures using digital-age communication and collaboration tools

5. Engage in Professional Growth and Leadership

Teachers continuously improve their professional practice, model lifelong learning, and exhibit leadership in their school and professional community by promoting and demonstrating the effective use of digital tools and resources. Teachers:

a. participate in local and global learning communities to explore creative applications of technology to improve student learning

b. exhibit leadership by demonstrating a vision of technology infusion, participating in shared decision making and community building, and developing the leadership and technology skills of others

c. evaluate and reflect on current research and professional practice on a regular basis to make effective use of existing and emerging digital tools and resources in support of student learning

d. contribute to the effectiveness, vitality, and self-renewal of the teaching profession and of their school and community

Source: National Educational Technology Standards for Teachers, Second Edition, © 2008, ISTE® (International Society for Technology in Education), www.iste.org. All rights reserved.

NETS-A

Table 2.6	NETS for Administrators 2009

1. Visionary Leadership

   Educational administrators inspire and lead development and implementation of a shared vision for comprehensive integration of technology to promote excellence and support transformation throughout the organization. Educational administrators:

   a. inspire and facilitate among all stakeholders a shared vision of purposeful change that maximizes use of digital-age resources to meet and exceed learning goals, support effective instructional practice, and maximize performance of district and school leaders

   b. engage in an ongoing process to develop, implement, and communicate technology-infused strategic plans aligned with a shared vision

   c. advocate on local, state and national levels for policies, programs, and funding to support implementation of a technology-infused vision and strategic plan

2. Digital-Age Learning Culture

   Educational administrators create, promote, and sustain a dynamic, digital-age learning culture that provides a rigorous, relevant, and engaging education for all students. Educational administrators:

   a. ensure instructional innovation focused on continuous improvement of digital-age learning

   b. model and promote the frequent and effective use of technology for learning

   c. provide learner-centered environments equipped with technology and learning resources to meet the individual, diverse needs of all learners

   d. ensure effective practice in the study of technology and its infusion across the curriculum

   e. promote and participate in local, national, and global learning communities that stimulate innovation, creativity, and digital-age collaboration

3. Excellence in Professional Practice

   Educational administrators promote an environment of professional learning and innovation that empowers educators to enhance student learning through the infusion of contemporary technologies and digital resources. Educational administrators:

   a. allocate time, resources, and access to ensure ongoing professional growth in technology fluency and integration

   b. facilitate and participate in learning communities that stimulate, nurture, and support administrators, faculty, and staff in the study and use of technology

(Continued)

Table 2.6	(Continued)

c. promote and model effective communication and collaboration among stakeholders using digital-age tools

d. stay abreast of educational research and emerging trends regarding effective use of technology and encourage evaluation of new technologies for their potential to improve student learning

4. Systemic Improvement

Educational administrators provide digital-age leadership and management to continuously improve the organization through the effective use of information and technology resources. Educational administrators:

a. lead purposeful change to maximize the achievement of learning goals through the appropriate use of technology and media-rich resources

b. collaborate to establish metrics, collect and analyze data, interpret results, and share findings to improve staff performance and student learning

c. recruit and retain highly competent personnel who use technology creatively and proficiently to advance academic and operational goals

d. establish and leverage strategic partnerships to support systemic improvement

e. establish and maintain a robust infrastructure for technology including integrated, interoperable technology systems to support management, operations, teaching, and learning

5. Digital Citizenship

Educational administrators model and facilitate understanding of social, ethical, and legal issues and responsibilities related to an evolving digital culture. Educational administrators:

a. ensure equitable access to appropriate digital tools and resources to meet the needs of all learners.

b. promote, model, and establish policies for safe, legal, and ethical use of digital information and technology

c. promote and model responsible social interactions related to the use of technology and information

d. model and facilitate the development of a shared cultural understanding and involvement in global issues through the use of contemporary communication and collaboration tools

Source: National Educational Technology Standards for Administrators, Second Edition, © 2009, ISTE® (International Society for Technology in Education), www.iste.org. All rights reserved.

Other ISTE Standards: TF and TL

Two more sets of standards bear mentioning as they focus on preparing technology experts for schools: the ISTE/NCATE National Educational Technology

Standards for technology facilitation (TF; 2001a) and technology leadership (TL; 2001b). **NETS-TF** and **NETS-TL** comprise eight topic areas, listed below:

1. Technology Operations and Concepts

2. Planning and Designing Learning Environments and Experiences

3. Teaching, Learning, and the Curriculum

4. Assessment and Evaluation

5. Productivity and Professional Practice

6. Social, Ethical, Legal, and Human Issues

7. Procedures, Policies, Planning, and Budgeting for Technology Environments

8. Leadership and Vision

The performance indicators are different as the TF standards foci are on practices at the school-building level while the TL standards foci are at the district, regional, state, and national levels. These standards as with other NCATE standards are written as program- or practice-based standards that are earmarked by the fact that they are measurable, as found in rubrics. According to Williamson and Redish (2009),

> the TF/TL standards are nearly identical in structure and content to the NETS-S (2007), NETS-T (2008) and NETS-A (2002) except for the performance tasks [$n = 78$] and rubrics . . . the NET-S, NETS-T and NETS-A do not have performance tasks attached to them. (p. 9)

What do these standards mean to the school leader? How one will encourage implementation and/or expectations for students, teachers, and leaders in reaching the goals of these standards is what the leader should be focused on. For example, how are standards linked with everyday practice? Modeling behaviors expected (displaying personal use of technology), providing professional development opportunities (encouraging staff to attend technology workshops), and ensuring access for students (using clickers in a large class) are but a few of the ways to think of the connections between standards and practices.

Clearly, there is no dearth of standards. Studies show that leadership is second only to classroom instruction in influencing student outcomes (CCSSO, 2008). How the school leader is able to stay knowledgeable of the standards requires a great degree of effort. Additionally, using only behaviorist outcome-based foci learning does not serve students or teachers as it too narrowly defines the curricular path. The innovations in teaching and learning have "artful" actions as well as those easily and narrowly measured. Technology is an opportunity to embrace the risk-taking hero in our leadership. Today's reality within schools means that a sometimes messy and playful leadership process that encourages cutting-edge technology use for optimal student learning is allowable, doable, and encouraged.

For example, is it technology innovation that makes the difference? Or is it the highly effective teacher delivering the instruction through technology that makes the impact?

The Leader's Tool Kit

Educational leaders need to know that national curriculum standards exist as well. To name just a few, consider the National Council of Teachers of English Standards for the English Language Arts (http://www.ncte.org/standards), the National Council for Geographic Education National Geography Standards (http://www.ncge.org/i4a/pages/index.cfm?pageid=3314), the National Council of Teachers of Mathematics Principles and Standards for School Mathematics (http://standards.nctm.org/document/index.htm), *Moving Into the Future: National Standards for Physical Education* published by the National Association for Sport and Physical Education (http://www.aahperd.org/naspe/template .cfm?template=ns_index.html), the National Council for the Social Studies' *Expectations of Excellence: Curriculum Standards for Social Studies* (http://www .socialstudies.org/standards), and so on.

It is often said that if all you have in your tool kit is a hammer, then everything in the world looks like a nail. Adult learning practices tell us that adults learn on a need-to-know basis: The adult learner has a focused need to learn something, and that something is the exact place to start. No one size fits all learners. Children are not so different, as technology practices have shown. Yes, they are compelled to go to school and learn and master certain subjects to continue through the required pre-K–12 path. The educational leader needs to be able to facilitate and guide teachers in expanding their tool kits from a fairly individualized perspective. That is, teachers should be encouraged to use different teaching strategies with tools that make sense for the learner.

A teacher's tool kit needs to have strategies for facilitating student learning within an active learning environment from introduction to mastery of topics. The creation of rubrics for measuring some of the standards/functions makes sense. Other features of a tool kit are not easily measured. ISTE rubrics help teachers develop strategies and methods that will guide a student from an introductory stage to mastery. ISTE (2008) defines this rubric scale as moving from Beginning level to Developing level to Proficient level and finally to Transformative level.

- The Beginning level teacher is a beginner in the use of technology tools and his or her ability to effectively use technology to improve his or her teaching and to help students learn.

- The Developing level teacher is becoming more adept and flexible in his or her use of technology tools.

- The Proficient level teacher is one who uses technology tools effectively in the improvement of student learning.

- The Transformative level teacher uses technology tools in collaboration with the active student learner that address the global and digital environment we live in today (ISTE, 2008).

For standards to work they must mesh. NETS-S and NETS-T must mesh with NETS-A and ultimately ISLLC 2008. What are the essential conditions for arranging an effective learning environment for all students? Standards give us a road map, a framework from which to delve into a rapidly moving field of free (Web 2.0) and costly software and hardware.

There is an old saying: *Just because you can, does it mean you should?* Don't go overboard using technology tools just because they are available. Are all the bells 'n' whistles of said software required to be used? Is the latest a must to purchase? This chapter began with the AASA Code of Ethics from which standards originated. The ability to measure learning is not the only reason to use technology tools. If we focus our teachers on student-centered learning opportunities and ask them to assess and formatively evaluate them, we are supporting an environment that supports the learning success for all students, à la ISLLC 2008. The educational leader should serve as the facilitator and motivator for formative change. A shared vision with your teachers and staff leads to a commitment of establishing flexible student groups of learning. How we wrestle with learner skills and innovation (information, media, technology for life and career skills) leads to themes important to all of us in the educational community, such as global awareness, civic literacy, health literacy, and so forth.

As we began this chapter, we recognized that the move from good leader to great leader can be a quantum leap. Technology can play a significant role as technological literacy is critical to the 21st-century understanding of student engagement. Tool kit leadership strategies include finding the courage to stay the course; using your voice in a plan; creating thought and actions in exploring the barriers and possible solutions; conducting formative assessments that allow for play activity learning; communicating with all stakeholders seeking transparency through blogs, wikis, podcasts, tweets, and so forth; and committing your artful leadership skills to your teachers in ways that foster their teaching experimentation in a safe environment to optimize student learning strategies for all learners. Educational leaders lead in the hopes of being inspiring. As was noted in the beginning of this chapter, how we build a learning ecosystem for both students and teachers will define us as good educational leaders or great educational leaders.

Conclusions

Clausen, Britten, and Ring (2008) wrote, "To create essential conditions for effective technology use in schools, there needs to be an increased emphasis regarding both the knowledge and support administrators provide to teachers who want to integrate technology with instruction" (p. 20). Building-level administrators who use the technology standards to help frame curricular decisions will ensure that teachers are prepared. Encouraging teachers to work in collaborative teams that review student data, curriculum strategies, and activities will enhance the curriculum mapping that ensures a coherent implementation of both NETS standards and practices for all students. These are topics that are covered in subsequent chapters in this book.

An empirical study done several years ago (Anderson & Dexter, 2005) found

the concept of school technology leadership was operationalized and aligned to technology goals, policies, budgets, committees, and other structural supports for improving technology's role in learning. Although this was not a test of the validity of the NETS-A standards [ISTE, 2002], the findings are consistent with and reinforce standards. (p. 72)

This research confirmed what we know is true about leadership and curriculum and staff development: Principals/superintendents must *walk the talk* and play a pivotal role in providing leadership in the use of technology.

A great educational leader energizes the learning environment using tools and teaching strategies for success of all children. The learning environment is student centered, is collaborative, fosters creative thinking, ensures digital global citizenship, integrates assessment practices, and encourages learner-constructed knowledge from multiple sources and experiences. Standards (and codes) serve to ensure the incentive and ethical posture that will aid the educational leader in modeling creativity and innovation.

Key Principles for Leaders to Know

- The use of codes/standards improves student, teacher, and staff performance.

- The integrity of the learning environment requires the leader to have both a global and a micro understanding of effective teaching practices and learner skills.

- A robust Digital Age learning culture has the ability to inspire.

| CASE STUDY 2.1 | Strategies to Meet Technology Standards With Limited Funding |

You are the superintendent of a small rural school district with two main problems: lack of funding and lack of infrastructure.

1. The small town has extremely archaic phone/data lines and is isolated, which makes bringing fiber to your area cost prohibitive.

2. The limited funding previously available has now been eliminated due to the country's and your state's severe cutting of funds to schools. You do not want your principals and teachers to lose sight of the technology goals you still have for the students and learning environment of the schools.

Discussion: Discuss with your administrators a strategy or strategies to help keep your district on track while having no additional funds and keeping in mind the ISLLC 2008 and NETS-A (ISTE, 2009) standards. Possible topics to cover include cancellation of a district technology training workshop, soft capital budget being frozen, no new technology upgrades, and so forth.

Does the district have a vision in preparing students to "meet the demands of a new age"? What policies or plans have been adopted/adapted recently?

Activity: Design a district plan that meets the needs of the community and considers discussion points noted above within the setting of lack of available funds and infrastructure. Use the ISLLC 2008 and NETS-A (ISTE, 2009) standards to guide in the design of your plan.

| CASE STUDY 2.2 | Efficacy of Online Education |

You are a superintendent of a growing district with 60,000+ students that is facing large budget cuts due to declining state support. You are being forced to cut teachers in addition to making cuts in all other aspects of the curriculum, textbooks, and so forth. In order to maintain advanced college placement classes, you want your principals to consider offering

(Continued)

(Continued)

online education across all grade levels. As part of your discussion you want to emphasize that holding true to the standards of the profession for students, teachers, and administrators undergirds the considerations required by the ethical administrator.

Discussion: Consider the "how to" question in thinking about ranking ISLLC 2008 based on improving student achievement, based on developing a technology-focused school culture, or based on supporting the district's change initiatives. Rank the NETS-A, NETS-T, and NETS-S standards. In a group, compare the lists and discuss an action plan to achieve the agreed-upon top three standards and their functions.

Activity: Using the standards (ISLLC 2008 and refreshed NETS-A/T/S), outline a plan that you will use to convince principals that online education is broader than just remedial education for K–12 students.

Web Resources

The **American Association of School Administrators** (http://www.aasa.org) is the premier organization for educational leaders.

The **American Association of School Administrators Code of Ethics** (http://aasa.files .cms-plus.com/PDFs/GovDocs/CodeofEthicsApprovedGB030107.pdf) is critical for educational leaders to be aware of.

The **American Society for Ethics in Education** (http://www.edethics.org) provides leaders with a broad view of what leadership means to parents, students, and teachers.

The **Center for the Study of Ethics** (http://www.uvu.edu/ethics) focuses the educational leader on curricular dimensions of education.

The **Center on Education Policy** (http://www.cep-dc.org) is a national independent advocate for public education and more effective public schools.

The **Council of Chief State School Officers** (http://www.ccsso.org) published the ISLLC 2008 standards for educational leadership policy.

The **International Journal of Educational Leadership Preparation** (http://www.ijelp .expressacademic.org) is a wealth of juried current research from both practitioners and professors that will help educational leaders lead.

ISTE NETS-A (2009; http://www.iste.org/Content/NavigationMenu/NETS/ForAdministrators/ 2009Standards/NETS_for_Administrators_2009.htm), *ISTE NETS-S* (2007; http:// www.iste.org/Content/NavigationMenu/NETS/ForStudents/2007Standards/NETS_for_ Students_2007.htm), and *ISTE NETS-T* (2008; http://www.iste.org/Content/Navigation Menu/NETS/ForTeachers/NETS_for_Teachers.htm) provide technology standards educational leaders need to be informed about.

ISTE Technology Facilitation (2001a; http://www.iste.org/Content/NavigationMenu/ NETS/ForTechnologyFacilitatorsandLeaders/Technology_Facilitation_Standards .htm) and *ISTE Technology Leadership* (2001b; http://www.iste.org/Content/Navigation Menu/NETS/ForTechnologyFacilitatorsandLeaders/Technology_Leadership_Standards .htm) are standards educational leaders should be aware of for use with technology experts.

Learning Point (http://www.learningpt.org), formerly North Central Regional Educational Laboratory, works to improve teaching and learning in schools.

Mid-continent Research for Education and Learning (http://www.mcrel.org) is a resource center offering practical, research-based solutions and resources.

The **National Association for Multicultural Education** (http://www.nameorg.org) informs education leaders on the latest research and practices in multicultural education.

The **National Association of Elementary School Principals** (http://www.naesp.org) is the premiere organization for elementary school leaders.

The **National Association of Secondary School Principals** (http://www.nassp.org/s_nassp) is the premiere organization for secondary school leaders.

The **National Council for Accreditation of Teacher Education** (http://www.ncate.org/ public/standards.asp) is the accreditation body for university teacher preparation, which includes leadership programs.

The **National Council of Professors of Educational Administration** (http://www .ncpeaprofessors.org) is the premiere organization for professors of educational administration/leadership.

The **National Policy Board for Educational Administration** (http://www.npbea.org) is a national consortium of major stakeholders in educational leadership and policy.

The **National School Boards Association** (http://www.nsba.org) is the premiere organization for school board leaders.

The **Parent Teacher Association** (http://www.pta.org) provides involvement strategies and resources.

PaTTAN, the Pennsylvania Training and Technical Assistance Network (http://www.pattan .k12.pa.us/teachlead/E_ectiveInstructionToolKitSearch.asp), provides educational leaders with effective instructional strategies that help teachers focus on success for all students.

The **Public Education Network** (http://www.publiceducation.org) provides resources and strategies for engaging the public in public education.

The **Southwest Educational Development Laboratory** (http://www.sedl.org) is a private, nonprofit, research and development, and dissemination institute dedicated to improving teaching and learning.

The **U.S. Department of Education** (http://www.ed.gov/policy/elsec/leg/esea02/index.html) provides an overview of Elementary and Secondary Education Act/No Child Left Behind methods and resources.

References

American Association of School Administrators (AASA). (2007). *Code of ethics.* Retrieved March 5, 2009, from http://aasa.files.cms-plus.com/PDFs/GovDocs/CodeofEthicsApproved GB030107.pdf

Anderson, R. E., & Dexter, S. (2005, February). School technology leadership: An empirical investigation of prevalence and effect. *Educational Administration Quarterly, 41*(1), 49–82.

Babo, G. (2009, February). Principal evaluation and leadership standards: Using the ISLLC 2008 "functions" as a perspective into the evaluation of building principals by New Jersey chief school administrators in suburban school districts. *NCPEA Education Leadership Review, 10*(1), 1–12.

Clausen, J. M., Britten, J., & Ring, G. (2008, September/October). Envisioning effective laptop initiatives. *Learning & Leading with Technology, 36*(2), 18–22.

Council of Chief State School Officers (CCSSO). (2008, June 3). *Educational leadership policy standards: ISLLC 2008* [Press release]. Washington, DC: Author.

Creighton, T., & Young, M. (2003). A conversation with Fenwick English: Standards without standardization. *NCPEA Education Leadership Review, 4*(1), 33–36.

International Society for Technology in Education (ISTE). (2001a). *Technology facilitation standards.* Retrieved February 5, 2009, from http://www.iste.org/Content/NavigationMenu/ NETS/ForTechnologyFacilitatorsandLeaders/Technology_Facilitation_Standards.htm

International Society for Technology in Education (ISTE). (2001b). *Technology leadership standards.* Retrieved February 5, 2009, from http://www.iste.org/Content/NavigationMenu/ NETS/ForTechnologyFacilitatorsandLeaders/Technology_Leadership_Standards.htm

International Society for Technology in Education (ISTE). (2002). *National educational technology standards for administrators 2002*. Retrieved August 14, 2009, from http://www.iste .org/Content/NavigationMenu/NETS/ForAdministrators/2002Standards/NETS_for_ Administrators_2002_Standards.htm

International Society for Technology in Education (ISTE). (2007). *National educational technology standards for students* (2nd ed.). Washington, DC: Author.

International Society for Technology in Education (ISTE). (2008). *National educational technology standards for teachers* (2nd ed.). Washington, DC: Author.

International Society for Technology in Education (ISTE). (2009). *National educational technology standards for administrators*. Washington, DC: Author. Retrieved July 5, 2009, from http:// www.iste.org/Content/NavigationMenu/NETS/ForAdministrators/2009Standards/NETS_for_ Administrators_2009.htm

National Policy Board for Educational Administration. (2006–2007). *Updating educational leadership professional standards in a changing public education environment.* Washington, DC: Council of Chief State School Officers.

Williamson, J., & Redish, T. (2009). *ISTE's technology facilitation and leadership standards: What every K–12 leader should know and be able to do.* Washington, DC: International Society for Technology in Education.

Chapter 3

ADMINISTRATION OF TECHNOLOGY

Teaching, Learning, and Resource Management

Ric Brown

There is a false dichotomy that exists between **leadership**, which constitutes exercising influence usually while interacting with others for mutual goal attainment, and **management**, which involves setting objectives and engaging in activities to meet those objectives (Brown, Noble, & Papa, 2009). Good managers need to have some leadership traits, and good leaders need to know how to manage. The two concepts are not mutually exclusive. In measurement parlance management skills are necessary but not sufficient for leadership. You can't keep the trains running on time (management) if you don't know where they are going (leadership). Conversely, being a good train manager is useless if trains are no longer needed.

This chapter attempts to consider the characteristics that will make you a leader, manager, and administrator of educational technology. On any one of the numerous topics broached in this chapter, you'll need to be reasonably fluent in the language of technology but, more important, know how to keep yourself informed—or know someone you can trust to keep you informed—on the pervasive influence of technology in education.

The following questions are addressed in this chapter:

- What are the aspects leaders should be focused on for optimizing high-quality **student outcomes**, or the skills and knowledge acquired by learners?
- What key aspects of development and training are major parts of any technology plan?
- How can adult personnel be made a part of their learning processes including use of previous experiences, prior knowledge, and individual learning styles and choices?
- What aspects of leadership will need to be problem centered and use all available tools and strategies?
- How can leaders use teamwork, mentoring, and support networks in professional development and training?
- What are the integral aspects required for the assessment and evaluation components of your technology plan?

What Kind of Educational Technology Leader Are You?

We need to start with some self-reflection. What kind of leader are you? This general question will certainly be reflected in your leadership and administration of technology (see Chapter 1 on entrepreneurial leadership) for your school, district, or unit within a college or university.

In the complex educational settings of today, you will need to emerge as a leader who is comfortable promoting and working with teams, who is serious about group problem solving, and who finds ways to support innovation within constantly changing landscapes.

In fact, Fullan (2008) argues that learning to manage change may be the most important skill for leaders of the 21st century. His six guidelines to effect change essentially include creating conditions for employees to succeed, creating conditions for effective and purposeful peer interaction, building capacity in personnel, learning to improve the work that one does, setting the conditions for easy access (vs. secrecy) to information for all, and developing many leaders to work in concert. Learning and practicing these guidelines allows for the development of an organization that is always in the process of transforming itself.

You need the freedom to think and to consider the possibilities. But, at the same time, you must keep perspective given some of the realities you will encounter. You cannot allow yourself to get lost in trying to be technologically sophisticated.

You'll need to find a way to remain on the cutting edge without falling off the cliff. This is especially critical in the fast-paced, ever-changing, and sometimes overwhelming field of information and educational technology. You must at the very least understand the general ideas of communication in a digital world; technology integration; data-driven **decision making**, or engaging in selection of various choices for action; and technology and the act of teaching and learning.

The fact that it can be done doesn't mean it should be done or needs to be done by you or your department, school, district, or university. The fact that the technology exists for fade-in, fade-out, color-rich PowerPoint slides delivered at a breakneck pace doesn't mean that you as the district or school site leader need to make such a presentation at the board meeting or teacher meeting. You really don't need to do it if you can't do it on your own. You're a technological professional sitting to the side of the stage.

You need to be tech savvy, not tech enamored or, at worse, a tech dilettante.

As the leader, unless you are as fully versed as your technological experts (unlikely), you need someone who can discuss with you the pros, cons, and other ramifications of technology decisions that need to be made.

As with any enterprise, large or small, articulate and skilled personnel are essential to an effective and efficient operation. With that in mind, let's introduce a new title for use in this discussion pertinent to your leadership. The term *techsperts*, meaning individuals who are very knowledgeable regarding hardware, software, and related applications, will be used to identify a class of individuals who are the experts when it comes to technology. *Expert* in this case means awareness and the "how to" when it comes to technology, old and new. It does not necessarily mean that they are experts in terms of pedagogy, management, or **professional development** (in technology)—activities designed to provide knowledge and skills to users of technology.

Without overgeneralizing or stereotyping, techsperts are typically very bright individuals who really enjoy technology and are always up-to-date on the latest hardware, software, games, networking systems, and so forth. Like all other individuals, they vary dramatically in personality. Don't believe the old joke that you can distinguish extroverted techsperts by the way they look at your shoes when they speak to you.

However, remember your techsperts may not look beyond the capabilities of the technology or, worse, may ignore the potential downsides of the latest versions or models that they desire. As well, they may not have the requisite management skills if they are in administrative positions.

In fact, what are the skills that need to be possessed by these individuals to deal with the ever-changing and rapid landscape of technology? Adams (2008) suggests management skills (budgeting, customer service, selection and retention of employees, etc.), comprehensive knowledge of Web-enabled technology (online learning, voice-over protocols, etc.), remote access management (technical resources to address the problems wherever they reside, site-level repairs, refreshings, understanding of centralized and decentralized services, etc.), security (hacking, unauthorized use, Web predators), management of data (databases, benchmark systems, longitudinal databases, etc.), electronic information delivery and access (grading, communication, etc.), and wireless systems.

As well, it is essential that there be someone on your team with the technical expertise (not simply a user of technology) to discuss/argue the salient points with the pure techsperts. There is nothing worse than to be in a decision-making position holding a discussion with someone speaking *technolese,* with no one able to translate it or put it into context.

You'll also need to be well versed or well briefed on the standards of technology for leaders (see Chapter 2). While some see the standards movement as the death knell of education, standards are a part of the reality of today. It is a misnomer that standards and regulations stifle creativity and innovation. They can also drive creativity and innovation.

As well, professional development for site administrators and district office staff is essential. The typical exposure to short-term topics by motivational speakers or the transfer of knowledge from "experts" to practitioners may be the least effective way for ongoing and substantive behavior change. Harris-John and Ritter (2007) suggest e-based professional development. The electronic format provides a plethora of topics, delivered in potentially interesting formats, at any time to any place (rural sites, remote sites, etc.). Additionally, the development of professional learning communities, enhanced through technology, may provide opportunities for ongoing networking and professional development.

You will have to consider that everyone has immediate access to you through e-mail. You must also know that you need not respond immediately or even at all to the panoply of communication. E-mail wars just escalate a nonissue. You'll have to pick and choose wisely and know when to answer, when to ignore, and/or when to pass the information to someone else to respond.

As a leader, ethical decision making is critical. Ethical behavior is not an esoteric quality but is the way we conduct ourselves. While specific definitions may vary, studies have shown some basic behaviors that are seen as part of one's ethical makeup (National Council of Professors of Educational Administration [NCPEA], 2007). These behaviors include honesty, fairness, caring, consideration, reliability, respect, professionalism, open-mindedness, and accessibility. Ethical administrators consistently do what is best for students, teachers, staff, and their communities without concerns for personal or professional gain.

With respect to all decisions you make, you must always ask:

- Who benefits?
- Who is hurt?
- What are the long-term effects of my decision today?

Salient Factors to Consider in Managing Educational Technology

The curricular and administrative/personnel mission and priorities must drive any technology planning and/or implementation. As well, you must focus on the intersection of academic, administrative, and personnel outcome and needs. You cannot implement technology solutions in isolation of the people who must interact with the technology.

For example, a new software solution for employee timekeeping, however elegant in its design, cannot be implemented if the employees who will keep time cannot successfully use the software and/or it is too complex for efficient and effective use. Or, a new academic software tool for grading or tracking student progress will only be effective if users find it more efficient and less time-consuming than paper-and-pencil methods.

As changes in the academic, administrative, and personnel mission and priorities occur, **technology planning and implementation**—preparing for activities to meet objectives of a goal and the subsequent monitoring of those activities to ensure they are used—must be facile enough to change in concert.

Curricular Outcomes and Needs

Academic outcomes, tight budgets, and stewardship are factors most often recognized as key to reforms in the governance of **academic technology**, which includes technology applications and tools focused on the acts of teaching and learning. Student needs must be the driving force in any technology planning and/or implementation.

The Teacher Perspective

It must be recognized that it is the quality of teaching that is critical, not simply throwing a lot of technology into the classroom. We have all experienced the 30-minute presentation by someone proficient in PowerPoint but not proficient in teaching. The half-hour consists of 120 slides at such a pace that blinking causes 10 missed slides. This is *not* **teaching using technology**, or teaching practices that use technology! Academic technology is the use of technology tools to enhance the teaching and learning process. It is teaching using technology, not technology used in teaching.

As noted, just having the technology is not enough; you must have professional development for teachers and the appropriate support personnel. A sound program in professional development requires a coordinated effort between teachers interested in enhancing their teaching *using* technology and the techsperts (trained in adult learning principles; see Chapter 5), continuous follow-up, and availability of resources. There are numerous publications and Web sites regarding the intelligent use of educational technology (see Web Resources).

For example, Hall (2008) notes that leaders need to build a professional culture of learning that is ongoing and a shared responsibility. That is, everyone participates equally in learning activities. A few suggestions include 10- to 15-minute microlessons that are focused on specific topics at the beginning of staff meetings or during working lunches, book study teams working on a few chapters of a particularly relevant book, learning logs consisting of brief notations of professional development efforts and outcomes, and attendance at professional development conferences with appropriate sharing with colleagues to better institutionalize the knowledge gained. In another example, Arns (2008) suggests staff development in a comfortable environment with collaboration, individual focused time, energy, and food.

The academic technology effort must be as tailored to the individual teacher as is possible and delivered at the time desired (both synchronous and asynchronous). Thus, providing generic workshops on a scheduled basis throughout the year will be less effective, given what is known about the adult learner and meeting individual needs.

An onsite technology coach of sorts can provide different methods of instruction, different technologies in instruction, and general follow-up as needed. Technology use cannot be forced on teachers. The best strategy involves planting the seeds by starting with volunteers and then waiting for interest to become infectious by word of mouth. Then, peer mentoring can provide an effective process for assisting teachers to use technology.

Effective teaching includes the complexities of connectivity: access to online services and resources, d-learning (distance learning), and m-learning (mobile learning). Teachers must be familiar with learning systems, individualized and individual devices. They must be well versed in whole-class instruction using technology, Web uses, wiki text, embedding of audio/video/interaction tutorials, simulations, edu-games, and so forth. Having software is just the beginning. Effective use includes proper planning and implementation. Sawtelle (2008) argues that 10 essential factors are needed for effective software implementation. These are objectives before planning, planning before implementation, involvement of stakeholders, an evaluation design and criteria for judgment, leadership in implementation management, appropriate physical environment and equipment, adequate training, prerequisite knowledge and skills, monitoring of implementation, and evaluation.

In sum, there must be sound curricular frameworks built with the decisions as to what tools are needed and why their use aids in providing all students with a greater opportunity for success. Teachers for tomorrow need to be familiar with software for all levels of students, remedial as well as enrichment.

The Student Perspective

Many teachers and administrators are embarrassed to note that their students seem to be more tech savvy than they and/or the students' parents. This is certainly true if *tech savvy* only refers to the *use* of technology. What junior high school student cannot take pictures with his or her phone, send a text message, or post on Facebook or Twitter to convey what's on today's test to the next-period students? However, the link between those skills and learning the essential knowledge to compete in today's economy is a loose one. In fact, some would argue (Marcovitz, 2008) that the instant gratification provided by technology may impede the deep thought and attention necessary for certain topics. Contradicting that view, Son (2008) argues that technology has the power to capture imagination and attention to make learning interactive and fun.

Jackson and Crawford (2008) suggest that because students spend a great deal of their time in a digital world of computers, cell phones, video games, and music devices, this represents a beginning point to changing the horizon of learning. They note that preferences for knowledge for the digital student have gone from nonownership to self-ownership, from linear to nonlinear, and from unresponsive when one does not understand to trying again. And, as important, the digital student is comfortable with network building as he or she reaches for information and social contact. Cilesiz (2009) notes these same phenomena in an international setting.

- Are students able to complete the three basic components that are essential for school and career/life success: research, production, and presentation?

- *Research.* They can Google, go to Wikipedia, and cut and paste information. But can they verify their information, correctly cite their sources, and coherently define a problem to study? Learners for tomorrow still need to go beyond only information gathering to learning higher-order thinking and reflective problem solving.

- *Produce.* They can send a picture of an embarrassing moment to all their friends and family or post a picture on Facebook. But can they put together a PowerPoint presentation highlighting key facts regarding global warming?

- *Present.* They can blog (factually or not) and tweet ("OMG, I'm eating a Pop-Tart!"), but can they use information to piece together a coherent report on a relevant topic?

We must not confuse mere technological facility with the higher-order concepts of synthesis, analysis, and evaluation. And social networking (MySpace, TeacherTube, Facebook, etc.) can be a powerful teaching tool that leads to team building and team solutions.

As a leader, you need to ask yourself about your support for technology for student learning. A recent study (Clausen, Britten, & Ring, 2008) of building-level administrators in Indiana provides conflicting results with respect to the technology environment in which we live. While all teachers were reported to use some form of technology daily (e-mail, word processing, PowerPoint) and up to a third were reported to use moderate technology (digital video, Web activities), only a few teachers were reported to be using high-end technology (computer simulations, universally designed instruction). Interestingly, while approximately half of the administrators reported respectively that their teachers sought assistance and support for technology use in the classroom, that they would provide technology training over other options, and that they considered technology use by teachers for student learning a priority, fewer than half reported that technology is a priority in their budget!

Does your library/media center include appropriate technology tools and support? Does it foster the world of intersecting communities? Is there at least a complete technology lab in each school with an interactive whiteboard, laptops for checkout, printers, digital cameras, and so forth? Does it include teacher/staff monitoring and student/teacher development?

If most students are comfortable using technology out of the school setting, how supportive are you about using technology in school?

Administrative Outcomes and Needs

The key concepts that influence decisions in this area include standardization versus heterogeneity, autonomy versus state/centralized mandate, funding formula versus straight allocation, "one model fits all" versus tiered structure, and performance goals versus academic freedom to explore alternative concepts.

A common dilemma in any large, noncorporate entity (school district, community college, etc.) will be the competing interests of the central office and individual units (school sites, departments, etc.). This is often referred to as the "enterprise" versus **decentralized configuration**, or technology management that is implemented at a unit/department level—that is, resources, personnel, and fiscal matters to be handled by the central administration versus delegation to some extent (all or part) to the various units within the organization. You will be amazed that a compromise solution can be difficult to achieve.

Typically in the **enterprise configuration**, a highly centralized model of technology management, the techsperts in the central office hold the decision-making authority regarding all, or most all, of education, communication, administration, and computing. Security concerns, bulk buying (good deals and equipment for their use or those they serve?), and sometimes a "we are the experts" mentality are given as reason for this configuration. Individual units must comply with the central office decisions and services, but some efficiencies and control are gained. However, some would argue if compliance and accountability are too tightly controlled, the outcome is alienated employees who become passive and do not continue to seek creative solutions to problems.

In the decentralized model, there is more local discretion, within some broad parameters concerning equipment purchase, software, and so forth. In this model, creativity in problem solving and opportunities for individualized solutions are enhanced. Certainly, functions handled more efficiently and effectively (e-mail service as an example) are left to the central office. However, if the district-level mission is too loosely coupled in the search for individuality, mission drift and confusion may occur.

As with much in school, it is a struggle of resources and philosophy. The techsperts (those who deal with campus hardware, e-mail, business computing, security, etc.) will often see themselves as experts in academic technology as well. Their understanding of technology and software will lead them to assume they are competent to provide classroom uses. They may be correct in a few cases if they have had some sort of adult learning and pedagogical training. If not, they may prove to be very handy with the hammer, but they only see nails and cannot really build anything useful.

For example, a technology director in a district may feel that he or she is the ultimate expert on academic technology. However, his or her idea of helping faculty is to schedule a series of classes on the use of various hardware and software packages. Faculty will likely report that these classes are "one size fits all" and express a strong preference for more individualized assistance.

There are a variety of administrative functions that must be successfully managed. These include:

- Financial management (general ledger, expenditures, revenues, accounts payable, accounts receivable, fixed asset accounting, material supplies inventory, etc.)

- Procurement (what to buy and for what purpose, obsolescence, software site licenses, etc.)

- Personnel/human resources (personnel data, payroll, position control, hours, salary administration, timekeeping, hiring and applicant tracking, communication, student activities, etc.)

- Grant writing and contract management services

- School management (bell systems, scheduling, average daily attendance, digital signage, etc.)

- Security and safety (cyber misconduct, cyber harassment, issues of free speech/expression vs. libel defamation, slander, censorship)

- Emergency procedures (evacuation, video/audio/broadcasts, etc.)

- Compliance issues (handicapping conditions, etc.)

- Data management (test reporting, tracking students individually and across schools, individual education program uses, assessment and diagnosis, etc.)

- Risk management (field trip procedures, data theft issues, etc.)

- Emerging technologies

Evaluating Your Educational Technology Decisions

Evaluation includes more than just assessment and data collection. It also means making sense of the data so that decisions based on the assessment can be made.

When doing technology planning and/or implementation, be clear about what data are to be collected to evaluate the effectiveness of your efforts. Such data need to be complete and comprehensive. Be sure the data collected are inexplicably linked to the mission and priorities. As well, the data collected should be based on operational definitions with fairly observable characteristics to ensure reliability (consistency across time and place) and validity (degree to which you are sure you are measuring what you intended to measure).

A good start might be an audit of the instructional programs in your district and/or site especially with respect to technology integration (Brooks-Young, 2004). A useful tool in such an audit would be an instrument developed using the

National Educational Technology Standards for Administrators (Chapter 2). Think of an instrument with each standard and skill listed down the left side of a page. After each skill would be a response format indicating your degree of use or level at which you actually support the skill. For example:

Standard 2: Establish a Robust Digital Age Learning Culture			
I model and reward the frequent, purposeful, and effective use of technology for learning.	Always	Sometimes	Rarely

Conducting such a process with respect to each standard will provide you with a starting point to a fruitful integration of technology audit.

Conclusions

Think of your own daily life and your use of technology. Did you pay any of your bills online? Did you order your medications online? When you stopped for gasoline, did you use the automated pay-at-the-pump feature? Did you fly through the toll plaza on the highway with your E-ZPass?

Now, walk into your district office or school site. For example: Is it as up-to-date as society? Are your teachers and students taking full advantage of technology to teach and learn? Are your bus schedules, ordering processes, and payment processes efficient and effective? If you have to think more than 5 seconds about these questions, you need to reconsider your technology plan and strategies.

To use some old clichés, you must walk the talk, practice what you preach, and model behavior you want. It is no longer enough to have a few zealous teachers who know technology or the one techspert business office employee. Schools of the 21st century need leaders with a comprehensive technology plan and a strategy to implement such a plan. Issues of instructional strategies, classroom materials professional development, hardware and software acquisition, data-based decision tools, and security require a knowledgeable leader/manager and an institutionalized commitment to appropriate and cutting-edge technology usage.

You must have a sense of where your district/school needs to go (sometimes called a vision) and a plan to implement that vision (management/administrative skills). You personally need to be committed to those ends, be aware of teaching and learning using technology, understand the change process, and be able to surround yourself with a team of knowledgeable individuals dedicated to the same outcomes.

Key Principles for Leaders to Know

- Your major focus should be on student outcomes, the skills and knowledge acquired by learners.

- Use appropriate data to develop and adjust program planning and implementation.

- Be aware of your teacher and staff interests and the factors serving to motivate them.

- Ensure that appropriate development and training are a major part of any technology plan.

- Adult personnel must be a part of their learning process including use of previous experiences, prior knowledge, and individual learning styles and choices.

- Administration will need to be problem centered and use all available tools and strategies. As well, to the maximum extent, include as many individuals in program development as possible.

- Teamwork, mentoring, and support networks are key to professional development and training.

- It is essential that technology planning and implementation be based on the student and employee needs and not solely on your desires, preferences, and/or biases.

- You need to be maximally aware of the social, legal, and ethical implications of decisions you make.

- Assessment and evaluation must be an integral component of your technology plan.

CASE STUDY 3.1 | Assessing Software

One of your information technology employees has just returned from a conference with knowledge of a new piece of administrative software that, while expensive, is purported to reduce costs in the long run.

Discussion: Discuss the steps you would take to investigate whether the software is appropriate in your particular environment. Include issues such as cost, constituencies to be consulted, training and professional development, short- and long-term perspectives, coherence with your mission and goals, and so forth.

Activity: Using the above discussion points and the Web resources found in this chapter, outline the assessment you will undertake to evaluate the effectiveness of your choices.

CASE STUDY 3.2 | Personnel Issues in Hiring a Technologist

As the new superintendent of a school district, you have the opportunity to hire the new director of technology services. While you do have some basic understanding of the technological world, you are by no means an expert.

Discussion: In light of your current setting, design the job announcement for the new position. What are the minimum skill expectations, the desired expectations, and the requisite professional background?

Activity: Design a list of interview questions you would ask of the finalists based on the class/group discussion. Consider the potential ramifications for student learning, staff morale, and so forth. Describe all the constituents (players), their concerns, and your possible solutions.

Web Resources

Ed Tech Action Network (http://www.edtechactionnetwork.org) provides educators with important issues for U.S. policy and tools to be a part of the political process.

Edutopia (http://edutopia.org/tech-tips) provides tips for blending technology into lessons.

Google Blog Search (http://blogsearch.google.com) is a search engine to find blogs on particular topics.

The **International Journal of Educational Leadership Preparation** has published such articles of interest as "Authentic Problem-based Collaborative Learning Practices for Professional Development in Teacher Education" (http://ijelp.expressacademic.org/article.php?autoID=210&issueID=64), "Digital Learners: How Are They Expanding the Horizon of Learning?" (http://ijelp.expressacademic.org/article.php?autoID=192&issueID=64), "e-Based Professional Development for Effective Teaching and School Leadership" (http://ijelp.expressacademic.org/article.php?autoID=157&issueID=63), and "Implementing Network Video for Traditional Security and Innovative Applications: Best Practices and Uses for Network Video in K–12 Schools" (http://ijelp.expressacademic.org/article.php?autoID=191&issueID=64).

ISTE's Professional Development Services (http://www.iste.org/profdev) help improve teaching and learning.

ISTE's Research and Evaluation department (http://www.iste.org/research) provides a dissemination site for cutting-edge research in educational technology.

ISTE School 2.0 (http://www.iste.org/school) provides access to resources for a district's strategic planning process.

ISTE Technology Facilitation (2001a; http://www.iste.org/Content/NavigationMenu/NETS/ ForTechnologyFacilitatorsandLeaders/Technology_Facilitation_Standards.htm) and *ISTE Technology Leadership* (2001b; http://www.iste.org/Content/NavigationMenu/ NETS/ForTechnologyFacilitatorsandLeaders/Technology_Leadership_Standards .htm) are standards educational leaders should be aware of for use with technology experts.

The **K–12 Instructional Media Center** (http://www.k12imc.org/iste) provides resources for designing, implementing, and lesson planning for teaching and curriculum.

The **National Educational Technology Standards** (http://www.iste.org/nets) provide standards for administrators, teachers, and students.

References

Adams, J. (2008). The essential skill set. *Edtech, 6*(2), 28–31.

Arns, J. (2008). Staff development: Café style. *Learning and Leading with Technology, 36*(3), 12–15.

Brooks-Young, S. (2004). The electronic briefcase for administrators. Eugene, OR: International Society for Technology in Education.

Brown, R., Noble, P., & Papa, R. (2009). *So you want to be a higher education administrator?* Lancaster, PA: Proactive Publications.

Cilesiz, S. (2009). Educational computer use in leisure contexts: A phenomenological study of adolescents' experiences in internet cafes. *American Educational Research Journal, 46*(1), 232–274.

Clausen, J. M., Britten, J., & Ring, G. (2008). Envisioning effective laptop initiatives. *Learning and Leading with Technology, 36*(2), 18–22.

Fullan, M. (2008, June). The six secrets of change. *Scholastic Administr@tor,* 59–63.

Hall, D. (2008). Professional learning: Making it work for you. *Learning and Leading with Technology, 36*(3), 10.

Harris-John, M., and Ritter, S. (2007). *E-based professional development (e-pd) for effective teaching and leadership.* Retrieved February 20, 2009, from http://cnx.org/content/ m15069/1.1

International Society for Technology in Education (ISTE). (2001a). *Technology facilitation standards.* Retrieved February 5, 2009, from http://www.iste.org/Content/NavigationMenu/ NETS/ForTechnologyFacilitatorsandLeaders/Technology_Facilitation_Standards.htm

International Society for Technology in Education (ISTE). (2001b). *Technology leadership standards.* Retrieved February 5, 2009, from http://www.iste.org/Content/NavigationMenu/ NETS/ForTechnologyFacilitatorsandLeaders/Technology_Leadership_Standards.htm

Jackson, S. H., and Crawford, D. (2008). *Digital learners: How are they expanding the horizon of learning?* Retrieved February 20, 2009, from http://cnx.org/content/m17218/1.2

Marcovitz, D. (2008). Is educational technology shortening student attention spans? *Learning and Leading with Technology, 36*(1), 8.

National Council of Professors of Educational Administration (NCPEA). (2007). *Ethical administrators: Tools for the trade.* Retrieved February 20, 2009, from http://cnx.org/content/m14495/1.1/

Sawtelle, S. M. (2008). Does this really work? *Learning and Leading with Technology, 33*(8), 12–15.

Son, J. D. (2008). Is educational technology shortening student attention spans? *Learning and Leading with Technology, 36*(1), 8.

Chapter 4

DESIGNING AND USING ACADEMIC INFORMATION SYSTEMS

Providing Decision Support Systems for Educational Leaders

Stephen Lawton

Educators have long been masters of data collection. Student files are filled with grades, test data, vital statistics, absence records, and the like, and voluminous reports are sent from schools to districts, from districts to states, and from states to the federal government. Most record keeping is transaction based—recording what occurred—and executed in order to comply with legal obligations. No Child Left Behind and state accountability systems have increased the sophistication of data collection and management, but educational leaders still do not have real-time data at their fingertips that can be analyzed on a timely basis for administrative and learning decisions. Fortunately, recent developments in **student information systems**, which contain student data; **learning management systems**, which provide content and assessment to the learner; and **Internet-based applications**, application software available over the Internet, are beginning to address this problem; however, for these systems to fulfill their promises, several questions need to be addressed.

First, how should one design an information system so that it will satisfy not only regulatory requirements but also the needs of educators and policymakers at all levels—classroom, school, district, state, and nation? Second, what types of systems currently exist that meet some or all of the needs of decision makers? And third, how does one select and implement one or more applications in a cost-effective manner? In addressing these questions, it is important to recognize that individuals at each level of the educational system may have very different needs. Often, the temptation exists for those at each level to design a system for their own needs, ignoring the needs of those at other levels and assuming that the same information would be sufficient for all parties, regardless of their positions. To counter this myopic tendency, each of the questions is answered by first stating a principle that is then illustrated through vignettes and discussion that reflect a diversity of viewpoints and a variety of examples. The goal is to describe a single integrated system that can provide information appropriately tailored to a variety of end users.

In this chapter, a variety of terms are used to refer to information systems, including ***academic information system***, devoted to curriculum and learning data; *student information system*; *student management system*; *learning management system*; and so forth. Terms are not standardized in this field, but by using the term *academic information system* we wish to draw a contrast with a "business information system." An academic information system would include all information needed to administer the academic site of information, including curriculum, instructional protocols, student data, teacher data, school data, and academic standards. The goal is to bring the same level of sophistication to the administration of education by the use of information systems that other fields of endeavor such as retailing, accounting, and manufacturing have already achieved.

The following questions are addressed in this chapter:

- How can leaders use knowledge of observable characteristics, which is inherently more valid and reliable than knowledge based on inferences about unobservable characteristics?

- How can leaders sort the measurable characteristics that have precise and widely acceptable definitions from those that are difficult to define, difficult to measure, or unique to a situation?

- What can leaders do in the collection and maintenance of all data on students, schools, and district characteristics in an information system that facilitates real-time and longitudinal analyses?

- How can leaders ensure standards reflect the developmental stage and natural variability of individuals and groups?

System Design

Ralph Wheeler, principal of a K–6 school in the deserts of the Southwest, had some time to kill while waiting for the next speaker at an education conference. He took out his file on fifth-grade student test results. One list, which he had just received from the testing company, had students' names with the bench-mark test he had had the teachers administer the previous month. The second list was of the students' proficiency classification on the previous year's state test. Wanting to know if the two scores were related, he carefully drew a four-by-four table—not proficient, approaching proficiency, proficient, excelling—and began writing each student's name in the appropriate box. Jan was proficient on both, so he placed a tally mark in the box with "proficient" in both the row and the column heading. Carlos was "excelling" on the benchmark but "proficient" on the state test, so a tally went in the appropriate box. As the speaker began—it was an official from the state department—Ralph continued with his tally.

Ralph's "information system," two lists from data 1 month or 6 months old, a pencil, and the back of a conference program, was quite effective in its own way. As he placed each tally, he pictured the student in his mind's eye—Jan was a charming young lady who lived in a foster home not far from the school; Carlos was rather thin and a killer on the basketball court. Only tallies showed in the table, but his personal knowledge meant that anomalies or surprises were evident. Carlos was now testing higher than he had the previous year. Good for him! Jan was a reader who consumed books, a fact not really reflected in her "proficient" performance. However, the data were not really current, and he rarely had the time to actually do a cross-tab to see whether benchmark scores correlated with the state tests. He was pleased with the result, however, since 75% of all scores fell into boxes with the same headings on both tests.

When we think of educational information systems, we tend to think of data on individual students. Beyond the individual student, though, we may be interested in classroom-level, school-level, district-level, or state-level data. We might be interested in groups distinguished in other ways—boys versus girls, Hispanic versus Anglo versus Asian versus Black, or charter versus traditional public schools. Hence, before data are collected, a number of questions need to be asked to ensure that the data can be used in all the ways intended (Lawton, 2001). Each of these questions leads to a principle to be followed.

- What is the person or thing being measured?

- What are its characteristics?

- How are the characteristics defined and measured?

- Which characteristics should be measured? Why?

- What are the relationships among characteristics?

- Can a standard be set by which to judge a given value?

Once these critical questions are answered, then one can address the other questions noted above: What types of information systems exist, and how can an educational leader acquire and implement an appropriate system?

Who or What Is Being Measured?

Principle 1: It is necessary to be clear about who or what is being measured and to collect data for the smallest entity possible, such as the individual. Information about larger entities such as schools or districts can be derived from data collected at the most **elemental level**, a unit that is at the most disaggregated level.[1]

Ralph Wheeler tested his school's students and analyzed the data to learn if the benchmark test being used reliably related to the state test scores. If the scores were not related, then the benchmark was a waste of time. His superintendent, Dr. Elsie Macaray, had another issue: The percentage of proficient students in the district's largest schools consistently lagged that of the district's smallest schools. She wondered if school size was a problem. The district was thinking of consolidating small schools due to enrollment declines. But if the students got lost in the big schools and their performance declined, then such a step would be regressive. Ralph focused on the individual student; he took school size as a given. Elsie, in contrast, focused on the school and its performance.

Clearly identifying the entity being measured—an individual, a school, a classroom, a census tract, and so forth—is critical. Some characteristics are inherently attributable to individuals (e.g., test score), some to groups (e.g., ethnicity), and others to institutions (e.g., size). For groups and institutions, some characteristics are aggregated or derived from the characteristics of their members; for example, individual test scores for the members of a group may be averaged, or the number of teachers relative to students in a school may be expressed as a pupil-teacher ratio. While this observation may be obvious, it is in fact a critical and often overlooked distinction: It is important to know the unit of analysis for both the design of information systems and the analysis of data.

Collecting data on the most elemental unit is very important in creating an information system. One can imagine, for example, a series of spreadsheets with data for a school district. One spreadsheet might have data on all students in the district, with information on their birth dates, grades, and so forth. The second might have information on all employees of the district—teachers, administrators, support staff, and so forth. Characteristics recorded for them might include their birth date, first year of employment, and so forth. A third might have data for every location of the district, including schools, offices, maintenance facilities, and so forth. A fourth might have all equipment in the district, from school buses to computers. Ralph would need information only from the student spreadsheet for his analysis, but Elsie would need to aggregate data from the student spreadsheet to the school level in order to link student performance to school size.

Database construction is not easy, but the results can be powerful. For example, the equipment and student spreadsheets could be connected. One could link the school bus a student rides to his or her absence rate, the amount of time he or she spends logged on to computers to his or her math test scores, or the number of math courses teachers have completed to their students' math performance. The possibilities are endless but only practicable if the database has been designed to provide the information needed to answer such questions.

One phenomenon of importance in analyzing relationships is what is termed the **ecological fallacy**, the assumption that a relationship at one level of analysis holds at another level of analysis. The fallacy is the assumption that a relationship that exists at one level of aggregation (e.g., among individuals) automatically holds at another level of aggregation (e.g., at the school level). This fallacy is often overlooked, and it is assumed, say, that if student absences are related to reading test scores at the individual level, with those with low absenteeism outperforming those with high absenteeism, it will also be true at the school level; that is, schools where students average fewer days absent would automatically have higher average test scores than schools with higher rates of student absence. But if one thinks for a minute, the fallacy is obvious: What if all schools had exactly the same absence rates? In that case, there would be no variation in this variable at the school level, and hence there would necessarily be no correlation between absenteeism and test scores at the school level. Thus, the often tacit assumption that a relationship that exists at one level of aggregation automatically exists at other levels is not justified.

Complementing the first principle is an important corollary: Collect data just once for each trait of an entity. In a properly designed information system, if a piece of information such as a birth date or phone number is collected once, it should never be collected again. Redundant data collection (often leading to errors due to minor variations such as the spelling of a name) is one of the great inefficiencies that, with proper planning, can be avoided.

What Characteristics Are Being Measured?

*Principle 2: Knowledge of **observable characteristics**, or directly observable traits of individuals, is inherently more valid and reliable than knowledge based on inferences about **unobservable characteristics**, a synonym for inferred characteristics, since the definitions of observable characteristics are less open to question and are more easily verified.*

Any individual, school, or other entity has many more characteristics than can be recorded, some of which are fundamental and directly observable, some of which are fundamental but not directly observable, and yet others of which are derived from fundamental characteristics. For example, a person's height and weight can be observed and measured directly while the individual's body-mass index can be calculated from these. With the concern about student obesity and studies relating health to student performance, recording such information makes sense, along with other observable data related to student conduct such as tardies, absences, and suspensions.

One particular school characteristic, the dropout rate, can be derived from aggregated student data and is of obvious importance to schools. On a pragmatic level, students who drop out are like clients lost to a business—their revenue leaves with them. As well, schools and districts with high dropout rates may be perceived as ineffective. At the individual level, individuals who drop out of school tend to earn less during their lifetime than students of comparable ability who do not leave school before graduation; they are also less likely to be employed and more likely to be incarcerated.

Unobservable characteristics are also important, although often more difficult to measure reliably since they must be inferred from the behavior or appearance of individuals. Critical in education are mental characteristics such as reading or mathematical abilities. For example, while we generally infer students' mathematical problem-solving ability from their performance on exams or standardized tests, we cannot independently verify that they cannot solve problems because they do not do so. Bored or disinterested students often perform below their potential. There are techniques to boost the reliability and validity of inferred traits; student engagement is higher, for example, when assessments affect grades and graduation than when they do not.

In practice, both observable and **inferred characteristics**, unobservable traits one infers from a person's behavior, including responses on tests, are important. No one would seriously design an academic information system based only on observed behaviors, yet there is a tendency to overvalue assessments of knowledge. Deportment, for example, is as relevant to success in the workplace as academic performance.

How Are Characteristics Defined and Measured?

Principle 3: It is better to measure characteristics that have precise and widely acceptable definitions than those that are difficult to define, difficult to measure, or unique to a situation. Precise and valid measures that yield data that are comparable across different settings and times are required.

Although terms like *reading level*, *dropout rate*, *pupil-teacher ratio*, and so forth are spoken of daily by educational leaders, teachers, and the media, their precise definitions are rarely stated. There are two reasons for this lapse. First, the operational definitions needed to record data on a routine basis are often difficult to develop and sometimes surprisingly complex; second, different individuals and groups often disagree on the best definition, resulting in the use of a single term for what, in fact, are many different phenomena (Pring, 2004).

The question as to how dropout rates should be measured is a good example. In 2005, the National Governors Association signed a nonbinding compact defining graduation rates (the converse of dropout rates) by dividing the number of graduates in a given year by the number of first-time ninth graders 4 years earlier (Dillon, 2008). How might such a formula affect reported dropout rates? In North Carolina, the new formula would increase the dropout rate from 5% (an annual dropout rate) to 32% (a cohort rate); in New York the new formula would change the rate of 23% to 35%. Why states might be reluctant to adopt the new formula is evident: It would tend to make their school systems look less effective. Equally evident is the importance of agreeing upon and applying a single definition if the calculated rates are to be used for comparative purposes or to diagnose the need for and effectiveness of educational interventions.

The National Center for Education Statistics has created the National Forum on Education Statistics to assist in standardizing and promoting uniform definitions of key educational variables for use in all states. Its Attendance Task Force, which is to issue its final report in late 2009, is developing "an exhaustive and mutually-exclusive list of attendance codes to provide the basis for accurate comparisons between districts and states. The attendance codes will also categorize reasons for nonattendance" (National Center for Education Statistics [NCES], 2008a). The center's more inclusive PK–12 Data Model Task Force is developing a conceptual model for data definition and collection that includes the teaching, learning, and business functions of school districts. It too will be reporting in late 2009 and will work to disseminate its model on a national basis (NCES, 2008b).

Agreed-upon definitions of observable characteristics, attendance (vs. absence), and graduation (vs. dropout) rates have not yet been developed, but reaching agreement on the definition of most academic skills is even more challenging. Different learning theories can lead to different definitions and measurement of the mathematical skills of students. In addition, there is the challenge of measuring attitudinal, emotional, and other value-related traits, which are sensitive personally and politically. In practice, most states have adopted academic standards and developed tests to measure progress toward these standards. At the national level in the United States, there is the National Assessment of Educational Progress and a variety of standardized tests, including the SAT and ACT. For the foreseeable future, local educational leaders will be expected to maintain data on a number of academic measures mandated at the district, state, or national levels. However, questioning the validity and the reliability of these measures is necessary to ensure that they are appropriate for local students and for use in making sound decisions.

Why Measure a Characteristic?

Principle 4: Measurement should focus, first, on observable characteristics that are linked with desired outcomes—social, cultural, and economic—and, second, on inferred characteristics, including test scores, which are both less certain and more likely to be misused than observable traits.

As a practical matter, educational leaders must ensure that their organizations have the data—personal, financial, and academic—required by legislation and policies at the local, state, and federal levels. Data on the highly qualified status of teachers, proficiency levels of students, Title I expenditures, and so forth must all be captured and available for reports. The amount of data required solely for compliance purposes is surprisingly large.

At the same time, for decision-making purposes, it is helpful to have a broader perspective and employ a conceptual framework or theory that explains educational success. That is, having a clear vision for a school or district is as relevant to planning information systems and deciding what needs to be measured as it is to planning academic programs. If we agree that the ultimate aim is for all students to develop into individuals who have rich and productive lives in cultural, social, and economic terms, then a number of characteristics that should be measured can be identified. These characteristics are found in correlational and longitudinal studies that have sought to explain the personal well-being of students in terms of their personal characteristics and experiences in and out of school. That is, the outcomes of education are not just test scores but also include healthy living, social success, artistic skills, and employability. Issues such as childhood and adult obesity, high rates of incarceration, and failure to maintain employment are the negative complements of the desirable traits we hope to instill.

Variables associated with success (or failure) include observable characteristics such as absenteeism on both an individual and a school level. Lower rates of absenteeism are associated with higher levels of academic achievement, lower rates of dropping out, higher rates of employment, and lower rates of criminality. Deportment, as reported by teachers, is also a strong predictor of social and economic success, as are participation in school and cultural activities, having both parents at home, and family economic status.

While test scores are often used as measures of educational outcomes, they can also be used for formative purposes to assess the effectiveness of learning programs and student efforts, even in the early grades. Ideally, measurements should be used to diagnose the learning problems that students or schools may encounter so that these may be remedied rather than used for ratings that stigmatize schools.

So much data collection goes on in schools simply for reasons of compliance; often data are used to rate students and schools or as the basis for allocation of funds. In contrast, data collection should be guided by a broad understanding of educational processes and outcomes so that the data may be used to monitor progress and to diagnose the need for intervention. For this to occur, we must reach beyond the narrow list of outcomes mandated by state testing programs (Rothstein, Jacobsen, & Wilder, 2008).

What Are the Relationships Among Characteristics?

Principle 5: Data on students, schools, and district characteristics should be collected and maintained in an information system that facilitates real-time and longitudinal analyses. Such analyses can be used for assessing the need for intervention or for research on program effectiveness.

Knowledge of the relationships among characteristics is the heart of the process of using data to inform decision making. Is size of school related to student performance? Do teachers who earned their credentials through alternative certification programs such as Teach for America teach their students as effectively as teachers who are trained in traditional schools of education? The number of questions that might be asked of relationships that are relevant to educational decisions in the classroom, school, state, and nation is literally unlimited.

In schools and classrooms, accurate knowledge of relationships is critical, particularly of those relationships for which there is evidence of a causal relationship. Why is this important? Consider student absenteeism. As noted earlier, students who are often absent are less likely to have high test scores, more likely to drop out, and more likely to become unemployed than students who are rarely absent.[2] It is reasonable to conclude that being absent is one cause of academic difficulties. An information system can be designed with automatic alerts to teachers, counselors, and administrators when critical student measurements enter the danger zone, as would be the case if a student started skipping school on a regular basis. Such an alert could be followed by swift action to determine the reasons for the change in behavior and to plan an appropriate intervention. As well, regular follow-up could ensure the intervention was effective and, if it was not, lead to an alternative plan.

It is critical for the information system to be designed to provide easy access and easy investigation of relationships. Historically, most data are collected for transactional purposes and are not stored in a manner that allows them to be easily retrieved. To achieve the goal of using information to support decisions in an interactive environment, this will not suffice.

How Can Standards Be Set to Assess Data?

Principle 6: Standards should reflect the developmental stage and natural variability of individuals and groups. Standards should be tied both to external criteria reflecting the social, cultural, and economic goals of education and to the norms observed in other contexts.

Simply collecting and reporting data are not enough; judgments have to be made. What rate of absenteeism is acceptable, and what is not? What test scores indicate proficiency? These judgments should never be arbitrary, and to avoid this pitfall, one of two methods of setting standards for decisions is commonly used. One approach is to link the level of student performance with the performance levels observed for adults in their roles as employees and parents. For example, a certain level of literacy is needed to read a daily newspaper or complete a job application. Linking the notion of being "proficient" in reading to a test score achieved by individuals who can complete these tasks would be a valid approach. The second approach is simply to compare levels observed in one setting with those typically observed elsewhere in other schools, districts, and states. One might conclude that an observation in the top half of a desirable characteristic's distribution such as reading scores or graduation rates is acceptable. These two approaches to setting standards are typically referred to as "standard-based" and "norm-based," respectively.

Simply basing judgments on snapshots of the performance of one or more students or schools is insufficient. Education is primarily concerned with individual growth and development over time. Measures of growth are critical. But not all children develop physically, mentally, or behaviorally at the same rate. There is always dispersion or variability: Children differ in weight and height, as well as math and language test scores. One needs to track average rates of change for both individuals and groups of children as well as the extent of dispersion that is observed. Identifying **outliers**, or observations outside the expected range on a control chart, can be useful in identifying those with either exceptional performance or exceptional need. The same notion is valid when applied to schools; continuously assessing their characteristics allows one to use what quality experts refer to as **control charts**, which show whether an activity is proceeding within acceptable bounds, to spot unusual changes (Brassard & Ritter, 1994).

One critical set of external standards in the academic realm comprises those set by state boards of education. If properly designed, these standards reflect the education outcomes needed for an individual to fully participate in the social, political, and economic life of the community.

Applying the Principles

Applying the six principles developed in response to the six initial questions to the design of an information system used to support the decisions of educational leaders is relatively straightforward at a conceptual level. The system must identify who or what is being measured (Principle 1), include both observable and inferred characteristics (Principle 2), and so forth. The result is the conclusion that a successful academic information system must

1. include data collected from the most elemental entities possible, including all individual students, teachers, principals, officials, schools, and school districts, and store data in a set of **relational databases**, a collection of databases linked for data analysis, or incorporate a **data warehouse**, a repository of an organization's electronically recorded data;

2. facilitate the aggregation and analysis of data at different levels—classroom, program, school, district, and state;

3. include data on key characteristics with information collected frequently to ensure relevancy and currency;

4. incorporate online analytic capability and preset indicators to identify tolerable ranges of behavior that, when violated, issue immediate notification to appropriate individuals;

5. place primary emphasis on observable characteristics of demonstrated reliability and validity;

6. ensure all data on inferred characteristics are reasonably stable, reliable, and valid; and

7. provide access to all parties—parents, teachers, education officials, guidance staff—appropriate to their roles and in a manner that protects individual privacy via a user-friendly interface with analytic capabilities.

Moving from these descriptive criteria of what a system ought to look like to developing and implementing such a system is a far more difficult task. As the capabilities of computers have increased and the Internet has become a daily tool for communication, a number of educational systems and private developers have worked to realize the vision suggested. Initially, a number of stand-alone applications were developed; overtime, consolidation, and integration have meant that the potential of the vision is beginning to be realized in practice.

Existing Information Systems

Educational leaders have to contend with variety information systems serving state, local, school, and classroom activities. For the most part, actual decisions about the design of these systems are made by others, particularly directors of information technology or, in the case of learning management systems, directors of assessment or curriculum.[3] The purpose of this section is to review the state of the art in regard to national,[4] state, district/school, and classroom academic information systems.

State Level

The federal government, through No Child Left Behind (the Elementary and Secondary Education Act) and other programs, has promoted the development of **every student databases** at the state level to facilitate both the provision of timely and reliable educational statistics throughout the nation and the ability of state governments to effectively monitor their educational systems. At least 47 states "have data systems in place that include five . . . essential elements" including individual student identification codes and the ability to track a student's test score from one year to the next (Davis, 2008).

One example of a statewide educational information system is Arizona's Student Accountability Information System (SAIS), which the state initiated in 2000 and which became active in the 2002–2003 academic year. SAIS has two primary purposes: The first is to collect data pertinent to school funding. The state allocates approximately $3 billion per year to local education authorities (LEAs) based on student registration data. The second purpose of SAIS is to collect data on student achievement, which are used to determine schools' adequate yearly progress (AYP) and other measures of success (Arizona Department of Education, 2000). Data on students include student identification (a unique identification number for each student), demographics, student membership (e.g., enrollment in a particular school and LEA), student needs and related program enrollment (e.g., special education), and student achievement. Every data element is authorized by particular legislation or regulations (Arizona Department of Education, 2007), and the system is compliant with the Family Educational Rights and Privacy Act. The system is designed so that data collected by an LEA can be encrypted and transmitted over the Internet to a computer maintained by the Arizona Department of Education. Student management system (SMS) used by LEAs must include an automated interface to upload data to SAIS to facilitate the process.

SAIS is a complex system, and the guidelines for data collection and coding require considerable expertise if the data captured are to be valid and reliable. For example, the critical variable related to student enrollment, which is used in determining the size of state grants to LEAs, includes 17 different codes: for example, E1—first Arizona enrollment this school year for a student returning to this school, E2—first Arizona enrollment this school year for a student from another school in this district, E3—first Arizona enrollment this school year for a student from another district in Arizona, and so forth. There are also 14 codes for student *ending* enrollment in a school: for example, W1—transfer to another school, W2—withdrawal due to chronic illness, and so forth (Arizona Department of Education, 2006). Such detail is needed to track students in order to ensure that the proper LEA receives funding for the student. However, such data can also be used to track student mobility within and among districts, to study trends in reasons for withdrawal, to study trends in dropout rates, and so forth, all of which are important indicators related to student achievement in academics, employment, and adult life in general.[5]

In 2005–2006, the State of Arizona Office of the Auditor General (2006), as part of its periodic review of state agencies, made a number of recommendations to the Arizona Department of Education's information technology division to improve security and the quality of data on SAIS. At the time, 29% of responding LEAs expressed concern about data reliability. Student management systems (which are also referred to as student information systems, or SISs) used by LEAs come from over 20 providers, including private vendors and systems internally developed by LEAs. While some SMSs were more than 99% accurate, at least one had an error rate exceeding 30%. While the Arizona Department of Education has implemented security enhancements, budget constraints at the state level have delayed improvements in testing of SMS software packages. LEAs, therefore, are largely self-sufficient in their design and acquisition of information systems that are critical to the efficient and effective function of K–12 education in the state.[6]

District Level

School district student information systems do far more than collect data for state departments of education; they are multifaceted resources that include gradebooks for teachers; "**dashboards**," which summarize the performance of schools by reporting key indicators; individual education programs for special education students; and reports on school status in regard to AYP. Access to these resources over the Internet is on a "need-to-know" basis. That is, parents can view their children's grades, homework assignments, test scores, and school's performance but not the information on other children; teachers are able to view information for all of their students but not for students in other teachers' classrooms; principals are able to access data for all teachers, students, and staff in their school but not in other schools; and so forth.

While some school districts will develop their own student information systems for use in schools, many choose to purchase systems from vendors. The market for such systems is still developing. Many vendors began as small companies that developed administrative systems using proprietary software or Web-based interfaces for schools. Increasingly, small companies with popular SIS/SMS programs have amalgamated or been purchased by large corporations, and the programs have migrated to Internet-accessible portals run on servers provided by the corporations, so-called **applications service providers**, or firms providing Internet-based applications. The latter approach saves districts the expense of maintaining their own servers with staff who are responsible for installing updates, archiving data, and so forth. However, because systems are still being developed to be more inclusive in their scope and more easily tailored to local needs, their purchase is not as simple as purchasing a copy of Microsoft Office. Committing to a particular vendor's SIS is more a marriage than a friendship; the relationship is demanding and unflagging for both parties.

Table 4.1 lists a number of currently available SIS programs aimed at the school district and school levels. A number of these programs can be scaled up and have been adopted at the state level, either for use by the state department of education alone or for use by both the state and its local districts (e.g., Administrative Assistants, Ltd.'s eSIS).[7] However, most customers are at the district level. Some systems are popular among smaller districts and cannot be scaled up above a threshold such as 10,000 students. Others employ "industrial strength" database systems such as those provided by Oracle. Though more expensive, these can handle hundreds of thousands of students.

By way of example, one large secondary school district in Arizona adopted Infinite Campus. Its functions include administration (attendance, behavior, enrollment, health, etc.), curriculum (course catalog, graduation planning, online registration, scheduling, standards management, etc.), instruction (assessment, gradebook, individual learning plans, special education), schools services (fee management, food services, locker management), communications (e-mail, form letters, mobile interface, parent/student portal, parent/student/staff survey), and

Table 4.1	List of Student Information Systems and URLs of Vendors
Student Information System	*URL*
CIMS Student	http://www.hammer.net/
eSIS	http://www.aalsolutions.com/
¡Estudiante!	http://www.charterdata.com/charterdata/
WinOSCAR	http://www.oscarsoftware.com/
PowerSchool Premier	http://www.pearsonschoolsystems.com/
SASIxp (being discontinued)	http://www.pearsonschoolsystems.com/
Schoolmaster	http://www.schoolmaster.com/
SILK	http://www.exlogica.com/
SIRS & SchoolLogic	http://schoollogic.com/
STI	http://www.sti-k12.com/
GENESIS & GENESEA	http://www.edupoint-media.com/
Infinite Campus	http://www.infinitecampus.com/
SchoolMAX	http://www.schoolmax.net/
Skyward Student Management Suite	http://www.skyward.com/
eSchoolPLUS	http://www.sungard.com/publicsector/
Star_Base School Suite	http://www.centuryltd.com/
eDistrict Unified	http://www.edistrict.net/
openSIS	http://www.os4ed.com/opensis/
SIS K–12	http://www.sisk12.com/

reporting and analysis (integrated state reporting, SQL reporting, standard reporting, data analysis and visualization, and data warehousing).[8]

The data warehousing feature can be particularly important. Since not all information systems in a district may "speak" to one another directly or be part of a relational database, a district may choose to set up a data warehouse, which receives data from a variety of sources, both internal and external to the district. Typically, data warehouses are designed to support **online analytical processing (OLAP)**, real-time analysis of data, which provides very fast response times. Analyses similar to those provided by Excel's pivot tables (Figure 4.1) but referred

Figure 4.1	Example of Excel Pivot Table for Student Height, Weight, and Waist by Gender (Simulated Data)		
	Gender		
Data	Female	Male	Grand Total
Height	63.42	72.80	68.11
Weight	132.50	200.50	168.75
Waist	30.50	36.10	33.30
N	15	15	30

to as "OLAP cubes" can be carried out almost instantaneously. However, in the interests of efficiency, data on all variables may not be imported into the warehouse during weekly, monthly, or annual updates. In contrast, similar analyses done within relational databases may be slower since data need to be retrieved and aggregated, but all data elements in the system are available for analysis at any time. Both approaches facilitate cross-sectional, correlational, and experimental research that assesses the relative effectiveness of specific educational interventions (Hsieh et al., 2005).

While Infinite Campus provides a data warehouse option, there are in fact over 20 independent vendors of data warehouses for school districts (McIntire, 2004). Table 4.2 provides a list of some of the more popular products.

Table 4.2	List of Data Warehouse Systems and URLs of Vendors
Warehouse System	*URL*
eScholar Complete Data Warehouse	http://www.escholar.com/
IBM Insight at School	http://www.ibm.com/
SAS Enterprise Intelligence Suite for Education	http://www.sas.com/
SchoolNet Instructional Data Warehouse	http://www.schoolnet.com/
TetraData K–12 Performance Data Management Platform	http://www.tetradata.com/
Education Analytics	http://www.claraview.com/
Edustructures SIFWorks Platform	http://www.edustructures.com/
D3M—Data Driven Decision Making	http://www.espsg.com/
AssessMart	http://www.otised.com/
SKOPUS Data Warehouse Solution	http://www.pcgus.com
EDU Analytics & Dashboards	http://www.q3solutions.com/
InformationNOW	http://www.sti-k12.com/

A second example is provided by a rapidly growing K–12 district in Arizona that had long used Win School and Mac School from Chancery Software as its SIS before the latter company was purchased by Pearson Education, Inc. Now the district is transitioning from the earlier software to PowerSchool Premier, a new integrated SIS that Pearson has launched to replace not only Win and Mac School but also PowerSchool Pro and SASI. Pearson advises that PowerSchool Premier, "when paired with Pearson Inform, a data analysis and decision support tool . . . , give[s] you a dashboard view into student performance, enabling you to measure student progress and improve district performance."[9]

Classroom Level

Information systems for classroom use offer capabilities only dreamed of in the 1960s when the notion of instructional sequence and programmed learning was developed (e.g., Gagné, 1973). The new resources, variously referred to as dynamic assessment, instruction and practice, assessment and diagnostics, learning management, or educational management systems, provide teachers with online resources for assessing students' performance on state standards.[10] At their best, these systems provide diagnostic, formative assessments that can identify areas in which students need additional growth. They can also prescribe material including online presentations and practice exercises, reassessment using tested online questions, and predictions as to how well a student will perform on state assessments. While these systems provide both students and teachers with opportunities for individualization, they can also be used on a school-wide or district-wide basis for assessing student progress in a variety of programs using either online testing or student test booklets prepared automatically with the names and identification numbers of students. While online testing is intuitively preferable—no paper, no scanning of documents, no delays—the logistics of accommodating thousands of students on computers, including the dissemination of individualized passwords and high volumes of data transfer, make the paper option more practicable in many circumstances.

Two widely used learning management systems are ASPIRE Assessment System, developed by Northrop Grumman and now promoted by ASCD (formerly the Association for Supervision and Curriculum Development),[11] and Galileo developed by Assessment Technology, Inc.[12] Both are works in progress, but they already have an installed base serving hundreds of thousands of children.[13]

To complement its Infinite Campus SIS, the Arizona secondary school district previously discussed uses Galileo to perform formative assessments and benchmarking of students with tests that predict student success on the Arizona Instrument to Measure Standards. It has used Galileo to assess over 4,000 students in a physical education program. Using online testing employing an instrument developed by the teachers to meet state standards in physical education, it used the online testing module and item analysis of test questions. With data downloaded from Infinite Campus to Galileo, staff could conduct complex statistical analyses to look for differences among schools, types of students, types of teaching resources, and so forth.

This district also adopted an innovation supported by Galileo, eInstruction's Classroom Performance System (CPS), which uses **student response pads**—also known as "clickers," or handheld devices that record responses in **student response systems**, or information collection, analysis, and presentation systems used in real time in classroom settings to assess student comprehension—for students to respond to teachers' multiple-choice questions; data are compiled immediately on the teacher's computer and may be displayed on an LCD projector.[14] Questions may be developed by the teacher, along with lecture notes for projection to students, or they may be selected from Galileo's data bank of over 60,000 items. In either case, teachers may use the results to support dynamic teaching, with immediate clarification of materials with which students have difficulty by reteaching portions or by prescribing additional study. They may also upload quiz data into Galileo in order to add to information on the current level of understanding of students.

To validate the use of these technologies, faculty and staff in the district conducted a research project comparing the relative effectiveness of options such as interactive whiteboards,[15] online testing using Galileo, and a student response system (eInstruction's CPS) (Tracy, Hendrix Miner, Clark, & Ziker, 2008). They assessed the effects of various combinations of e-resources on student participation, engagement, and achievement. Among their conclusions were that students preferred online assessments to paper-and-pencil assessments by a ratio of 9:1, that a similar ratio liked using the student response system, that student engagement increased, and that in most cases students' growth in knowledge over a period of time was positive. Students particularly liked the student response system, with one commenting, "Feels like I'm text messaging my teacher." While this one study does not prove the cost-effectiveness of integrated educational information systems, it does demonstrate the feasibility of linking daily classroom data on student learning to the vast array of data collected within the school district.

No one academic system currently can satisfy all possible needs of states and school districts. A leader with a clear understanding of a system's possibilities, critical characteristics required for success, and available options is needed before action to adopt a system can be taken. The examples provided in this section illustrate that academic information systems offer many possibilities and that educational leaders should plan with the future—not the present—in mind.

Selection of an Academic Information System

The ideal academic information system is a vision, not a reality. In practice, educational leaders must begin by assessing where they are in terms of **decision support systems**, information systems with data and the analytical capability required for informed decisions, and where they wish to be. In most states, departments of education will have developed some type of SIS that imposes constraints on systems adopted at the district or school level. Local academic information systems must be compatible with the state system; that is, they must be able to upload data to the state system, unless it is an online system used directly by districts and schools.

There are at least six stages to the adoption of a new academic information system: (a) identify stakeholders and their role in the process, including students, teachers, community members, and board members; (b) determine district goals for the system; (c) define criteria for selection; (d) establish timelines and selection processes; (e) compare technology solutions; and (f) move from decision to planning for implementation, which would include careful attention to district and state purchasing procedures (e.g., requests for proposals).

For the fifth stage, conducting research on the experiences of other districts in similar situations is helpful. In some cases, professional consulting firms may have resources available that can be purchased that evaluate various systems' relative effectiveness (e.g., Rust, 2008). In other cases, state, university, or district consortiums[16] may have studies available. Also helpful is the Electronic Learning Assessment Resources (ELAR),[17] a project of the California Department of Education and a valuable resource that includes a facility for comparing the attributes of various resources and a guide for assessing the alignment of a district's goals with the attributes of potential resources. Table 4.3 presents an ELAR-derived comparison of two electronic assessment resources, Galileo K–12 Online and Pearson Benchmark. Although only a portion of the full comparison is presented, the table demonstrates the inclusive nature of Galileo with its links to state standards, dropout rates, AYP, and so forth, in contrast to the assessment-focused character of Pearson Benchmark. Pearson does have more inclusive products; this comparison is meant only to illustrate ELAR's functioning.

Table 4.3	Electronic Learning Assessment Resource (ELAR) Comparison of Two Dynamic Assessment Systems[18]				

● = Feature Part of ELAR   ⊘ = Feature Not Part of ELAR   🔍 = Major Focus

ELAR Title and Publisher	Galileo K–12 Online (Assessment Technology, Inc.)		Pearson Benchmark (Pearson Assessments)	
ELAR Features	Contains Feature	Major Focus	Contains Feature	Major Focus
A. Sources of student academic assessment data				
1. State-administered norm-referenced test. (CAT/6)	●	🔍	⊘	
2. California Standards Test (CST)	●	🔍	⊘	
3. California High School Exit Exam (CAHSEE)	●	🔍	⊘	
4. California English Language Development Test (CELDT)	●	🔍	⊘	
5. School or district performance tests	●	🔍	●	🔍
6. Assessments incorporated in the district- or school-adopted textbooks	●		●	
7. Student grades	●	🔍	⊘	
B. Sources of relevant background data that could impact achievement				
1. Student ethnicity	●	🔍	●	
2. Student gender	●	🔍	●	
3. Socioeconomic background of students (free and reduced lunch, etc.)	●	🔍	●	
4. Dropout rates and/or attendance data	●	🔍	⊘	
5. Student participation in special programs (Title I, Sp. Ed., GATE, ELL, etc.)	●	🔍	●	
6. Adequate yearly progress (AYP) rating for the school/district	●	🔍	●	

Source: Copyright © California Department of Public Education. Reprinted with permission.

One particular characteristic education leaders should insist upon in an SIS is certification by the **Schools Interoperability Framework (SIF) Association**:

> The SIF Association is a non-profit membership organization whose members include over 1400 software vendors, school districts, state departments of education and other organizations active in primary and secondary (PK–12) markets. These organizations have come together to create a set of rules and definitions which enable software programs from different companies to share information. This set of platform-independent, vendor-neutral rules and definitions is called the SIF Implementation Specification. The SIF Specification makes it possible for programs within a school or district to share data without any additional programming and without requiring each vendor to learn and support the intricacies of other vendors' applications.[19]

Also critical are planning for implementation, installation and implementation, and staff development to ensure users have the expertise needed to fully use the potential of contemporary academic information systems. Other chapters in this book deal with these issues.

Conclusions

A reader's response to the question "What's your Achilles' heel?" appeared in the online publication *School CIO: Strategies for K–12 Technology Leaders*[20]:

> I spent the last three years . . . assisting educators as they struggle to understand and implement a vision of data-driven decision making (D3M). . . . Misconceptions abound regarding how to successfully approach such an important and intrinsically complex initiative. The complexity arises not from information technology, but from the expectation that D3M offers an off-the-shelf solution to low student achievement. . . .
>
> Recently I was on the verge of helping a district begin their D3M trek when we came to an abrupt halt. The stop sign was erected by the district's instructional and administrative leaders, not the IT [information technology] organization. . . . IT was not able to allay fears that the "right" data had been identified and was available.
>
> The hurdle facing educators . . . is their own need to acquire knowledge of performance management principles before they are asked to define their requirements for data and technology-based decision support tools. As usual, professional development should come first before the first brick of a data warehouse is laid.

Our emphasis on six key principles and seven characteristics of good academic information systems addresses some of the issues raised by this respondent. We consider data on observable characteristics that can be verified and related to important educational outcomes to be the "right" data. Equally important, though, is what one does with the data and analyses. Implicit throughout this chapter are theories of school improvement and student learning. That is, it is assumed that there are cause-effect relationships among characteristics and that making and evaluating changes is a good approach to assisting both schools and students.

The experience of one school-level data coach illustrates this pragmatic approach to improvement. Using data from Galileo, he discovered that benchmark testing for one group of students—African Americans—did not successfully predict the groups' performance on statewide tests; the average score for the group was lower than predicted. Drilling down on attendance data, he discovered several members of the group had been suspended several times, including the period during which benchmarking tests were given. However, they participated in the statewide tests, and their low performance dragged down the group's performance. In response, the school eliminated out-of-school suspensions and substituted in-school suspensions. These actions would ensure, at the very least, that the students would be available to take benchmark as well as statewide tests, ensuring more accurate prediction. Hopefully, with the in-school suspension program, which incorporates time with tutors, these students' performance would improve as well.[21]

While well-designed and -implemented academic information systems will not prescribe interventions, they can be expanded to include a knowledge base of options to be considered. At the same time, if constructed in a flexible manner, data could be used to assess the impact of the intervention selected. Of course, changing a student's attitude about school, even improving the student's life and future success, might not show up in state test scores, which have become the central focus of school evaluation. We tend to prefer evidence based on observable data like school attendance, absences, and disciplinary referrals. Changes in these behaviors are necessary if not sufficient conditions for improving school academic performance and are related to being successful as parents, community members, and employees, which are the ultimate goals of education.

Key Principles for Leaders to Know

When designing and selecting academic information systems,

- be clear about who or what is being measured and that data are collected for the most elemental entity possible;

- be aware that knowledge of observable characteristics is inherently more valid and reliable than knowledge based on inferences about unobservable characteristics;

- measure characteristics that have precise and widely acceptable definitions rather than those that are difficult to define, difficult to measure, or unique to a situation;

- focus measurement, first, on observable characteristics that are linked with desired outcomes—social, cultural, and economic—and, second, on inferred characteristics, including test scores;

- collect and maintain all data on students, schools, and district characteristics in an information system that facilitates real-time and longitudinal analyses; and

- ensure standards reflect the developmental stage and natural variability of individuals and groups.

CASE STUDY 4.1 | Developing Student Information Systems

In your role as academic curriculum director at a school district's sole high school, you've been appointed to a district committee to select or develop a new student information system for the district. The existing system was developed internally with consultation from a small consulting firm that has ceased operations. The district chief information officer (CIO) insists she can continue maintaining and developing the current system, which lacks a portal for teachers and parents, which has only 10 reports that are run once each semester, and which runs on Windows XP installed on a computer in her office. She insists new systems are not worth the money, but she has not provided information on costs and capabilities of systems available from vendors.

Discussion: What five questions would you put to the district CIO at the first meeting of the SIS committee? Explain why you have selected each of these questions in terms of their importance.

Activity: Based on the questions developed in the discussion, the committee decided you should prepare a list of options for the district in terms of the purchase of a new SIS. How would you approach this task? Outline your steps and the resources (especially online resources) you would draw upon. How would you present your report to the committee? Why? (Note: Do not do a report; just describe the process.)

CASE STUDY 4.2 | Academic Information Systems and Data Usage Issues

Focus on your experience with academic information systems in your educational setting and the ways you work with data.

Discussion: Discuss the following:

1. How do I make use of data from the system?
2. How do I analyze the data?
3. How have my analyses affected my behavior and with what results?
4. How could I make better use of the information system?
5. What types of professional development would I need to improve my usage?

Activity: Now, reflect on your experience with academic information systems. List the changes in the system you would recommend. Design a plan on how to proceed to bring these changes to reality.

Web Resources

Administrative Assistants, Ltd. (http://www.aalsolutions.com/), is a major provider of student information systems.

The **Arizona Student Accountability Information System (SAIS)** (http://www.ade.az.gov/sais/) is an example of a state-level student information system.

ASCD ASPIRE (http://www.ascd.org/programs/ASPIRE_Assessment_System.aspx) is an example of a state-of-the-art assessment system.

Assessment Technology, Inc. (http://www.ati-online.com/), is the provider of Galileo, an online instructional management and assessment system.

The **California Learning Resource Network** (http://www.clrn.org/home/about.cfm), the home of ELAR, is an excellent resource for researching different types of online systems for academic, instructional, and administrative information systems.

The **Education Data Exchange Network** (http://www.ed.gov/about/reports/annual/2005report/2h/edlite-2h2-plans.html) is the current mode of creating a national data resource in education.

The **Educational Pipeline** (http://www.highereducation.org/reports/pipeline/) facilitates the tracking of students as they move through the educational system.

eInstruction (http://www.einstruction.com/) is the source of a leading student response system that provides immediate feedback on student learning.

Electronic Learning Assessment Resources (http://www.clrn.org/elar) is an excellent resource for researching different types of online systems for academic, instructional, and administrative information systems.

Infinite Campus (http://www.infinitecampus.com/pages/product_menu/district-edition .php) is a major provider of online academic information systems for schools and districts.

The **National Center for Education Statistics** (http://nces.ed.gov) is the key source of statistics on education in the United States.

PowerSchool (from Pearson; http://www.pearsonschoolsystems.com/products/powerschool/) is a leading provider of student information and assessment systems to schools and school districts.

School CIO: Strategies for K–12 Technology Leaders (http://www.schoolcio.com/) is a site for IT professionals and chief information officers in schools and educational institutions.

The **Schools Interoperability Framework Association** (http://www.sifinfo.org/general-overview.asp) is the leading group for facilitating the development of standards for school-related software to ensure software packages can "talk" to one another.

SmartBoards (http://www.smartboards.com/) is a provider of interactive whiteboards for instruction.

Wireless Generation (http://www.wirelessgeneration.com) is a firm focused on moving educational technology from wires to wireless communication.

References

Arizona Department of Education. (2000, December). *SAIS: Student data base system.* Retrieved November 2, 2008, from http://www.ade.az.gov/sais/Downloads/PresentationForAASBO.pdf

Arizona Department of Education. (2006, December 4). *Student database transaction requirements.* Retrieved November 2, 2008, from http://www.ade.az.gov/sais/codevalues/DataTransaction Code Values_FY07.doc

Arizona Department of Education. (2007, June 7). *SAIS collection authorities.* Retrieved November 2, 2008, from http://www.ade.az.gov/sais/downloads/saiscollectionauthorities.doc

Bosworth, K., & Ford, L. (2005, April 11–15). *Implementing NCLB provisions in Arizona: An evaluation of fifteen Alternative-to-Suspension Programs.* AERA Annual Conference, Montreal, Quebec, Canada.

Brassard, M., & Ritter, D. (1994). *The memory jogger II: A pocket guide of tools for continuous improvement and effective planning.* Methuen, MA: GOAL/QPC.

Davis, M. R. (2008, January 23). *Finding your way in a data-driven world.* Retrieved August 6, 2009, from http://www.edweek.org/dd/articles/2008/01/23/3data.h01.html

Dillon, S. (2008, April 1). *U.S. to require states to use a single school dropout formula.* Retrieved August 5, 2009, from http://www.nytimes.com/2008/04/01/education/01child.html?scp=1& sq=U.S.%20to%20require%20states%20to%20use%20a%20single%20school%20dropout% 20formula&st=cse

Gagné, R. M. (1973). Learning and instructional sequence. *Review of Research in Education, 1*(1), 3–33.

Hsieh, P., Acee, T., Chung, W., Hsieh, Y., Kim, H., Thomas, G., et al. (2005). Is educational intervention research on the decline? *Journal of Educational Psychology, 97*(4), 523–529.

Lawton, S. B. (2001, June). The ideal educational information system: Is it possible . . . or desirable? *School Business Affairs, 67*(6), 15–18.

Maxwell, L. A. (2008, July 22). *70 districts compare practices on collecting, analyzing data.* Retrieved August 25, 2009, from http://www.edweek.org/login.html?source=http://www .edweek.org/ew/articles/2008/07/30/44apqc.h27.html&destination=http://www.edweek.org/ew/ articles/2008/07/30/44apqc.h27.html&levelId=2100

McIntire, T. (2004, August 16). *Eight buying tips: Data warehouses.* Retrieved August 26, 2008, from http://www.techlearning.com/story/showArticle.php?articleID=26806926

Medina, J. (2008, October 20). *Report cites chronic absenteeism in city schools.* Retrieved August 25, 2009, from http://www.nytimes.com/2008/10/21/nyregion/21attend.html?scp=1&sq=Report% 20cites%20chronic%20absenteeism%20in%20city%20schools&st=cse

National Center for Education Statistics (NCES). (2008a). *National Forum on Education Statistics: Attendance Task Force.* Retrieved September 18, 2008, from http://nces.ed.gov/forum/ attendance.asp

National Center for Education Statistics (NCES). (2008b). *National Forum on Education Statistics: PK–12 Data Model Task Force.* Retrieved September 18, 2008, from http://nces.ed.gov/forum/ pk12_data_model.asp

Pring, R. (2004). *Philosophy of educational research* (2nd ed.). London: Continuum International Publishing Group.

Rothstein, R., Jacobsen, R., & Wilder, T. (2008). *Grading education: Getting accountability right.* Washington, DC and New York: Economic Policy Institute and Teachers College Press.

Rust, B. (2008). *MarketScope for K–12 student information systems in the United States* [ID No. G00161247]. Stamford, CT: Gartner, Inc.

State of Arizona Office of the Auditor General. (2006). *Arizona Department of Education– Information Management* [Report No. 06–07]. Retrieved August 25, 2009, from http://www .auditorgen.state.az.us/Reports/State_Agencies/Agencies/Education_Department_of/Performance/ 06-07/pa06-07.htm

Tracy, B., Hendrix, J., Miner, K., Clark, T. & Ziker, C. (2008). *The impact of technology on the participation, engagement, and achievement of high school students.* Glendale, AZ: Glendale Union High School District.

Walker, M. (2008, October 23). *Parents can keep high-tech tabs on Des Moines students.* Retrieved November 9, 2008, from http://www.desmoinesregister.com/article/20081023/NEWS02/ 810230383

Notes

1. An analogy from science might be helpful. The periodic chart of the elements lists each element: hydrogen, helium, lithium, and so forth. Atoms of elements combine to form molecules. For educational databases basic, elemental, or atomic entities normally would be individuals. Data on individuals can be aggregated to yield a characteristic of a larger unit, such as a classroom or school.

2. Medina (2008) states, "More than 90,000 of New York City's elementary school students— roughly 20 percent—missed at least a month of classes during the last school year." The problem is worst in poor and minority communities, and it "puts [these] students behind their middle-class peers."

3. Information technology is a rapidly changing field, and even by the time this chapter is published, the field will have changed. In particular, the rapid adoption of smart phones, including both BlackBerrys and iPhones, and Web-based access on other mobile devices are likely to play an increasing role in accessing data. Information on the performance of individual students, teachers, and schools likely will be at leaders' fingertips (or thumbs) regardless of time of day or location. See, for example, products and services from Wireless Generation at http://www.wireless generation.com.

4. For states to forward data to the U.S. Department of Education there is the Education Data Exchange Network (EDEN). See http://www.ed.gov/about/reports/annual/2005report/2h/edlite-2h2-plans.html. See also, on the Educational Pipeline, http://www.higheredinfo.org/analyses/Pipeline%20Article.pdf.

5. Student mobility is a major problem for LEAs. Students leave without notice, register in new schools in other districts with different names, move out of state, and so forth. Often, a school may not know a student has enrolled in a new school until, weeks after the event, a request for an academic file is received. Given that most states now assign "every student" numbers, it would appear possible to create a national "every student" number.

6. As part of the American Recovery and Reinvestment Act (2009), the U.S. federal government has allocated $250 million to assist states with improving their student information systems.

7. See http://www.aalsolutions.com/.

8. Infinite Campus (http://www.infinitecampus.com/pages/product_menu/district-edition.php) also comes in a state edition.

9. See http://www.pearsonschoolsystems.com/products/powerschool/. Home access to such portals provides parents with the ability to track their children's progress, download assignments, and e-mail teachers. Anecdotal reports indicate some parents may be persistent and overly anxious, creating problems for teachers and administrators. These "helicopter" parents may overstep proper bounds. See http://en.wikipedia.org/wiki/Helicopter_parent and Walker (2008).

10. California's Electronic Learning Assessment Resources classifies data management resources in five categories: data warehouse, data analysis and reporting system, curriculum management system, instruction and practice system, and assessment and diagnostic system. See http://www.clrn.org/elar.

11. See http://www.ascd.org/programs/ASPIRE_Assessment_System.aspx.

12. See http://www.ati-online.com/.

13. Other providers include CTB/McGraw-Hill (http://www.CTB.com), Datawise, Inc. (http://www.datawise-ed.com), Wireless Generation (http://www.wirelessgeneration.com), DataDirector (http://www.datadirector.com/), LearningStation (http://www.learningstation.com), and Provost Academy (http://www.provostsystems.com/). Also see Table 4.2.

14. See http://www.einstruction.com/.

15. See, for example, http://www.smartboards.com/.

16. For example, the Houston, Texas-based nonprofit APQC (formerly the American Productivity and Quality Center) partnered with school districts to use its benchmarking process to collect information about what types of data the districts collected, the software programs they used to manage and analyze data, and how much time they spend weekly analyzing data at the district, school, and classroom levels. See Maxwell (2008).

17. See http://www.clrn.org/home/ and http://www.clrn.org/elar/findRightElar.cfm.

18. Shown in Figure 4.1 is a partial reproduction of a table resulting from a search using http://www.clrn.org/elar/search.cfm.

19. See http://www.sifinfo.org/general-overview.asp.

20. See http://www.schoolcio.com/shared/printableArticle.php?articleID=192203398.

21. Other theories of school change and learning would suggest other approaches for intervention. For example, Bosworth and Ford (2005) evaluated alternatives to suspension that involved different types of community service and found these alternatives helped change student behavior. Invariably, there are multiple interventions that may be devised to address a given problem or different definitions of an issue. Academic information systems support decisions; they do not make them.

PART II

Leadership Teaching and Learning

In Part II, the book provides depth for issues of teaching and learning using technology. **Chapter 5: Leading Adult Learners** outlines various styles of the adult learner. **Chapter 6: Planning, Designing, Implementing, and Evaluating Technology** continues the theme by moving to the school site to plan, design, and implement technology solutions. **Chapter 7: Web 2.0 Learning Environments in Distance Learning** and **Chapter 8: Design of Creative Online Learning Spaces** expand the teaching and learning perspective beyond the school site, both geographically and into cyberspace.

Chapter 5

LEADING ADULT LEARNERS

Preparing Future Leaders and Professional Development of Those They Lead

Rosemary Papa and Jessica Papa

Two key questions begin this chapter: What are the changing dynamics for faculty teaching today that prospective educational leaders need to know? And, what are the primary challenges prospective administrators face in professional development and optimally managing teachers who are using technology in their respective settings? It is critical for those faculty instructing prospective educational leaders to understand the adult learner to maximize teaching and learning. In this chapter **adult learning theories**, or theories about how adults learn, and how we engage **adult learners**, or adults in a learning environment, set the stage for managing and using technology in subsequent chapters.

Learning is the acquisition of knowledge through experiences with the result of a change in behavior. Learning theories focus on how one learns. Learning theories originated with a focus first on the study of children and adolescents and more recently on adult learning. It is common today to think of learning as being lifelong: from the cradle to the grave. The maze of learning theories provides no single answer to define how one learns but does permit a substantial perspective to the process of learning. Some learning theories are more appropriate to **adult learning and pedagogy**, or teaching strategies for how adults learn.

The following questions are addressed in this chapter:

- What can leaders do to acknowledge the adult learner's motivation and interests?

- How can leaders learn to mentor the adult learner?

- How can leaders give professional development choices in planning training activities for optimal learning experiences?

- How can leaders provide problem-centered activities for professional training activities?

- How can leaders lead using different approaches and strategies?

Learners of All Ages

Attention and **motivation**—the degree with which the learner approaches learning—and how we use these are critical to understanding how we approach classroom experiences for our learners. If we know how a learner approaches the acquisition of knowledge, then we can arrange classroom strategies that will enhance his or her learning. Various theories focus on the motivations of the learner: Are they internal or external in their locus of control? What motivates a person to want to learn? External motivation in the early years of schooling requires children in most countries to attend school, so the motivation to be there is one of first family approval and expectation and then legal requirement. As one ages through middle and high school to college, the motivation to attend schooling unto itself becomes the motivation. Externally, the factor may be to get a well-paying job or gain respect from one's family. Internally, one may seek greater knowledge because he or she is inquisitive and curious. It can also be a combination of both external and internal factors. As is the case with children who begin life with their ever-expanding curiosity to learn about the world, this individual nature to learn reemerges with passion when adults are no longer required to attend school yet choose to keep learning. So, now that we have them in their seats, how do we keep their attention?

Often in the learning cycle, because students are required to be in front of us during elementary and middle school or until high school, we as educational leaders often fail to see the student as a complex learner different from the other students. We tend to focus on delivering the content usually following the latest fad in education tied to knowledge standards established by our country's policymakers, which influences the textbooks we use. In adult education, the similar conundrum may also exist.

How we then approach the years from high school to the lifelong learner becomes quite complex, both from a social-political perspective and from a learning theory choice perspective. With no clear road map of acceptance by research and theory, we hope to persuade the reader that strategies from a variety of learning perspectives should be of benefit to the educational leader who seeks to be the best he or she can be. Of course, from our perspective, the best educational leader is one with a focus on managing, leading, and teaching the adult learner as an individual. As the saying goes, "When the learner stops being attentive, I am no longer leading or teaching."

Is the 18- to 23-year-old similar to the 30- to 40-year-old or the 50- to 60-year-old? Common sense tells us that life experience greatly influences our motivation, our ability to learn, and the attention we choose to give learning. From the time we exit mandatory schooling and transition to learning that we choose, such as continuing into college or working at a job we are happy with, we begin adult learning. Adult learning is learning done on a continuum from the adolescent-adult stage forward.

Adult Learning Theories

How we learn and help others learn is the subcontext for this chapter. Some—à la Bandura (1986), Bloom (1965), Brown (1990), Dewey (1938), and Glasser (1990)—tie learning to personal motivators. Others—à la Gardner (1983, 1999a, 1999b, 2006) and Guilford (1950)—focus on innate individual differences. And for others **behaviorism or learning as cognitive constructivism**, in which learners construct knowledge based on previous knowledge, is of prime importance to defining learning. Learning-based theories describe the learner from a variety of key points. Presented in Table 5.1 are the learning theories by category listed by the key researcher and the approximate time his or her theories were developed.

Table 5.1 Learning Theories and Timeline of Theory Development
Behaviorism
Watson (1900–1930) and Skinner's (1940–1980) Behaviorism: The study of objective behavior and learning as a response to positive or negative stimuli.
Cognitive Constructivism
Freud (1880+) and Erikson (1959+): Stages of the life cycle included adult development beyond adolescence. Erikson took Freud's work that ended with adolescence and developed theory that reached to old age.
Piaget and Cognitive Constructivism (1920+): Four stages of development: Formal Operations, the final stage (ages 11–15), assumes this age reaches adult cognition and conceptual reasoning abilities. Knowledge is constructed through individual experiences.
Bruner (1950+): A founding father of constructivism found that learners construct ideas based on previously learned knowledge.

(Continued)

Table 5.1	(Continued)

Bloom's Taxonomy of Educational Objectives (1965+): Learning occurs both cognitively (knowledge) and affectively (beliefs, values, and attitudes).

Lave (1990+) and Wenger's (1999+) Communities of Practice: Situated learning and engagement in communities of practice for adults are the focus of their theory.

Social Constructivism

Vygotsky and Social Cognition (1920+): Development of the individual occurs first on a social level and later on an individual level. The potential for development occurs when children participate in social behavior. This is called the Zone of Proximal Development.

Bandura's Observational Learning (1960+): Operant view of learning that comprises four steps: attention, retention, reproduction, and motivation.

Humanism

Maslow (1930+): Experiential learning with an emphasis on choice, creativity, values, self-realization, and dignity.

Rogers (1960+): Inclusion of feelings and emotions in learning. Learning occurs at a personal level.

Motivation

Dewey (1930+): Experiential learning leads us to more learning.

Glasser Control Theory (1990+): The theory of motivation and what a person wants most at any given time. Choice is at the heart of this theory.

Brown Locus of Control (LOC) (1980+): Internal and external LOC factors that influence how we view ourselves and others.

Gilligan (1980+): Feminist voice given to adult learning and cognition.

Levinson (1970+): Male and female adult life stages are identified.

Intelligence

Guilford's Structure of Intellect (1950–1980): The intellect comprises operations, content, and products, with a focus on creative abilities.

Gardner's Multiple Intelligences (1980+): Individuals possess distinct forms of intelligence in varying degrees.

Adult Learning and Pedagogy

Knowles (1970+): Founding father of adult learning views learning as cyclical: Experience leads to reflection, which leads to action, which leads to concrete reflection, and so on. Andragogy refers to adult learning while pedagogy focuses on children.

Cronbach and Snow Attitude Treatment Interaction (1970+): Learning is best achieved when strategies are geared directly to the learner's specific abilities.

Cross (1970+): Characteristics of Adults as Learners (CAL) model views learning as lifelong.

Freire (1970+): The critical analysis of experience and acting on that analysis lead to more learning.

Behaviorism

Beginning with Behaviorism, Watson (1928) and subsequently the famous B. F. Skinner (1974) believed that behaviorism was the key to learning through the use of positive or negative stimuli. Behaviorism is limited in its range for addressing adult leaner needs as it does not consider cognitive and affective processes.

Cognitive Constructivism

Numerous perspectives have contributed to **cognitive constructivism**, or the construction of knowledge based on previous knowledge. Piaget (1970) viewed cognitive construction as having four stages. For the purposes of this textbook, we are focused on Stage 4, Formal Operations for ages 11 to 15, which assumes that this age reaches adult cognition and conceptual reasoning abilities. Knowledge from this point forward is constructed through individual experiences. Because of his work with children, some consider Piaget the inventor of the field of cognitive development (Gardner, 2006). Criticism of Piaget has been found in his lack of acknowledging individual differences and in minimizing cultural and social factors and ignoring motivational factors.

Bruner is considered to have been one of the original thinkers in cognitive constructivism. Learning is an active process. Learners construct new ideas based on their existing knowledge. Bruner (1983) stated, "Knowing how something is put together is worth a thousand facts about it" (p. 183).

Parallel to Piaget and Bruner, personality theory from the mid-1950s in adult research began to take the view that all learning does not end with adolescence. In personality theory, Erik Erikson's eight stages of life expanded Freud's view of five stages and challenged the notion that development ended with adolescence. Erikson (1959, 1968) took Freud's original five stages and expanded them to eight to include adult development. These additional stages are Stage 6—young adult (late teens through 20s), characterized by intimacy versus isolation, seeking partners and friends; Stage 7—middle adult (30s to 50s), characterized by generativity versus self-absorption, seeking a meaningful home and workmates; and Stage 8—old adult (60s and beyond), characterized by integrity versus despair.

Bloom's (1965) contribution to learning was to define the cognitive (knowledge) domain in unison with the affective (attitudes, beliefs, values) domain. His taxonomy for educational objectives is widely used today for developing and helping students categorize test questions.

Lave and Wenger (1991) have defined their learning research as adult learning theory. They have recently identified that as we grow older engaging in communities of practice increases our ability to analyze our experiences. They call this intentional reflection. This is a commonly used process today in adult learning.

Social Constructivism

For Vygotsky (1978), learner development occurs first at the social level and later on an individual level. The idea of **social constructivism**, further explored in Chapter 7, is defined as a theory that supports co-construction of knowledge, which is a more student-centered approach to learning. Vygotsky's Zone of Proximal Development is the potential for learning when children participate in social behavior. His work, which began in the 1920s, was embraced during the later part of the 20th century for its contribution to cultural understanding in how we learn.

Approaching it from another perspective, Bandura (1986) puts motivation at the heart of the observational learning theory. His four steps are attention, retention, reproduction, and motivation.

Humanism

Humanist learning theory—or **humanism**, the idea that learning occurs at the personal level—focuses on the emotional and affective aspects of the learner. Maslow's (1943) research was centered on the need for experiential learning. Experiential learning emphasized one's ability to choose and encouraged creativity, values, and self-realization. Personal dignity in learning was at the heart of this theory. Rogers (2002, 2004) also believed that learning should be at the personal level. Learning should include one's feelings and emotions along with the cognitive. Overemphasis of the cognitive was not conducive to good learning.

Motivation

Motivation impacts learning in interesting ways. Glasser's (1990) Control Theory is a theory of motivation that ties learning to what a person wants most at any given time. Brown (1990; Brown & Marcoulides, 1996) identifies the internal or external motivators that drive a person's locus of control. This locus of control impacts how a person attributes success or failure and, thus, one's motivation to learn. Dewey's (1938) theory found experiential learning leads us to more learning. Experiential learning motivates us to learn. Rogers (2004) stated that motivation is the single most important factor for the learner: "Unless you are motivated you will not and cannot learn" (p. 15).

Adult learning combined with personality psychology continued to expand during the late 1970s and 1980s. Levinson's (1978) seminal work *The Seasons of a Man's Life* and Carol Gilligan's (1982) *In a Different Voice* brought further attention to adulthood relative to age, gender, and culture. Female development up to this time had been researched as though complete adult development was inaccessible to the female by virtue of gender characteristics. These studies countered that thinking and elevated that girls do learn differently than boys.

Intelligence

Guilford (1950) believed that the intellect comprised operations, content, and products. His interest was creativity and how one develops this ability.

Creativity and how we engage the learner are supported by Gardner's (1983) theory of multiple intelligence. He has to date identified nine intelligences:

- Verbal/Linguistic: reading, writing, speaking, and listening
- Logical/Mathematical: working with numbers and abstract patterns
- Visual/Spatial: working with images, mind mapping, visualizing, drawing
- Musical/Rhythmic: using rhythm, melody, patterned sound, song, rap, dance
- Bodily/Kinesthetic: processing information through touch, movement, dramatics
- Interpersonal: sharing, cooperating, interviewing, relating
- Intrapersonal: working alone, self-paced instruction, individualized projects
- Naturalist: spending time outdoors, sorting, classifying, noticing patterns
- Existentialist: wondering people, philosophical, seeking the bigger picture

Gardner's (1983, 1999a, 1999b, 2006) work continues to redefine the learner and what attributes he has identified have led to specific learner strategies. Influences from Bruner and Piaget are found in Gardner's work.

Adult Learning and Pedagogy

The "founding father of adult learning" title is often attributed to Knowles. Knowles (1990) uses the term *andragogy* for adult learning distinguished from *pedagogy,* which is children based. Knowles suggested an endpoint to adulthood, as noted by Rogers (2002), that occurs when individuals perceive themselves to be essentially self-directing. Knowles (1990) identified the following principles:

- Adults need to participate: plan and evaluate their instruction.
- Experiential learning activities should be provided.
- Topics must be relevant to their jobs or personal life.

Learning for adults should be problem centered versus content oriented.

Cronbach and Snow (1977) identified attitude at the heart of their theory. Learning, they said, is best achieved when strategies are geared directly to the learner's specific abilities. Their theory is called Attitude Treatment Interaction.

Adult learning contains critical reflection characteristics that require analysis for the learner (Freire, 1972) and are action based for the learner (Knowles, 1990). As stated by Alan Rogers (2002), "Freire . . . suggested that learning is accomplished by critically analyzing experience and acting on the basis of that analysis . . . [and for] Knowles . . . action is an essential part of the learning process, not a result of the learning process" (p. 107).

K. Patricia Cross's (1981) Characteristics of Adults as Learners (CAL) model contains guidelines for adult education programs. These guidelines are practical and situational for adult learning with attention to characteristics such as full-time versus part-time, required (compulsory) versus voluntary, and so forth. Cross's three principles of adult learning are (a) learning should capitalize on one's experience, (b) age of the learner is a factor, and (c) challenge the adult to continue to grow. Choices on how the learning is organized are important to the adult learner.

Engaging Adult Learners

All the learning theories mentioned in the preceding brief summary have impacted the evolution of adult learning and pedagogy, some to a greater degree than others. Cognitive and social constructivisms are strong underpinnings to adult learning, as are humanist and motivation-personality theories. Figure 5.1 depicts the relationship of learning theories to adult learning and pedagogy.

Understanding adult learning and pedagogy requires us to know the adult learner differs from the child learner and that adult motivations and experiences require us to know different strategies to keep adults' attention. The best adult strategies are found foremost in the work of Cronbach and Snow (1977), Cross (1981), Knowles (1990), and Lave and Wenger (1991). The evolution of these theories can be found in cognitivism, social constructivism, motivation theory, intellect theory, and humanism.

Today, adult learning can only be studied through a complex arrangement of factors. Learning styles and the psychological theories of learning allow us to acknowledge that learning is neither stagnant for adults nor easy to describe by a single learning theory.

How we lead the adult learner is greatly impacted by knowledge of both the context and the learner him- or herself. Contextual understanding by the educational leader is as critical as the transfer of knowledge and how it is transferred through strategies and activities. One's skill and ability as an educational leader is tested now by both knowledge of how adults learn and the tools available today that were not available even 10 years ago.

Figure 5.1	Learning Theories' Relationship to Adult Learning

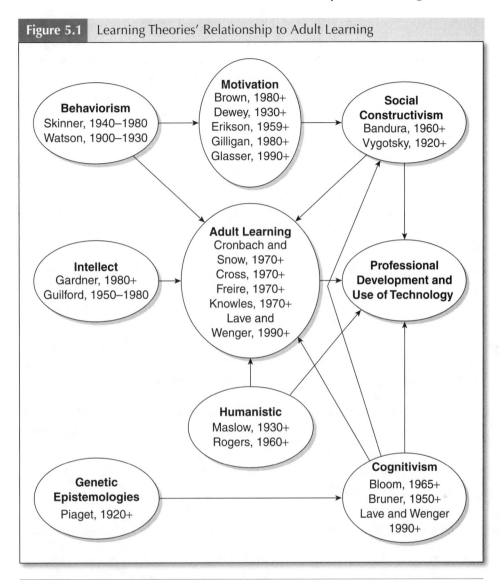

Note: Dates reflect the approximate time each scholar's theories were being developed.

Mentoring Adult Learners

The former role of the educational leader, the benevolent authoritarian, is now being transformed to the *mentor/coach*. Papa (Papa-Lewis, 1984, 1987) has researched extensively as an organizational theorist how mentoring adults influences their learning. **Mentoring**, the most complete human skill to acquire; teaching; coaching; facilitating; and other such similar descriptors describe a process for adult learning. Building upon the work of Erikson

(1959, 1968), Gilligan (1982), Glasser (1990), Lave and Wenger (1991), Levinson (1978), Maslow (1943), Rogers (2002, 2004), and Vygotsky (1978), cultural, linguistic, and gender nuances are additional factors that comprise the adult learner and that the educational leader must understand when working with adults. In understanding the communication patterns of the individual the following eight stages represent in descending order of ability how adults communicate both at work and in their personal lives: mentoring, negotiating, instructing, supervising, diverting, persuading, speaking-signaling, and serving. Mentoring is considered the most complete human skill to acquire immediately followed by negotiating and instructing. Papa's (2002a, 2002b; Papa-Lewis, 1984, 1987) research combines adult learning, the research of Cross (1981) and Knowles (1990), and characteristics of mentoring in the following manner.

- Adults are motivated to learn as they develop needs and interests that learning will satisfy. An adult's (protégé's) needs and interests are an appropriate starting point for mentoring.

- Adult orientation to learning is life or work centered. The appropriate frameworks for organizing mentoring are life- or work-related situations rather than theoretical subjects.

- Experience is the richest resource for adult learning. The approach for mentoring involves active participation in a planned series of experiences, the reflection of those experiences, and their application to work situations.

- Adults have a deep need to be self-directing. The role of the mentor is to engage in a process of inquiry, reflection, and decision making with the protégé rather than transmit knowledge and then evaluate the protégé's conformity to it.

- Individual differences among adult learners vary with age, gender, culture, language, and experience. Mentoring must make optimum provisions for differences in style, time, setting, and pace of learning.

Shifting the educational leader's role from passive to engagement of the learner forces the educational leader to understand the role of mentoring adults. Papa (2002b) has adapted Knowles's (1980, 1990) work on how adults learn best: Some adults learn best by listening and taking notes; some adults learn best by working in groups with other students; some adults learn best by reading rather than listening to lectures; and some adults learn best by doing specific assignments based on the material covered.

Combined with mentoring skills, according to Papa (2002a), the educational leader should (a) provide alternative models, showing how a problem can be approached in a variety of ways; (b) communicate questions, to aid in comprehension of the issues; (c) try to give a sense of the various strategies that were rejected as well as those that were adopted, as one can imagine that educational leaders sometimes lead without reference to situation, context, people involved, and so forth; (d) share his or her intentions (How do you analyze the problem? What are you trying to accomplish? Why are you adopting this strategy? Don't just let them observe you; explain in advance the context, what you understand the problem to be, what you expect to accomplish, what obstacles you anticipate, etc.); (e) conduct mutual debriefing, with the leader willing to share mistakes as well as successes; (f) provide an opportunity for both him- or herself and the adult learner to learn; (g) work at the relationship, which does not just "happen"; (h) provide successful experiences for those involved; (i) recognize this is not cloning and that a fundamental respect for the views, experiences, and sensitivities of those you are leading must be preserved; and (j) develop mutual trust and befriending. Peer-to-peer instruction and mentoring-based leadership are skills the educational leader should practice.

Teaching and Leading Adult Learners

Great teaching is defined by the ability to inspire learners. Motivate the learner and you will grab his or her attention. Keeping a learner's attention is more difficult. Educational leaders need many strategies at their fingertips to keep others' attention.

Adult learners by the nature of their characteristics will learn best when in a mentoring environment. In this environment the educational leader acknowledges that he or she is a learner as well. Figure 5.2 describes how adults can be taught reaching all learners. This chart has the educational leader understand that by changing the strategies for the learner, all adult learners are engaged. Hearing something said, saying something, doing something, and seeing something acknowledge that adults learn differently. The goal is to keep the learner's attention: To optimize engaged learners demands the use of strategies and techniques that support the varied learning styles of adults.

To say one leads the way one was led is not entirely true. More precisely, one leads the way he or she learns best. How one learns best keeps his or her attention. It may not keep the attention of those one is trying to lead. Introducing concepts from a variety of strategies ensures all learners are engaged. Papa's (2002b) practices for adult learners are easy to remember: See the concept, hear the concept, say the concept, and apply the concept. The following figure describes the strategies that can be used for each of these four areas. *Hear It* focuses on the learner who needs to read and write the concepts in order to learn the content. *See It* offers a visual for the learner, such as writing on a board or using PowerPoint. *Say It* refers to learners who must talk about the concept and are frequently those who ask a lot of questions. This strategy is good for peer-to-peer work and group work. *Do It* is the hands-on application that allows for trial and error. It is especially important that we discuss mistakes.

Figure 5.2	Adult Learning Characteristics

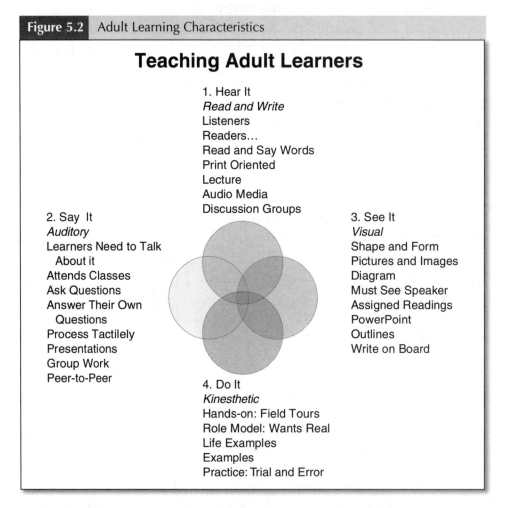

Teaching Adult Learners

1. Hear It
Read and Write
Listeners
Readers…
Read and Say Words
Print Oriented
Lecture
Audio Media
Discussion Groups

2. Say It
Auditory
Learners Need to Talk
  About it
Attends Classes
Ask Questions
Answer Their Own
  Questions
Process Tactilely
Presentations
Group Work
Peer-to-Peer

3. See It
Visual
Shape and Form
Pictures and Images
Diagram
Must See Speaker
Assigned Readings
PowerPoint
Outlines
Write on Board

4. Do It
Kinesthetic
Hands-on: Field Tours
Role Model: Wants Real
Life Examples
Examples
Practice: Trial and Error

Conclusions

This chapter has focused on the adult learner, how one learns, and the need for educational leaders to understand these dynamics. What are the multimedia applications that connect to the visual, auditory, verbal, and kinesthetic learner? How do the changing technology practices impact the learner? The answers to these questions are found in the remaining chapters of this book.

Key Principles for Leaders to Know

Experiences of the adult learner continue to be the rich backdrop the educational leader can build upon. Also required is having educational leaders who are trained in learning theory—from a variety of perspectives, as found in this chapter.

Key principles for the educational leader to understand are to

- acknowledge the adult learner's motivation and interests;
- mentor the adult learner;
- consider strategies to participate in the adult learner's learning;
- use the adult learner's life experiences in the activities provided;
- give the adult learner choices in planning his or her learning;
- explore the adult learner's expectations for learning, work related and/or personal;
- provide problem-centered activities;
- analyze each individual for learning characteristics;
- lead using different approaches and strategies;
- create socialization opportunities in activities;
- demand the adult learner's attention through inspirational leadership; and
- practice learner-centered rather than educational leader–centered leading.

CASE STUDY 5.1 | Applying Adult Learning Theories

It is the first day back from summer break. As the new principal, you desire to know more about the teachers in the school. You decide to do a learning activity with the teachers that will help you begin to know them and, therefore, to lead them better. You ask them to think about their summer break. For example, did they travel? Did they teach summer school? Did they work at another job? Did they take flying lessons? Did they learn to scuba dive?

You ask them to respond to a specific open-ended question. Choose one style from the following four that most closely fits your style (that appeals most to you):

1. If you are a *cognitivist combined with intellect theory,* you might ask to describe how they learned something new from previous knowledge they already had. When did they realize they were constructing new ideas? Think outside the box. Ask them to provide rich detail in what they believed they learned.

(Continued)

(Continued)

2. As a *humanist,* you might ask to describe the most emotional day they had this summer and why it was emotional. What was the outcome? How did they feel? What did they learn from the experience?

3. If you are a *social cognitive constructivist and motivation theorist,* you might ask them to describe what they learned from their peers and how they personally felt about it. Did they go along? Did they resist doing what their peers did? Why did they join in or decide not to join in?

4. An *adult learner theorist* might ask them to describe something they learned this summer and what the steps that they did to learn were. What strategies did they use or have to learn? What skills did they master? Were they successful in learning it? If so, why? If not, why not?

Discussion: Which of the four styles listed above best describes your style? Why? Refer back to Table 5.1 to help explain your answer.

Activity: Using Figure 5.2, identify the most likely type of learning style(s) you have by examining your answer to the above discussion. Reflect on the types of strategies that best reflect your style.

CASE STUDY 5.2 | Self-Reflection and Professional Development

By identifying how adults learn, administrators are better able to arrange approaches to meet the learning styles of those they lead and arrange for professional development in their respective school settings. This insight will serve us well when we are seeking buy-in for new multimedia applications that will improve management aspects of the workplace and especially student success for all. Focus on a professional development situation in which you were a learner: a situation in which you were asked to learn a new concept. What was the concept? What was the setting in which you were to learn?

Discussion: In a group, discuss how you as the learner would respond to the following questions.

- How key was attention to the learning and the act of learning?
- What optimized your attention?
- What maintained your attention?
- What role did peer or personal motivation play?
- How much control as the learner did you have? Was it enough?
- How much did interest or need affect (your) learning?

Activity: Now plan a professional development activity by focusing on the following issues.

- How key is maintaining the attention of the learner in the act of learning?
- What would you do to optimize attention?
- What would you do to maintain attention?
- What role does peer or personal motivation play?
- How much control for the learner do you think is necessary?
- How much does interest or need of the learner affect your training?

Web Resources

Adult Education Quarterly (http://aeq.sagepub.com/reports/mfc1.dtl) is a scholarly refereed journal committed to advancing the understanding and practice of adult and continuing education.

Adult Learning (http://www.fsu.edu/~adult-ed/jenny/learning.html) is a site focused on adult learning characteristics.

The **California Distance Learning Project** (http://www.cdlponline.org/) provides teacher resources and student activities for adult education in California.

Community Partnerships for Adult Learning, U.S. Department of Education (http://www.c-pal.net/build/technology/index.asp), prepare adults for the demands of a changing economy and society.

The **Educational Technology Clearinghouse** (http://etc.usf.edu/adult_ed/index.htm) site has a variety of links to adult education materials, as well as links to other resources.

How Adults Learn (http://agelesslearner.com/intros/adultlearning.html) describes adult learning theory and where to find additional resources where you can learn more about how adults learn.

The **International Society for Technology in Education** (http://www.iste.org/AM/Template.cfm?Section=NETS) is the source for professional development, knowledge generation, advocacy, and leadership for innovation.

The **Iowa Professional Development Model** (http://tinyurl.com/dxpkup) is a collaborative effort of the Iowa Department of Education and a group of stakeholders representing area education agencies and providers of professional development in the state of Iowa.

Mentor Information and Materials (http://www.tr.wou.edu/bridges/adult.htm) are available for understanding adult learners.

Teaching Tips Index (http://honolulu.hawaii.edu/intranet/committees/FacDevCom/guidebk/teachtip/teachtip.htm) provides teaching tips for adult learners.

The **U.S. Department of Education's Office of Educational Technology** (http://www.ed.gov/about/offices/list/os/technology/index.html) is responsible for coordinating the development and implementation of educational technology policies, research projects, and national technology summits.

References

Bandura, A. (1986). *Social foundations of thought and action: A social cognitive theory.* Englewood Cliffs, NJ: Prentice Hall.

Bloom, B. S. (1965). *Taxonomy of educational objectives.* London: Longman.

Brown, R. (1990). The construct and concurrent validity of the social dimension of the Brown locus of control scale. *Educational and Psychological Measurement, 50,* 377–382.

Brown, R., & Marcoulides, G. A. (1996, October). A cross-cultural comparison of the Brown locus of control scale. *Educational and Psychological Measurement, 56*(5), 858–863.

Bruner, J. S. (1983). *In search of mind: Essays in autobiography.* New York: Harper & Row.

Cronbach, L., & Snow, R. (1977). *Aptitudes and instructional methods: A handbook for research on interactions.* New York: Irvington.

Cross, K. P. (1981). *Adults as learners: Increasing participation and facilitating learning.* San Francisco: Jossey-Bass.

Dewey, J. (1938). *Experience and education.* New York: Macmillan.

Erikson, E. H. (1959). Identity and the life cycle. *Psychological Issues, 1,* 1.

Erikson, E. H. (1968). *Identity, youth and crisis.* New York: W. W. Norton.

Freire, P. (1972). *Pedagogy of the oppressed.* Harmondsworth, United Kingdom: Penguin.

Gardner, H. (1983). *Frames of mind: The theory of multiple intelligences.* New York: Basic Books.

Gardner, H. (1999a). *The disciplined mind: Beyond facts and standardized tests: The K–12 education that every child deserves.* New York: Simon & Schuster.

Gardner, H. (1999b). *Intelligence reframed: Multiple intelligences for the 21st century.* New York: Basic Books.

Gardner, H. (2006). *The development and education of the mind: The selected works of Howard Gardner.* London, United Kingdom: Routledge.

Gilligan, C. (1982). *In a different voice: Psychological theory and women's development.* Cambridge, MA: Harvard University Press.

Glasser, W. (1990). *The quality school.* New York: Harper & Row.

Guilford, J. P. (1950). Creativity. *American Psychologist, 5,* 444–454.

Knowles, M. S. (1980). *The modern practice of adult education: From pedagogy to andragogy.* New York: Association Press.

Knowles, M. S. (1990). *The adult learner: A neglected species.* Houston, TX: Gulf.

Lave, J., & Wenger, E. (1991). *Situated learning: Legitimate peripheral participation.* Cambridge, United Kingdom: Cambridge University Press.

Levinson, D. J. (1978). *The seasons of a man's life.* New York: Alfred A. Knopf.

Maslow, A. H. (1943). A theory of human motivation. *Psychological Review, 50,* 370.

Papa, R. (2002a). *The art of mentoring.* Sacramento, CA: Center for Teaching and Learning.

Papa, R. (2002b). *How we learn.* Sacramento, CA: Center for Teaching and Learning.

Papa-Lewis, R. (1984). The mentoring relationship between major advisors and doctoral degree advisees (Doctoral dissertation, University of Nebraska–Lincoln, 1983). *Dissertation Abstracts International, 45*(2), 402.

Papa-Lewis, R. (1987). The relationship of selected variables to mentoring in doctoral level education. *International Journal of Mentoring, 1*(1), 22–26.

Piaget, J. (1970). Piaget's theory. In P. Mussen (Ed.), *Handbook of child psychology* (p. 1). New York: Wiley.

Rogers, A. (2002). *Teaching adults* (3rd ed.). London: Open University Press.

Rogers, J. (2004). *Adult learning* (4th ed.). London: Open University Press.

Skinner, B. F. (1974). *About behaviorism.* New York: Random House.

Vygotsky, L. S. (1978). *Mind in society: The development of higher psychological processes.* Cambridge, MA: Harvard University Press.

Watson, J. (1928). *The ways of behaviorism.* New York: Harper & Brothers.

Chapter **6**

PLANNING, DESIGNING, IMPLEMENTING, AND EVALUATING TECHNOLOGY

Shadow W. J. Armfield

The appropriate and powerful integration of **technology**—the application of hardware intended to be used with or through a personal computer (Windows or Mac OS) or an electronic device that can aid in accomplishing a specific task, such as learning a concept or researching a term—into the classroom must be done in a purposeful and supportive manner. The technologies and the way they are used must support the goals of the administration, the teachers, and the students. Because each school is unique in its needs and goals, it is paramount that each school begins to develop a plan for the most appropriate technologies and how they should be used. This chapter delves into the ways the administrator can develop a strategic plan allowing for the advancement of **technology integration**, the use of technology in a learning environment to enhance understanding of curricular content, into the daily activities that permeate the school.

Current classroom teachers are a generation of "digital immigrants" preparing a generation of "digital natives." Today's students have keen insight into the ways technology may be used to enhance their understanding both in and outside of the school system. Yet in most schools current technologies are used for traditional activities, such as writing papers and developing linear presentations, or worse, they are not used at all. To confound the situation, teacher autonomy keeps teachers removed from outside influences that may reinforce their students finding personal meaning and successes in their educations. This limited view of how technology may be integrated into the environment of **learning**, in which content and/or technologies are actively used to develop deeper understanding and further application, and the isolation of teachers produces a chasm between classroom use of technology and its potential.

The integration of technology into the learning environment must be both an individual and a school-wide priority. This chapter's focus will be on the development of a community that has the long-term goal of preparing teachers for technology integration. The chapter will begin by examining overarching ideas of what a learning community is, beliefs about the integration of technology into the learning environment, and challenges prevalent within each of these concepts. The final section of the chapter is concerned with strengthening the community and developing a shared vision of technology integration. The focal point is on utilizing long-term professional development to create a learning community with the purpose of planning, designing, implementing, and evaluating technology integration and innovation throughout the school.

The following questions are addressed in this chapter:

- What can leaders do to ensure use of technology is not reactive?

- How best can leaders develop themselves as mentors/facilitators?

- How can leaders ensure communities of practice support revolving growth?

- What can leaders do to ensure professional development is constant and cyclical?

- What skills does a leader need to have to ensure others embrace technologies knowing that technology needs will be ever-changing?

Transforming the School

The central processes of public schools tend to remain virtually unchanged for lengthy intervals, resulting in general functions and behaviors associated with schools being acculturated by those who have attended or worked in the system. As a result of this enculturation, reform tends to take place primarily on the surface, leaving classrooms and instruction relatively unscathed (Tyack & Cuban, 1995). Michael Fullan (2001) argues that reform is too often seen as simplistic and that deep and lasting change will be unable to find a foothold if it is conducted solely to meet the most current issue. Progress within the individual classroom will be limited unless there is a systematic change that progresses the entire culture surrounding that classroom.

The history of education predicts that a focus on change to meet the needs of a current crisis is likely to have little impact on the core structure of the educational system. Yet at the same time, it is evident that the explosion of technologies available to our students and the changing ways in which our students interact through technologies require some sort of action. To externally push for reform and further sequester our teachers in their classrooms, as has been done in the past, is clearly not a viable choice. Before beginning a discussion of beliefs about technology, the role it can play within the learning environment, and a systematic approach to successful implementation, an alternative method for promoting progress will be defined.

Communities of Practice

Kofman and Senge (1995) indicate that there are three areas of dysfunction for any organization (school or business) within the current culture. These are fragmentation, competition, and reactiveness. Fragmentation refers to the idea of breaking down whole systems into parts and focusing on one part. It is argued that fragmentation causes a breakdown in systems by focusing on overly specific goals. The idea of competition has to do with the overzealous individual working to continually stand out within the community. And reactiveness is action based solely on current and local problems without consideration for what that action might mean for the future or for the larger community. The idea of competition is not highly prevalent in the field of education, but both fragmentation and reactiveness are consistent in the field. In order to develop overarching educational goals that meet the needs of the administration, teachers, and students, a shift in our understandings of leadership must occur.

Communities of practice diverge from the conventional wisdom of schools that created a hierarchy in the system; students receive direction from the teacher who receives direction from the principal who receives direction from the superintendent and so on. New beliefs about school structure promote the idea of administrators, teachers, and, in some cases, students working together to develop a shared set of goals for a school. This community examines areas of success and areas that need improvement within the school structure and then works to create a change that will rectify the areas in need of improvement. Fullan (2001) indicates that through the building of a community all members of the school begin to have ownership and a meaningful connection in the process of change. Administrators who are looking to promote progressive and lasting change must look to teachers as partners in the process.

Through the implementation of a **community of practice**—an organizational structure of administrators, teachers, and, if possible, students and parents working collaboratively to understand school-wide needs and develop goals, plans, and activities—an administrator's role changes in the structure of the system. He or she is no longer deferred to for the final decision. Instead, he or she is a collaborator helping to set long-range and overarching goals, innovation, and guidance. The administrator begins to develop the community by bringing faculty into the decision-making process. This community is founded on collaboration, both within and outside of rank, and develops a plan for the future. Successful communities of practice not only focus on these future goals but also look to the present and past to understand the culture of the school. The past can be a great predictor of the school's future and may also produce understandings of failures to progress in the past (Schwartz, 1991). These insights are then worked into the plans for the future.

Communities of practice must provide a supportive environment where there is an openness and appreciation for new and unique ideas, where the individual is free to speak without worry of disparagement, and where the individual has time for **reflection**, or premeditated analysis of personal and community practice up to a specific point, on individual and collective information. As community members put new understanding into practice, clearly defined ways of sharing or debriefing must be developed. This collective intelligence is further used for reflection and the focus on further progress. Finally, the administrator must begin to actively listen, question, and prompt dialogue and debate. He or she must actively demonstrate his or her ability to reflect on alternative points of view and to infuse new ideas into his or her own practice (Garvin, Edmondson, & Gino, 2008).

While a community of practice might be a successful approach for all aspects of a school, this chapter focuses on building the community to develop understandings about the use and integration of technologies throughout the school. The administrator brings forth the idea of further developing technology's role, but the community of practice develops a collaborative belief about the role that technology will play in the school-wide community (Holland, 2001).

Technology Integration

Until the middle of the 20th century, school was a place of enlightenment where students went to develop an understanding of the world outside their immediate community. In the years since, the development of electronic and, recently, digital devices has given children in developed countries instant access to the world (Prensky, 2008). By 2002 there were approximately four students for each computer in the United States, and 98% of the schools in the United States were outfitted with computers and high-speed Internet (Market Data Retrieval, 2002). Unfortunately the rapid development of new technologies and the ensuing development of school infrastructures have yet to impact the pedagogy or content of the typical classroom.

As computers and networks have evolved, it has become increasingly clear that the application of technology in the learning environment must change as well. By 1980, Seymour Papert began to question the classroom application of the computer. He argued that computer-based learning activities previously controlled the student's learning but that future learning activities must be controlled by the student. David Thornburg (1999) concurred and shared that what is important is to think of technologies not as tools to supplement what we have always done but as tools to allow us to do things that we have never done.

Proponents of technology integration into the learning environment have often envisioned technology playing the same role within the classroom as it does within the greater society. At this point, that vision has yet to materialize. It is argued that this is due to the focus on the technology itself and not its usefulness in the learning environment. The constant and rapid change in technologies makes learning of current technologies only part of the point. Individuals must also grasp a generalized understanding of the tools so they are not left behind as new technologies come into play (Mishra & Koehler, 2006).

While technologies are constantly evolving and individuals (teachers and students) need to stay abreast of how to use the technologies, the focus in education is moving away from learning *about* toward learning *with* and *through* the technology. In order for technology to be integrated with any considerable impact, teachers must begin to examine their content, determine the best pedagogical framework for teaching that content, and then use technologies in a way that supports both the learning of the content and the pedagogical framework. This is no simple task considering the variables: the individual teacher, the specific content of the course, and the many different ways to approach teaching. One thing is clear: There is no one specific solution for integrating technology into the classroom (Mishra & Koehler, 2006; SIGTE Leadership and NTLS Program Committee, 2008).

Challenges

In one study, 75% of seniors leaving high school stated that their course work was not interesting or meaningful. Fifty percent believed that what they learned would have little use in helping them have a successful life. On the other hand, this trend appeared to slow by engaging students in personally meaningful activities through participatory media (Nussbaum-Beach, 2008). Does this mean that technology is the savior of education? That is highly unlikely, but it is one component of the entire system.

The challenge for administrators is to begin to move teachers to understand that technology is part of the solution in meeting the needs of 21st-century learners. They must work to develop overarching goals that can then be fleshed out by the community of practice. This must be done with the understanding that if the policy appears to have too narrow of a direction, it will be met with resistance and have only mild surface effects within the classroom (Fullan, 2001).

Further challenges are presented by the technologies themselves. As educators move to integrate technology into the learning environment, they face the following obstacles: (a) Teachers are resistant to using equipment and ideas for which they have little experience, (b) teachers do not understand how certain technologies can benefit them and their students, (c) students envision the use of technology differently than the teachers do, and (d) teachers are looking at the technologies as tools to replace old ones, not as tools that have not been available previously (Prain & Hand, 2003). These challenges can be reduced by including teachers in the development of school-wide goals and preparing them to use the technologies in ways that are both personally meaningful and at their stage of development. The following section examines using a community of practice to do both.

Professional Development: Building the Community

In Chapter 5 of this volume, Papa and Papa give a complete description of mentoring the adult learner. It is stated that the adult learner is motivated to learn when needed, learns in association with things personal or work related, learns through experience, and is self-directed but can be engaged in inquiry and that each learner brings with him or her a history that is unique from any other. This framework for the adult learner helps define why past iterations of reform have been minimal. The goals of the reforms were to change the system from without, but the research indicates that when working with the adult learner a change in the system must come from within. Change for an individual can have a grand effect on the change in a system. By engrossing each individual in personal professional development, a community of practice can be developed that moves the entire school to a new level of understanding.

Traditional school-wide or district-wide professional development has focused on the individual conducting the in-service. Limited positive results have been found in professional development requiring teachers to participate in in-services, which require them to use presented ideas in their classrooms but provide no follow-up (Darling-Hammond, 1997).

The current belief is that the goal of professional development is not to present the faculty and staff with large amounts of information and expect each piece to be implemented but to develop shared governance that creates an opportunity for the administration, faculty, and staff to develop a plan of action based on a particular school's and individual's needs. It begins with the creation and maintenance of the decision-making process that is consistent and accessible to all involved (Glickman, Gordon, & Ross-Gordon, 2001). Professional development is about generating change in the school. The National Staff Development Council's (2001) standards describe professional development as a collaborative process that develops a community focused on school-wide goals. They point out that this is a continuously involved and evolving group working to promote understanding of best practices through the alignment of content, pedagogy, and assessment.

Not only does the professional development need to be connected with the goals of the school, but it must also align with the individual needs of the teacher. Teachers must be able to define what those needs are and have input into how the professional development can help them the most. Learning best occurs not when information is given or demonstrated but when knowledge is gathered through the intimate work with a particular curriculum within a community. It is through the practice and the shared communication about the practice that learning occurs and that the community is moved forward (Guskey, 2000; Lave & Wenger, 1991).

Furthermore, professional development is an ongoing process. Studies have demonstrated that when conducted over time, with a dual focus on collaboration and authentic application, professional development gives the participants a deeper connection and desire to continue to develop their understandings (Giordano, 2007; Watson, 2006).

When the matter of professional development is technology, the learning of technologies and the integration of them into the learning environment must be considered. As described in the section on technology integration, the current consensus is that when technology is used in the learning environment, it should focus on supporting pedagogy and student understanding of content. But before teachers can support pedagogy and content they must feel comfortable with the technology. As a result, teachers must have some training, either formal or informal, on specific technologies. Training of the technologies themselves should be short, quickly followed by explorations into how they may be used in the learning environment (Guskey, 1985).

Schibei et al. (2008) suggest addressing the stages of the individual teachers before continuing to develop a plan for technology integration. Those who are uncomfortable with technology may want to begin with basic technology skills. Teachers with technology skills, but who have yet to move technology into the classroom, would want to focus on using the technology to support specific teaching activities. Individuals who have been using technology for teaching should begin moving toward a more student-focused use of technology within the existing curriculum. Finally, individuals who have worked with technology in the standard curriculum should look at how technology can transform the curriculum and change the culture of the school.

Finally, regardless of where individuals are in their abilities to integrate technologies into the classroom, they will benefit from personal, peer, and community reflection. These reflections help each teacher gain insight into his or her own teaching. When shared with peers and the larger community, the reflections become records of change within the school and continue the development of a shared vision.

The process that we are now moving into is developed with the purpose of giving teachers the opportunity to develop habits that allow for the incorporation of new technologies, new ways of thinking about learning, and reflection for the betterment of the individual classroom as well as the school as a community. The goal in this process is to change beliefs about new ways to approach learning and how technology may support these. There are five key ingredients to start the change process: Administrators and teachers must have open, public conversations about pedagogical beliefs; teachers must break into smaller communities to support and reflect on practice; teachers must vicariously experience using technologies in innovative ways; new technologies should be introduced progressively; and teachers must have continued technological and pedagogical support (Ertmer, 2005).

Figure 6.1 provides an overview of the professional development process. This process is built on the idea that reflection is the key to understanding the past and present culture of the school. Reflecting both individually and as a community

| Figure 6.1 | The Professional Development Process |

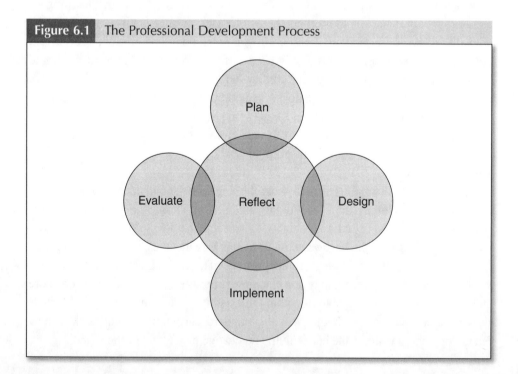

builds a pattern on which future plans may be built. Although the process is gone through in a specific order (planning, designing, implementing, and evaluating), it is indefinite. The end of one round of the process is the beginning of the next.

In order to see the process in action, subsequent sections will be followed with an example of the process. The process described here was used with 30 teachers and administrators from rural districts in southeastern Arizona. The entire professional development program lasted 3 years and demonstrated a consistent growth, even among the most resistant members of the group.

Planning

As the administrator begins to plan for the development of a community of practice focused on integrating technology into the learning environment, there must be a focus on what is already available within the school. Begin planning by starting at the end of the process. The end of the process is evaluation. What must be evaluated at the beginning of the process are the past and present uses of technologies in the building. There needs to be an inventory of what is available.

Building a community of practice is about involving all members of the community in the development of understandings and goals. The teachers have the technologies and can help create a vision of the school's current use of technology. Each teacher, including the media specialist (if the school has one), should document each piece of technology he or she has in his or her possession for instructional and/or learning purposes. The goal is building a community that focuses on both individual and school needs, so this inventory should be shared with the community.

How each technology in the inventory is used or not used expands upon the description of the community's beliefs about technology. Each member of the community should reflect on how the technologies are used. For some of the members this may be a long and detailed list; for others it may be very short. Members also need to reflect on the technologies that are not used and reasons they are not used. The reflections should be collected in the database with access for all members so they can see it shared at community meetings. The goal is not to embarrass or brag but to develop a community understanding of what is available, how it is used, and how it might be used.

The community also needs to think about what isn't available, why it's needed, and how it would be used. Whether purchase is possible or not is not the goal at this point. Predicting what would be beneficial for the community helps develop a long-term vision of technology's role in the school.

With the database of the technologies and how they are used developed, it is time to think about how the available technologies can meet the needs of the students, the faculty, the district, and the state. The teachers have a background in the content that must be taught in their classrooms but may not have been exposed to the ways technology can support their teaching and their classroom content. Teachers need to research both general information about technology integration and ways in which technology is integrated in specific content areas.

Examining professional journals and records of teacher practice, the teachers should document a number of innovative ways to integrate technology into the learning environment. In a community discussion, ideas should be shared about the research and whether or not such uses of technology can be accomplished in their school. This conversation should be based on the technologies available, teacher abilities, and district and state standards. The administrator must be prepared to ask questions requiring detailed thoughts and reflection on each teacher's own practice.

Based on these conversations, goals for developing technology-integrated activities should be set. For such an activity to be successful, teachers must be allowed to approach the use of technology at their comfort level. They need to think about technology and content standards and how the technology can support what they do in the classrooms, and then they need to learn that technology.

> Teachers in the workshop came from 13 different school districts, each with his or her own set of technology and goals for what he or she wanted to accomplish. Some of the individuals simply wanted to learn how to use technologies that they had not used before. For others the focus was integrating the technology into the classroom, while for some it was how to use technology for administrative activities. Regardless of his or her position or goal, each individual examined the technologies available and researched, with the support of the training staff, how those technologies might be used for his or her specific goal and how they could be used beyond his or her goal. Some of the participants were resistant to participation initially, but as they listened to and shared with the community they became part of it. Some of them required three to four meetings (1 month apart) before they fully engaged.

Learning the Technologies

In order for teachers to successfully use technologies in their classes, the administrator must ensure training and time for learning the technologies. The U.S. Department of Education (2003) found that by 2003, 85% of the teaching population was comfortable using technology for classroom instruction, but many (80%) were still interested in having a better understanding of integration. Even with this high level of comfort, expecting all teachers to develop and implement technology-integrated activities without time to learn or practice the technologies is setting them up for failure. It takes time to learn new technologies, and it is important that time be set aside for learning them. Even the most technologically advanced members of the community need time to perfect their use of technology. Teachers must be involved in learning technologies in a collaborative and hands-on environment (Rosenfeld, 2008).

There are a number of ways that teachers can begin to learn the new technologies. Some of the faculty may be able to learn it on their own by "playing" with it or by going through tutorials. Others may learn best by working in smaller groups and collaborating with peers with similar needs. This gives them the opportunity to focus on their needs without the threat of feeling too slow, too fast, or generally out of place (Schibei et al., 2008).

Advanced members of the faculty may also work with their colleagues to support them in developing skills. Martinez and Harper (2008) suggest that students may be able to support the faculty in the learning of technologies. While this requires a different way of looking at students, they suggest including students in the training or possibly allowing them to conduct the training. They argue that students are often aware of the teachers' feelings and are supportive in the process of helping the teacher learn the new technologies. Finally, if a technology is too new or too advanced, professional trainers may be used (even in this case, the training must focus on the teacher's individual needs).

The constant and rapid change in technologies makes learning of current technologies only part of the point. Individuals must also grasp a generalized understanding of the tools so they are not left behind when new tools come into play (Mishra & Koehler, 2006). The teacher must be the impetus for change in the classroom. Knowledge of how to use specific technologies is not enough to change the process, but it is a requirement if the teachers are to feel prepared for their integration. Once they have a grasp on the technology, they may begin to see how it may be used in combination with their content and pedagogical process (Giordano, 2007).

> The training site required that all members of the community learn to use the computer-based applications in the same room. This worked out well for this group as some of the members were very experienced with many applications and felt comfortable sharing their expertise with others. Although not all members were at ease using the computers (some struggled with saving documents to the correct place throughout the first year), each had the opportunity to learn and reflect on his or her learning. The community's conversations led to the knowledge that as a group its members were ready to try their skills in the learning environment.

Designing

Simply learning about how one might use technology in specific learning environments is not enough. Teachers must fully develop learning activities in which technology is used to better understand content and enhance teaching (Mishra & Koehler, 2006). The administrator needs to support the individual's progress toward this level of technology use by ensuring continuity in the community of practice. This must be done in terms of both maintaining consistent meetings and ensuring that the meetings are productive and thoughtful. The administrator must facilitate communication and support teachers in being clear about intended goals, obstacles, and possible consequences.

At this point in the process, the teachers have had the opportunity to explore the technologies they have available to them and how such technologies might be used in the classroom. The opportunity to learn new technologies, become more proficient with a technology, or help others learn new technologies is then given. Having learned how to use a specific technology, the teachers now have experiences on which they may reflect. Based on what they researched and their own experiences with the technology, they must examine whether or not using it in their classroom will be beneficial to their students' learning. This is a conversation that needs to be initially individual but eventually with the entire community. The community may help clarify how the technology might be used or why it should not be used in the manner presented.

It is important to think of technology integration on both the community and the individual level. As a community, the teachers and administration are supporting one another, but as individuals, the teachers are figuring out where they are on the continuum and in what ways technologies can serve them best. For them to be successful, teachers must be able to focus on the learning environment of their specific classroom. By developing within their own classrooms, the teachers find authentic connections that can then be continually reflected upon both individually and within the larger community (Schibei et al., 2008). They must ensure that they are focusing not only on the technology but also on how that technology may support pedagogy and content. It is at this juncture that the community may be most helpful.

Discussing the content to be taught, the way it will be taught, and how technology will be integrated so that the students may develop deeper understanding gives the individual a way to reflect before proceeding to the implementation. This reflection also gives the community of practice the opportunity to share and gather ideas. The continual conversation with the self and the community will ensure that technology is supporting the student's learning as well as meeting the school's needs.

The design process is not solely about the development of content but is also about the development of constructs to support that content. The teacher must make sure that the technology and resources are ready for student use. As the teachers are designing the learning activities, they can look, once again, to their students for help. Their students may be a great resource in helping make sure that the technologies and/or technology-based instructive supports are developed (i.e., presentations, videos, Web sites) (Martinez & Harper, 2008). They may even plan to engage the students as a resource during the implementation phase.

The design phase is primarily about the reflective process, making sure that the goals of the activity are clear, concise, and based on sound research and standards. This is all in preparation for the implementation and evaluation stage.

> As members of the community of practice entered the design stage, they created proposals describing how they would use technology to support learning in their classrooms. These proposals included specific goals for students, standards to be met, and how it would lead to their growth as a teacher. The proposals also included a detailed account of how they would accomplish each of these. Finally, the teachers included an evaluation plan. The goal of the evaluation plan was to help the teachers determine whether or not they were successful in meeting their goals. Each of these was shared among groups within the community. A facilitator sat in with each group to probe for clarification and further detail.

Implementing and Evaluating

Although change in beliefs and actions may be the goal of educational change, it appears that teachers are more fully equipped to discuss their beliefs only after the actual implementation of new practices in the classroom (Fullan, 2001). Traditional approaches in professional development have teachers take ideas from an in-service and implement them. There appears to be little worry about impact on learning. In this process, however, the administrator is engaging faculty in understanding what was planned, what actually occurred, what students learned in the process, and what the teacher learned in the process.

Before proceeding with implementation, the faculty member needs to develop a plan for evaluation. Such a plan must include specific information on how each teacher will assess progress in the integration of technology, its effect on student learning, and how the understanding may be used to develop technology-integrated activities in the future. Participating in a self-study allows the teacher to focus on activities that are in direct response to his or her class. The teacher can define the rationale, schedule, and flow of the classroom activities and the related research. Through the reflective activity the teacher can begin to understand whether espoused beliefs about his or her classroom intent align with the actual classroom activities (Louie, Drevdahl, Purdy, & Stackman, 2003).

Lambert (1995) points out that developing and implementing a plan of action are only the beginnings in understanding, whether or not the change process has begun to be effective. She maintains that the creation of meaning and knowledge needed to understand the individual's movement toward the indicated goal comes from individual and community reflection on the practice and experiences of, interaction with, and observation of colleagues and students. Evaluation is a collaborative process that must focus on reflection, analysis, and refinement. In this design it has a benefit not only for the individual and his or her classroom but also for the entire community as understandings are shared, questioned, and analyzed (Schoen, 2007). The community feedback is a place to provide support and stimulus but not to simply confirm the teacher's initial understandings. The community is asked to be encouraging while requiring the teacher to further examine the intent, the process, and the feedback. Teachers are to inquire about specifics and offer their own explanations. The goal of community feedback is to help the entire community grow. It is a model that requires teachers to assess their own classroom activities and share these with a larger community, giving both the individual and other members of the community opportunity to analyze practice and compare with research findings and their own beliefs and then move toward the development of new classroom norms that are congruent with both (Lim & Chai, 2008).

Members of the community of practice participated in a poster session to share their personal understandings of the activities that took place in their classrooms. In this poster session, the community was encouraged to question the teachers about why they chose to use specific technologies to support learning, whether or not they found the technology supported student learning, and how they might modify the activity if they were to do it again. Members had the opportunity to vicariously participate in nearly 30 other activities and, in the process, develop an understanding of what worked well, what didn't work well, and what had yet to be tried.

The Second Cycle

At this point, the teachers and the administration have been through one cycle of the process. This, of course, is not the end but rather the beginning. By now, all members of the community have a better understanding of both individual and school-wide technical needs. This is the time the community must take a second look at the technologies and how they are being integrated throughout the school and decide what is next. Community members must begin to plan for the role that technology will play in the school's future. They must examine how they see technology being used for teaching and learning, reexamine the technologies available, and determine what they don't have but need and what they do have but don't need. This plan must be concise, describing precisely how technology will be used by teachers, administrators, and, most important, students, and how these uses support the overall goals of the school.

Evaluating Technologies

While the evaluation of technologies is part of the overall process of school improvement and takes place within the cycle described above, as the community develops and makes technology a part of the curriculum, new technologies will be required. This section gives an overall view of what must be addressed when purchasing new or updated technologies.

The media barrage us with the newest and "most useful" technologies, but if the technologies don't actually support the content and the pedagogy of the classroom, they aren't much good (Hall & Pearson, 2009). Traditional tools used to evaluate technologies for the school were based on a checklist of features and comparisons of cost. While these may be important issues when it comes to the finer points, the overall question should be focused on whether or not the technology supports the goals set forth by the individual teacher or the school as a whole (Kelly, 2008).

The National School Board Association (n.d.) indicates that technologies must be examined under four specific criteria: technical, instructional, organizational, and ethical. The technical criteria allow the user to assess whether or not the technology is compatible with current and available technologies. An instructional criterion asks the reviewer to look at curricular pedagogical issues (i.e., how the tool supports students meeting standards or how the tool can be used for collaboration). The organizational criteria are focused on needs of faculty development and information technology support. Ethical criteria focus on meeting the needs of all learning populations. The technologies must also be examined for evidence of effectiveness, alignment with standards, appropriateness for students, and cost (i.e., purchase, maintain, etc.) (SRI International, 2002).

It is vital that a school go through the process of evaluating the technology not only from the theoretical standpoint but also from a standpoint of application. A pilot use of the technology should be conducted. In this pilot the evaluating team can examine whether or not it actually meets all of the criteria laid out in the theoretical construct: How suitable is it for student use, will it support meeting the requisite standards, does it work with available technologies, and does it support the community philosophy of quality teaching and learning practices (Kelly, 2008)?

The focus on continually reflecting on practice is needed for teachers to grow in a field that is ever changing. While the integration of technology into the individual classroom is a goal for the teacher, the administrator, with the help of the individual teachers, has the community goal in mind. While evaluating the implementation gives the individual the opportunity to see changes within his or her own classroom, it is the collegial and school-wide piece that helps build a community that grows and changes as needed (Lambert, 1995).

Currently the focus is on working to integrate technology into the support of pedagogy and predefined content. Prensky (2008) contends that as we move forward, schools must change what they do altogether. He insists that we shut our students down when they walk through the school door—that instead of supporting students' understandings of all of the information that they are gathering through their use of technology outside of the school, we ignore it and continue with an outdated curriculum. He maintains that the purpose of school must evolve from one where students go to get information to one where students go to apply, analyze, synthesize, evaluate, and communicate about all of the information to which they already have access. The development of a community of practice that consistently examines the needs of the students, the school-wide community, and the education system removes the need for reactiveness to such changes. They are able to grow and change as the system changes, ensuring that the students are prepared when they move on from the community.

Key Principles for Leaders to Know

Understandings of the ways to use technology to enhance pedagogy and content are continually evolving. By developing a community of practice, an administrator works to prepare his or her staff not only for the current view but also to change with the understandings.

- Current practices in technology integration will evolve.
- School use of technology must not be reactive.
- The administrator's role is as mentor and facilitator.
- Communities of practice support revolving growth.
- Professional development is constant and cyclical.
- Reflection leads to understanding and growth.
- Teachers must collaborate.
- Teachers must self- and community evaluate.
- Technologies and technology needs will change.

CASE STUDY 6.1 | Technology Resistance Among Teachers

As you are in the initial stages of determining the technologies available and how the teachers use them, you notice that one of the teachers has yet to share. Furthermore, the teacher seems to be disengaged with the conversation all together. When the community breaks for the day, you approach the teacher and ask her for her thoughts about the direction you put forth for community action. The teacher explains:

"This is good for the rest of the faculty, but in my course there is just no place for technology. The goals in my area are set around getting the students involved in physical activity. To place the students in front of the computer takes away from the much-needed activity."

You share with the teacher that you understand her concerns but continue the request that she engage in the community at future meetings. As you move into the planning stage, the teacher still seems to make no effort to share her own opinions about technology or its place in the curriculum.

Discussion: Discuss how you could work with other members of the community to engage and support this teacher as she works through the idea of using and integrating technology into her curriculum.

Activity: As a mentor and based on your understandings of the process outlined in this chapter, develop a flowchart with multiple scenarios showing how you might help this individual engage in her understandings of technology and its use in her classes.

CASE STUDY 6.2 | Technology Integration With Limited Funds

At the end of the first cycle of activity, you find that some of the teachers have been inspired by their first activities and are interested in further developing the integration of technology into their teaching and the curriculum. As they prepare for the second cycle, they find that the technologies they want to use to support their students' learning are not available. They come to you asking if they can be purchased.

Discussion: Based on your understanding of a community of practice, what is your role in this decision? How will you reconcile your role as a member of the community of practice with that of budget administrator?

Activity: As the new technologies are being discussed and tried out, what will the community need to look for to know whether or not it is getting the best possible technology for the intended goal? Outline what steps you require to demonstrate how the intended benefit negates the cost.

Web Resources

The **eduTecher** (http://edutecher.org/) Web site was set up as a resource for teachers and students as they work to begin the process of technology integration into the classroom. For the administrator this is a great site to share with the teachers to get them thinking about how they might integrate technology into their own classrooms.

The **National Staff Development Council** (http://www.nsdc.org) has set as its goal enhancing student achievement through professional development. At this site you will find resources on preparing for staff development including strategic plans, standards, and workshops.

The **Society for Organizational Learning's** (http://www.solonline.org/) motto "circles of inquiry . . . ripples of action" describes the focus of the content that can be found on its site. The site was set up as a resource for those who are working to develop communities of practice. On this site you will find publications that will further detail the idea and information about the foremost thinkers in organizational learning.

TPACK, Technological Pedagogical Content Knowledge (http://www.tpck.org), was designed as a support mechanism for those who are mentoring teachers on the integration of technology into the classroom. On this site the reader will find a detailed account of what TPACK is and current research into understandings of best practices for preparing teachers to integrate technology.

References

Darling-Hammond, L. (1997). *Doing what matters most: Investing in quality teaching.* New York: National Commission on Teaching and America's Future.

Ertmer, P. A. (2005). Teacher pedagogical beliefs: The final frontier in our quest for technology integration? *Educational Technology Research and Development, 53*(4), 25–39.

Fullan, M. G. (2001). *The new meaning of educational change* (3rd ed.). New York: Teachers College Press.

Garvin, D. A., Edmondson, A. C., & Gino, F. (2008, March). Is yours a learning organization? *Harvard Business Review, 86*(3), 109–116.

Giordano, V. A. (2007). A professional development model to promote Internet integration into P–12 teachers' practice: A mixed methods study. *Computers in the Schools, 24*(3/4), 111–123.

Glickman, C. D., Gordon, S. P., & Ross-Gordon, J. M. (2001). *Supervision and instructional leadership: A developmental approach.* Boston: Allyn & Bacon.

Guskey, T. R. (1985). Staff development and teacher change. *Educational Leadership, 42*(7), 57–60.

Guskey, T. R. (2000). *Evaluating professional development.* Thousand Oaks, CA: Corwin.

Hall, C. J., & Pearson, A. C. (2009). How to build for the future of technology in schools. *Independent School, 68*(2), 62–69.

Holland, P. E. (2001). Professional development in technology: Catalyst for school reform. *Journal of Technology and Teacher Education, 9*(2), 245–267.

Kelly, G. (2008). A collaborative process for evaluating new educational technologies. *Campus Wide Information Systems, 25*(2), 105–113.

Kofman, F., & Senge, P. M. (1995). Communities of commitment: The heart of learning organizations. In S. Chawla & J. Renesch (Eds.), *Learning organization: Developing cultures for tomorrow's workplace* (pp. 15–43). Portland, OR: Productivity Press.

Lambert, L. (1995). Constructing school change. In L. Lambert, D. Walker, D. P. Zimmerman, J. E. Cooper, M. D. Lambert, M. E. Gardner, & P. J. Ford Slack (Eds.), *The constructivist leader* (pp. 52–82). New York: Teachers College Press.

Lave, J., & Wenger, E. (1991). *Situated learning: Legitimate peripheral participation.* Cambridge, United Kingdom: Cambridge University Press.

Lim, C. P., & Chai, C. S. (2008). Rethinking classroom-oriented instructional development models to mediate instructional planning in technology-enhanced learning environments. *Teaching and Teacher Education, 24,* 2002–2013.

Louie, B. Y., Drevdahl, D. J., Purdy, J. M., & Stackman, R. W. (2003). Advancing the scholarship of teaching through collaborative self-study. *The Journal of Higher Education, 74*(2), 150–171.

Market Data Retrieval. (2002). *Technology in education 2002.* Shelton, CT: Author.

Martinez, S., & Harper, D. (2008, November). Working with tech-savvy kids. *Educational Leadership, 66*(3), 64–69.

Mishra, P., & Koehler, M. J. (2006). Technological pedagogical content knowledge: A framework for teacher knowledge. *Teachers College Record, 108*(6), 1017–1054.

National School Board Association. (n.d.). *Assessing technology tools.* Retrieved March 1, 2009, from http://www.nsba.org/sbot/toolkit/att.html

National Staff Development Council. (2001). *Standards for staff development, revised.* Retrieved March 1, 2009, from http://www.nsdc.org/standards/index.cfm

Nussbaum-Beach, S. (2008, February). No limits. *Technology and Learning, 28*(7), 14–18.

Papert, S. (1980). *Mindstorms: Children, computers, and powerful ideas.* New York: Basic Books.

Prain, V., & Hand, B. (2003, Summer). Using new technologies for learning: A case study of a whole school approach. *Journal of Research on Technology in Education, 35*(4), 441–458.

Prensky, M. (2008, March). Turning on the lights. *Educational Leadership, 65*(6), 40–45.

Rosenfeld, B. (2008). The challenge of teaching with technology: From computer idiocy to computer competence. *International Journal of Instructional Media, 35*(2), 157–166.

Schibei, R., MacCallum, J., Cumming-Potvi, W., Durrant, C., Kissane, B., & Miller, E. (2008). Teachers' journeys towards critical use of ICT. *Learning, Media, and Technology, 33*(4), 313–327.

Schoen, S. (2007). Action research: A developmental model of professional socialization. *The Clearing House, 80*(5), 211–216.

Schwartz, P. (1991). *The art of the long view: Planning for the future in an uncertain world.* New York: Currency Doubleday.

SIGTE Leadership and NTLS Program Committee. (2008, September/October). Realizing technologies potential through TPACK. *Learning & Leading with Technology, 36*(2), 23–26.

SRI International (under a task order from the Planning and Evaluation Service, U.S. Department of Education). (2002). *An educator's guide to evaluating claims about educational software.* Retrieved March 1, 2009, from http://www.ncrel.org/tech/claims/

Thornburg, D. D. (1999). *Technology in K–12 education: Envisioning a new future.* Proceedings of the Forum on Technology in Education: Envisioning the Future, Washington, DC, December 1–2.

Tyack, D., & Cuban, L. (1995). *Tinkering toward utopia.* Cambridge, MA: Harvard University Press.

U.S. Department of Education. (2003). *Federal funding for educational technology and how it is used in the classroom: A summary of findings from the integrated studies of educational technology.* Washington, DC: Office of the Undersecretary, Policy and Program Studies Service. Retrieved March 1, 2009, from http://www.ed.gov/rschstat/eval/tech/iset/summary2003.doc

Watson, G. (2006). Technology professional development: Long-term effects on teacher self-efficacy. *Journal of Technology and Teacher Education, 14*(1), 151–165.

Chapter 7

WEB 2.0 LEARNING ENVIRONMENTS IN DISTANCE LEARNING

Chih-Hsiung Tu and J. Michael Blocher

Distance learning has grown at meteoric rates over the past decade. Christensen Aaron, and Clark (2002) argued that distance learning is disrupting traditional education; this is the theory of **disruptive innovation**, an innovation that, by its implementation, disrupts the status quo. The theory of disruption can provide researchers, practitioners, and policymakers with a new perspective on increasingly effective, affordable, and accessible educational opportunities in our society. Distance learning is disruptive to traditional learning for several reasons:

1. It targets prospective students who in the past have been unable to access education because of the lack of time, money, and/or skills.

2. It targets prospective students who appreciate a simple educational and learning service.

3. It offers prospective students an easy and effective method to do what they are already trying to do.

Distance learning itself is not inherently sustaining or disruptive in nature; rather it is how and to whom this innovation is deployed that ultimately determines whether online learning will be sustaining or disruptive. The school administrator needs to be able to critically review technology tools that optimize learning and as well be a consistent advocate for teacher buy-in and accountability measures.

The following questions are addressed in this chapter:

- What are the key characteristics leaders need to have when integrating Web 2.0 tools to support learning?

- What are the products to deliver that leaders need to understand (i.e., how might teachers be trained so they understand correctly that online learning technology is to deliver knowledge and skills, not just content)?

- How can leaders encourage teachers and students to build differentiation/personalized learning?

- How can leaders provide effective training on a regular basis to assist teachers with integrating different Web 2.0 tools that support their learning and/or their work?

- How can leaders facilitate a learning community and **community learning**—that is, understanding, knowledge, or learning that grows beyond individual members of a community—to aggregate collective intelligence via social networking and connecting?

Mistaken Perceptions

There are a few misconceptions about distance learning that mislead educators, practitioners, and policymakers to plan, develop, and deliver effective instructions. Distance learning has been seen as fast learning, like fast food. Distance learning currently integrates computer and Internet technologies and is characterized by speed and immediacy—the ability to access a vast amount of information at the click of a mouse, coupled with multiple communication channels and social networks. This seems contradictory to traditional notions of education—the need to reflect, to build cumulatively on existing knowledge and develop individual understanding over time. Just as there has been a backlash against "fast food" with the "slow food" movement, some are arguing for the need to a return to "slow learning" as a counter to the speed and immediacy that digital learning appears to offer.

Many educational institutions perceive that distance learning is about putting all instructions online. Many schools and other educational institutions attempted to use the Internet to develop online courses involving two-way real-time communication between online teachers and students in a remote location. They were marketed as a comparable alternative to a "bricks and mortar" education. As many administrators, teachers, and students came to realize, however, initially the quality of the distance learning was found lacking when compared to traditional classroom-based instructions.

This mentality restricted the goals of distance learning to those of an "alternative" to traditional education. Distance learning was about convenience learning. Today, distance learning has attained the status of mainstream education. The misperception that it was a poor alternative to mainstream education is today not supported by research. When the option of traditional education was not available, it was necessary to satisfy the desire/necessity for learning through distance learning. Therefore, many people see distance learning as "second-best education." Again, this misperception is not supported by research.

Distance learning applies various computer technologies to make learning occur; therefore, people refer to distance learning as the "technology revolution," which is misleading. Frequently, distance learning institutions focus on technology development and revolution rather than people. It should be seen as a human revolution, a revolution in human capabilities (Batson, 2008). In the span of a few decades, humans have learned to think with their fingers, to imagine that a flat screen is really as big as the world, to create new personae for themselves, to expand their social interactions in number and kind, to write and design in new ways, to visualize complex concepts, to find information in seconds, and to incorporate that information into a constantly evolving awareness. People, not machines, are doing all of this.

Technology affords people to discover abilities, talent, and imaginations and expand human capacities. We humans are discovering aspects of our abilities and imaginations that we didn't know about before. Centuries ago, we discovered things that could make nice sounds, and we found the musical talents and abilities that we have. Now, we have discovered digital technologies that help us solve problems, communicate, and create in ways we didn't know about before.

The Net Generation

The extent of technology use by students, particularly by the **net generation**— people born after 1980, suggesting that these students fundamentally differ from previous generations in the way they process information, communicate, and learn—is a critical issue in distance learning. Kennedy et al. (2006) assert that educational institutions are ill equipped to educate a new generation of students whose sophisticated use of emerging technologies is incompatible with current teaching practice. The net generation's technology users create considerable implications for school policy and practice. Oblinger and Oblinger (2005) describe the characteristics of the net generation, arguing that these students are comfortable with technologies and suggesting that the ways in which they learn are task orientated and experiential.

These students prefer to receive information quickly and are adept at processing information, multitasking, and using multiple/multimodal communication channels to access information and communicate with friends and tutors. Net generation students are actively involved in codesigning their e-learning environments and have technical tools and skills that provide them with new opportunities for organizing and restructuring their own learning experiences (de Laat, Lally, Simons, & Wenger, 2006).

Current Use of Course Management System Software for Distance Learning

Many educational institutions perceive that **course management systems (CMSs)**, also known as learning management systems, or LMSs (see Chapter 4), include most or many of the learning tools for online learning and online communication (i.e., e-mail, discussion boards, chats, grading systems, student grouping systems) as part of their core provision and strategic plans, rather than instructional designs and strategies that focus school policy on the use of personalized, student-centered tools. In fact, most educational institutions' current CMS or LMS has been through several versions, such as Blackboard and WebCT; however, it has remained the same or lacked innovated improvement for distance learning. Even where the pedagogy is student centered, CMSs/LMSs are not—administrative processes and assessment practice remain firmly bound to hierarchical, differentiated educational structures.

Web 2.0 Disrupts Distance Learning

Web 2.0 technologies, which support, encourage, and provide Web space for content published by the user rather than the Web site designer or developer, have the potential to disrupt current distance learning technology and have long been promoted as disruptive (Sharples, 2002). Web 2.0 has become synonymous with this more interactive, user-generated, and collaborative Internet instrument (Alexander, 2006). Many argue that the new possibilities of these social networking tools result in a fundamental shift in the way students learn, consume, and produce new artifacts (Braun & Schmidt, 2006; Brown, 2000). In other words, researchers value the importance of whether students are given tools and opportunities to create personal learning space to enhance their own learning. This is validated by a Web 2.0 construct proposed by Tu, Blocher, and Roberts (2008).

Web 2.0 technology disrupts current distance learning technology as it offers more equity of participation and mutual negotiation. Conole, de Laat, Dillon, and

Darby (2008) ask critical questions: Will simply letting Web 2.0 loose on education be enough to bring about such changes, or is something more needed? Will the changes in social practice we have seen generally through adoption of Web 2.0 happen automatically, or is there something fundamentally different about education? Current distance learning technology is essentially more individualistic and objective while the philosophies inherent in Web 2.0 technology are more social and subjective.

Arguably, then, there has never been a better alignment of current thinking in terms of good pedagogy—that is, emphasizing the social and situated nature of learning rather than focusing on knowledge recall with current practices in the use of technologies (i.e., user-generated content, user-added value, and aggregated network effects). Despite this, the impact of Web 2.0 on education has been less dramatic than its impact on other spheres of society, use for social purposes, supporting niche communities, collective political action, and social commentary. This difference is due to a complex set of factors, technological, organizational, and pedagogical, that the administrator needs to be aware of.

Current distance educational systems are slow to change; the practice and process of teaching and learning are embedded in these systems. It is critical to think about how distance learning institutions must map different pedagogies to use Web 2.0 tools. Tu et al. (2008) proposed theoretical constructs for Web 2.0 learning environments to highlight four dimensions of learning that can be integrated to consider using different tools that afford online students to create, develop, and manage their own learning space.

Constructs for Web 2.0 Learning Environments

Web 2.0 learning environments are grounded in sociocultural learning. Online sociocultural learning is in a constant flux of cognitive development with the force of dynamic social interaction. It is in need of a construct to guide researchers and practitioners to elaborate how interaction occurs in Web 2.0 learning environments. A Web 2.0 construct is proposed by grounding online sociocultural learning (Tu & Yen, 2007), sociopsychological theories, communication theory, and others. Tu et al. (2008) proposed that the constructs of Web 2.0 learning environments contain four dimensions—cognitive, social, networking, and integration—to create and manage individual learning spaces in distance learning.

Cognitive Dimension

In a theater performance, actors create and/or follow scripts that direct their performance in their drama. The cognitive dimension serves a similar function in

Web 2.0 learning environments, as it refers to the process and development within sociocultural learning environments. This dimension focuses on the process of the individual thinking about his or her engagement in and the culture within the learning environment rather than products, performance, and biology. In other words, individuals think about what, how, and with whom they will contribute, which is then implemented as they generate their content through interactions. Furthermore, they may think strategically about this process, which could be viewed as a metacognitive element of this dimension. The metacognitive element of this dimension may impact how students interact within Web 2.0 learning environments as they may add, reduce, or modify elements of their "self" by strategically projecting an identity that may not be a totally transparent representation of their "self." In other words, students in this environment may create a script that directs their performance.

Psychological phenomena emerge from an interaction of processes (Cole, 1995). This process is observed as one attempts to understand the mental models of the other parties through mutual explanations by projecting different identities. A more effective explanation refers to sharing, self-reflecting, negotiating, and self-explanation, called elaborated explanation (Dillenbourg, Baker, Blaye, & O'Malley, 1996). Webb (1991) concluded that engaging students in elaborated explanation would lead to knowledge improvement because elaborated explanation ensures students progressively integrate the process into their knowledge structures. This can be validated by Vygotsky's (1962) deliberate semantics: the change required from maximally compact inner speech to detailed written speech.

Social Dimension

The social dimension refers to actors and their relationships to others. Sociocultural learning focuses on both the individual and the social contexts that constitute the relationships of individual, social, and cultural environments. This relation is explained by the causal two-way relationship between individual and social properties, including the internalization processes associated with the development and externalization processes whereby individuals affect social structure (Valsiner, 1998). Social linkage and human networks become critical in Web 2.0 learning environments.

Networking Dimension

The networking dimension refers to the network technology architecture/ stage that empowers actors/students with advanced mechanisms/props/tools to learn/perform. These technology mechanisms/props allow students/actors to design their clothing, to weave the fabric, to tailor their clothing, and/or to select a different wardrobe to present different characters in the drama that is unfolding on their theatrical stage, the individual learning space. These mechanisms create, edit, reflect, visualize, and organize social content in the platforms of flat structured, collaboratively navigated, and/or socially navigated systems and so forth. Wiki technology affords participants to weave, design, and tailor clothing; blog technology allows students to select different clothing; Second Life allows students to act on a virtual stage.

Although networking technologies are hard technologies, in social learning environments, they should be perceived as cultural tools. The objects/tools that are associated with social practices and acts should be considered cultural tools that are perceived, interpreted, and employed differently in different activities, contexts, events, and situations, since cultural practices are socially embedded. It should be seen as a situated and distributed learning system.

Web 2.0 technological forces shape students' networking practices (Boyd & Ellison, 2007). Instruments (hardware) and semiotic tools (text/language, user-generated content, mashups, RSS, and folksonomies) are employed to achieve online social interaction supported (Freire, 1994) by premeditated tools (wiki writing, blog reflection, and social annotation). Wertsch and Tulviste (1992) observed the relationship between the use of tools and the performance of actions as "individual(s)-operating-with-mediational-means" (p. 8). This is the evidence that social tools and the individual become one.

Integration Dimension

The integration dimension refers to actors/students performing/engaging in activities. Depending on the contexts, sometimes actors/students have many active and interactive acts/activities to perform/engage in while sometimes they may have less. It is critical that all interactions engage students in collaborative and community-related activities because acting/learning is a social ritual.

Collaboration

Collaboration could range from involving one's self to involving others in meaningful and authentic/situated activities. How schools collaborate with their community and the district is critical. Meaningful and authentic activities bond students and teachers collectively to catalyze social interaction into skills and knowledge acquisition. Learning is conceived as a property of the group (social and cultural) and is built up from the individual participants. Online sociocultural learning that emphasizes collaborative, meaningful, and authentic learning activities could provide effective strategies to improve learning. Situated cognition theory (Lave, 1988) states that the environment is an integral part of cognitive activity and not merely a set of circumstances in which context-independent cognitive processes/activities are performed. Sometimes each individual collaborates with him- or herself to manage his or her multiple identities to engage in more constructive (articulate/reflective) acts. Sometimes individuals collaborate with other students' multiple identities to engage in more active (manipulative/observant) acts. Ideal, meaningful, and authentic online activities should allow students to acquire ownership in negotiating, planning, and managing processes in collaborative and authentic project-based learning activities in a **learning community**, where the purpose of membership is for individual learning through the engagement with other community members.

Community

Online learning communities, by accentuating the scaffolding approach, could potentially create dynamic social interaction to engender positive social acts with others. Online students engage themselves with online technology in building partnerships with other learners. Online students are involved in a distributed model of cognition (Pea, 1993) that is embedded in cultural-historical tradition based on Vygotsky's (1978) theory.

A learning community goes beyond students getting together to learn. Four different types of learning communities (Carotenuto et al., 1999) are identified to obtain a better understanding of how community members process and engage in community activities: communities of interest, communities of purpose, communities of passion, and communities of practice. These four communities provide different sets/stages upon which students act based on their contexts (needs, intentions, and purposes).

District Structure and Processes

Web 2.0 technology emphasizes the fundamental shift from information to communication, more specific in social communication/interaction. Effective Web 2.0 integrations would require each individual student to manage his or her Web 2.0 tools to meet his or her learning goals. Distance learning institutions should be aware of Web 2.0 technology architecture and plan their technology learning structures and processes.

The aim is to provide an enabling learning architecture along with a series of exemplary learning applications that demonstrate how Web 2.0 principles can be applied in an educational context.

Architecture of Learning

A key characteristic of Web 2.0 is user participation—the "wisdom of the crowds," the "architecture of participation"—mashups, remixing, and co-construction are fundamental and widespread practices in Web 2.0. In contrast, despite the general increase in group collaboration in recent years, educational systems fundamentally revolve around individual testing—evidencing of attainment of a level of knowledge and understanding against a set of predefined criteria. Even where group work is encouraged, more often than not there are strategies to ensure recognition of individual contribution to some extent.

Authority Destructions

Social constructivism is a more student-centered approach to learning that emphasizes the need for coconstruction of knowledge (please see Chapter 5). Traditionally, education and the way teaching occurs are divided into subject fields with knowledge, on the whole, being static and unchanging. This model has been increasingly challenged in the last few decades as subject domains fragment and diversify and as knowledge seems to expand exponentially. It is no longer possible for any individual to be an expert in his or her field, with an understanding of the full scope of his or her domain. Web 2.0 by its nature copes seamlessly with a complex and changing knowledge domain; fundamental to Web 2.0 practice is that no one individual is expert and rather all individuals are part of a social network of others; the power of the Web enables knowledge to be co-constructed and hence continually changed as needed.

Personal Learning Space

Web 2.0 tools are available as free online services. What is also noticeable about these new tools is that many are multifaceted in nature. Their use in combination has led to a new paucity in the system; information can be transmitted seamlessly between systems, and functionality created in one tool can be embedded or be made available in another. For example, the "embed" function enables SlideShare presentations or YouTube videos to be incorporated into blogs and run in situ in that environment. This enables students to create their own personal environment and to consume information at a location and in a format they choose/control. The emphasis on the social and collaborative characteristics of these new tools is very prominent, as is the shift from desktop tools to Web services—emphasizing the assumption that there is near-ubiquitous access to the Internet.

It is evident that the new technologies now enable individuals to personalize the environment in which they work or learn, appropriating a range of tools to meet their interests and needs; such **personal learning environments** have been considered as an alternative to institutionally controlled virtual learning environments, such as CMSs or LMSs. Personal working environments and a mixture of institutional and self-selected tools are increasingly becoming the norm. Research looking at how students are appropriating technologies points to similar changes in practice: Students are mixing and matching different tools to meet their own personal needs and preferences, not just relying on institutionally provided tools; indeed in some instances students shun the latter in favor of their own personal tools.

Weller (2007a) strongly argued that CMSs/LMSs are dead and do not support effective distance learning strategies. Online students have been using and managing Web 2.0 tools based on their own learning preferences, communication styles, and so forth. The plethora of free and often functionally better tools now available is challenging the notion of an institutionally developed and controlled CMS or LMS.

Clearly there is tension between personalized tools and institutional tools, between integrated institutional systems and loosely coupled systems, and between what we should control and what students should control. The implications are profound, for institutional structures and processes, for individual roles and identities, and for the way in which we view learning and teaching.

The Strengths of Web 2.0 Tools

Web 2.0 tools normally have a few distinguishing features to support and enhance individual learning spaces.

- Appropriate tools: Because the tools are loosely coupled the educator and students can choose the ones they want, rather than being restricted to the limited set in a CMS/LMS.

- Collective eco-learning community: Compared with managing an individual space system, online learning would be integrating more actively with collaborative tools to promote cross online learning communities.

- Guests from outside the community: With student-controlled space, students are freely able to invite guests to participate in their online learning spaces. This kind of intracommunity collaboration is very limited in a CMS/LMS.

- Better-quality tools: Because offering each of these loosely coupled elements is what each company does, it is in each one's interest to make them really good. This means they stay up-to-date, have better features, and look better than most things produced by schools or districts.

- Friendly, similar interfaces: Related to the above, these tools often look better and similar, and also their use makes a course feel more user-friendly to a student who is raised on these tools compared with the rather sterile, dull systems encountered in higher education.

- Cost: Using collective tools to explore various effective learning tools is without cost or results in minimal costs.

- Avoids software sedimentation: While institutional systems tend to embody institutional practice, which becomes increasingly difficult to break, having a loosely coupled system makes this easier and also encourages people to think in different ways.

Planning Personal Learning Space

Personalization and appropriation of technologies are the keys to personal learning space. Personalization and a sense of control come across as key factors of success in the use of Web 2.0 technologies. Importantly, if students did not find the technology or platform provided by the school or district useful, they were in a position to bypass it in favor of their own personalized approach and preferred tools (Conole et al., 2008). This raises a challenge in terms of institutional policy on technologies.

These personalized tools are limited to one course or course use. Students can appropriate selected tools for another course or for noncourse uses. Below are a few examples that distance learning teachers and their principals can integrate to support individual students' learning spaces. This is not an exhaustive list for online learning activities.

- Social interaction: Integrate social networking sites (MySpace, Facebook, Ning) and online profiles to support social relationships and promote trust to build healthy online learning communities.

- Content with discussions: Wiki technologies allow the content to be uploaded; each page has its own forum, and students control the content and participate in active content discussions.

- Social communication: Integrate Twitter or Jaiku to create low-level, non-intrusive conversations between students. Discussion boards are appropriate as well.

- Virtual meetings: Integrate Flashmeeting and Skype and schedule regular sessions.

- Announcements (news and updates): Integrate teachers' blogs to which students subscribe via RSS.

- Quiz/informal assessment tools: There are many assessment tools available, such as Blog Quiz that can be embedded into course content wiki pages.

- Resources: Zotero and Delicious afford students to manage their online resources on a Web platform.

- Sharing: Collaborative sharing is the key to social learning. Google Docs, FileURLs, SlideShares, YouTube, and Diigo allow students to share their files, presentations, videos, and annotations online on different public and/or private levels.

Professional Development

For administrators to provide effective infrastructures for online teachers and instructional designers, professional developments for Web 2.0 technologies are needed. When principals plan and implement programs based on the human elements of the innovation, they are required to make sensible and wise plans. Students, not machines, are the agency for technology learning. People are in control and are the revolution and the emergent miracles. Technology professional developments are not just about technology skills. In fact, the success of Web 2.0 technology innovation depends on faculty members understanding what talents and abilities their students can discover in themselves when they distribute and appropriate different Web 2.0 tools. In other words, the faculty members themselves have to spend a semester integrating their own Web 2.0 tools to discover what talents and abilities in themselves come forward.

Three major steps are critical in teacher technology training. First, online teachers must become "performers," those who can facilitate online students to manage their individual learning spaces. This means online teachers would employ Web 2.0 technologies before assigning students to do so. Second, intuitions should assist teachers with identifying a purpose for adopting Web 2.0 technologies so they know how to design their curriculum effectively and then how to assess this innovation. Third, intuitions should assist teachers with relating Web 2.0 technologies to the goals of the course and help show how they fit in and benefit students.

Critical Issues

Integrating Web 2.0 tools to support distance learning has several weaknesses and issues (Weller, 2007b) to be resolved and further pondered.

- Authentication: Students are required to sign in each time a different Web 2.0 tool is accessed.

- Frustration: Frustration occurs when students are limited to certain tools despite an increased ability to cope with a range of tools.

- Support: Noncentralized technical support must be available.

- Reliability: Lesson control is needed in the server times and service level agreement for intuitions.

- Monitoring: There is a lack of ability to monitor students' learning progress.

- Distracting: Integrating multiple tools could be distracting from learning.

- Support from students: It is unclear whether a positive or negative impression occurs when students seek support from fellow students, rather than from the school or district.

Conclusions

The next generation of tools (Web 2.0 learning) is disrupting learning as it is disrupting CMSs/LMSs. Distance learning leadership should reflect from the past and look forward to establish distance learning for the future. As Shakespeare (1904) observed in *As You Like It*, "All the world's a stage, and all the men and women merely players" (p. 56). Web 2.0 environments afford online students the opportunity to learn by acting in a learning environment and thus to interact to accomplish their learning goals. Learning begins in a classroom where the teacher occupies "center stage" while students are the audience to absorb the lessons being presented. This soliloquy moves to a more interactive level where teachers invite students to share their own individual learning and performance space to interact with the teacher or other students through group activities.

Key Principles for Leaders to Know

When integrating Web 2.0 tools to support learning, it is critical to understand the key characteristics of Web 2.0 tools and their key values.

- Products to deliver: Provide training to teachers so they understand correctly that online learning technology is to deliver knowledge and skills, not just content.

- Web platform: Provide effective training via a Web platform to model effective educational services/pedagogy.

- Personalization and choice: Encourage teachers and students to build differentiation/personalized learning.

- User positioning: Allow and encourage teachers and students to take control of their own data to create personal learning environments.

- Services, not packaged software: Provide effective training on a regular basis to assist teachers with integrating different Web 2.0 tools to support their learning and/or their work.

- Architecture of participation: Allow and empower teachers to organize their learning model via participation, creating, editing, organizing, retrieving, and tagging contents.

- Remixable data source and data transformations: Schools should provide multiple Web 2.0 tools, but they may have duplicate functions to allow teachers to select their own tools. Assist teachers with aggregating and connecting various forms of data/content.

- Software above the level of a single device: One piece of software doesn't result in effective learning. Software should be seen as constant evolving services, rather than items that are updated or upgraded on a regular basis. Schools should update and identify new software to support teachers.

- Harnessing **collective intelligence**, or aggregate intelligence that develops through community learning via social networking and connecting within a learning community: Integrate various Web 2.0 tools to create and foster a healthy social learning community for teachers to learn from each other and exchange effective online technology strategies.

CASE STUDY 7.1 | Web 2.0 Learning Environments

You are a member of a technology advisory committee for your school or district. You and your committee members have been asked to present a system/model that integrates Web 2.0 technology to deliver online learning in the sense of a personal learning environment.

Discussion: Discuss how your school/district currently integrates CMS (Course Management System) to deliver electronic instructions.

Activity: Prepare a Web 2.0 system/model that supports the concept of the following four tenets found in this chapter: personal learning environment, online collaboration, online learning community, and social interaction.

CASE STUDY 7.2	Personal Learning Environment in Web 2.0

Now your superintendent agrees with your committee's presentation and wishes to implement Web 2.0 technology; however, your school or district would like to develop effective policies and practices for the implementation of Web 2.0 technology.

Discussion: Discuss how the development and implementation of policies and practices might be identified.

Activity: Develop a 3-year Web 2.0 technology implementation plan for your school or district. Remember to incorporate the ideas that you previously presented to your district administrator team.

Web Resources

Becta ICT Research (http://www.becta.org.uk/) is a government agency leading the national drive to ensure the effective and innovative use of technology throughout learning.

Building the Field of Digital Media and Learning (http://digitallearning.mac found.org/site/c.enJLKQNlFiG/b.2029199/k.94AC/Latest_News.htm), from the MacArthur Foundation, helps determine how digital technologies are changing the way young people learn, play, socialize, and participate in civic life.

EDUCAUSE (http://www.educause.edu/) is a nonprofit association whose mission is to advance higher education by promoting the intelligent use of information technology.

FutureLab (http://www.futurelab.org.uk/) supports transforming the way people learn through innovative technology and practice.

Horizon Reports (http://www.nmc.org/horizon) identify key emerging technologies.

O'Reilly Media (http://oreilly.com/) publishes the knowledge of innovators through various media. Tim O'Reilly initiated the term *Web 2.0.*

Teach Web 2.0 Consortium (http://teachweb2.blogspot.com/2007/09/teach-web-20-consortium-kick-off.html) purports to explore Web 2.0 social networking tools and determine their educational value.

Web 2.0 Summit (http://en.oreilly.com/web2008/public/content/home) brings the intelligence, innovation, and leadership of the Internet industry together to discuss the future of Web 2.0 technology.

References

Alexander, B. (2006). Web 2.0: A new wave of innovation for teaching and learning? *EDUCAUSE Review, 41*(2), 32–44.

Batson, T. (2008, November 5). *Machines are dumb.* Retrieved December 5, 2008, from http://campustechnology.com/articles/2008/11/machines-are-dumb.aspx?sc_lang=en

Boyd, D. M., & Ellison, N. B. (2007). Social network sites: Definition, history, and scholarship. *Journal of Computer-Mediated Communication, 13*(1), article 11.

Braun, S., & Schmidt, A. (2006). *Socially-aware informal learning support: Potentials and challenges of the social dimension.* Proceedings of the European Conference on Technology-Enhanced Learning (EC-TEL 06), Heraklion, Greece, October 2006. Retrieved December 11, 2008, from http://publications.professional-learning.eu/Schmidt_Braun_LOKMOL06_final.pdf

Brown, J. S. (2000). Growing up digital: How the Web changes work, education, and the ways people learn. *USDLA Journal, 16*(2), 10–11.

Carotenuto, L., Etienne, W., Fontaine, M., Friedman, J., Muller, M., Newberg, H., et al. (1999). *CommunitySpace: Toward flexible support for voluntary knowledge communities.* Paper presented at the Changing Places workshop, London. Retrieved October 28, 2008, from http://domino.watson.ibm.com/cambridge/research.nsf/0/0e8c8166a02d5338852568f800634af1/$FILE/community space.PDF

Christensen, C. M., Aaron, S., & Clark, W. (2002). Disruption in education. In *The Internet and the University: Forum 2001* (pp. 19–44). Boulder, CO: EDUCAUSE. Retrieved December 6, 2008, from http://net.educause.edu/ir/library/pdf/ERM0313.pdf

Cole, M. (1995). The supra-individual envelope of development: Activity and practice, situation and context. *New Directions for Child Development, 67,* 105–118.

Conole, G., de Laat, M., Dillon, T., & Darby, J. (2008). Disruptive technologies, pedagogical innovation: What's new? Findings from an in-depth study of students' use and perception of technology. *Computers & Education, 50*(2), 511–524.

de Laat, M., Lally, V., Simons, R., & Wenger, E. (2006). A selective analysis of empirical findings in networked learning research in higher education: Questing for coherence. *Educational Research Review, 1*(2), 99–111.

Dillenbourg, P., Baker, M., Blaye, A., & O'Malley, C. (1996). The evolution of research on collaborative learning. In E. Spada & P. Reiman (Eds.), *Learning in humans and machine: Towards an interdisciplinary learning science* (pp. 189–211). Oxford: Elsevier.

Freire, M. M. (1994). *A socio-cultural/semiotic interpretation of intercommunication mediated by computers.* Paper presented at the International Conference L. S. Vygotsky and the Contemporary Human Sciences, Moscow, Russia.

Kennedy, G., Krause, K., Gray, K., Judd, T., Bennett, S., Maton, K., et al. (2006). Questioning the net generation: A collaborative project in Australian higher education. In *Proceedings of the 23rd annual ascilite conference: Who's learning? Whose technology?* (pp. 413–417). Sydney: The University of Sydney. Retrieved December 11, 2008, from http://www.ascilite.org.au/conferences/sydney06/proceeding/pdf_papers/p160.pdf

Lave, J. (1988). *Cognition in practice: Mind, mathematics and culture in everyday life (Learning in doing).* Cambridge, MA: Cambridge University Press.

Oblinger, D. G., & Oblinger, J. L. (2005). *Educating the net generation: An EDUCAUSE e-book publication.* Retrieved December 11, 2008, from http://www.educause.edu/educatingthenetgen/5989

Pea, R. D. (1993). Practices of distributed intelligence and designs for education. In G. Salomon (Ed.), *Distributed cognitions: Psychological and educational considerations* (pp. 47–87). Cambridge, United Kingdom: Cambridge University Press.

Shakespeare, W. (1904). *As you like it* (p. 56). Boston: D. C. Heath & Co., Publishers.

Sharples, M. (2002). Disruptive devices: Mobile technology for conversational learning. *International Journal of Continuing Engineering Education and Lifelong Learning, 12*(5/6), 505–520.

Tu, C., Blocher, M., & Roberts, G. (2008). Constructs for Web 2.0 learning environments: A theatrical metaphor. *Educational Media International, 45*(3), 253–268.

Tu, C., & Yen, C. (2007). Online socio-cultural learning. *International Journal of Continuing Engineering Education and Lifelong Learning, 17*(2/3), 99–120.

Valsiner, J. (1998). *The guided mind: A sociogenetic approach to personality.* Cambridge, MA: Harvard University Press.

Vygotsky, L. S. (1962). *Thought and language.* Cambridge, MA: MIT Press.

Vygotsky, L. S. (1978). *Mind in society.* Cambridge, MA: Harvard University Press.

Webb, N. M. (1991). Task-related verbal interactions and mathematics learning in small groups. *journal for Research in Mathematics Education, 22*(5), 366–489.

Weller, M. (2007a, June 12). *The Ed Techie: My personal work/leisure/learning environment.* Retrieved December 5, 2008, from http://nogoodreason.typepad.co.uk/no_good_reason/2007/12/my-personal-wor.html

Weller, M. (2007b, August 11). *The Ed Techie: The VLE/LMS is dead.* Retrieved December 11, 2008, from http://nogoodreason.typepad.co.uk/no_good_reason/2007/11/the-vlelms-is-d.html

Wertsch, J. V., & Tulviste, P. (1992). L. S. Vygotsky and contemporary developmental psychology. *Developmental Psychology, 28*(4), 1–10.

Chapter 8

DESIGN OF CREATIVE ONLINE LEARNING SPACES

Mary I. Dereshiwsky

The **online classroom**, a place on the Internet where students and teachers log in to learn together and which contains links to learning modules, discussion forums, announcement posting areas, a question-and-answer posting area, quizzes, tests, and other online learning resources related to a given class, presents unique opportunities for leading-edge instructional delivery. With the growing popularity of Web-based courses, educational leaders need to be aware of the distinctive features of an **online course**, in which subject matter is offered for teaching and learning over the Internet in an online classroom, as compared to the traditional face-to-face course. What are the components of effective, creative online course design? This chapter will discuss best practices for design of instructional content and student **assessment**, or evaluation of teaching performance for its effectiveness. It will also explain some special areas for **posting**—that is, the composition and display of a message that can be viewed by some or all parties in an online course (other students and/or the teacher) or the submission of a course assignment in an online classroom—and how they are important to successful student learning online (see also Chapter 11). The role of the lesson plan will also be discussed. Finally, some creative ways of individualizing the online classroom will be shared.

The following questions are addressed in this chapter:

- How can leaders convey to others that individualizing online course design is feasible and doable?

- How can leaders work with others to understand one does not have to be a computer programmer to design a successful online course?

- How can leaders provide professional training in creating online instructional materials?

- What are the differences between an online course syllabus and a typical syllabus for a face-to-face course?

It's All in the Delivery: How to Effectively Package Instructional Content

Successfully translating instructional lectures to the visual online classroom format may take some careful planning. It's important to keep in mind the primarily *visual* medium of the online classroom. This means packaging what you have to say in a way that is appealing and understandable to your students. So, just like an architect sketches out the layout of a house before beginning to build it, you should also take some time to lay out the structure and flow of your online course before putting it up as Web pages in your online course area.

The **Certified Online Instructor (COI)** certification offered by the Learning Resources Network (LERN), which is based on completion of several courses on how to teach online, passing a review of one's online teaching, and passing a comprehensive exam covering online teaching and learning, uses the following quality criteria when reviewing online class lessons:

1. Break up your instructional materials into **modules**, or units of content in an online course that are equivalent to a cluster of chapters in a textbook, and topics.

   This is much like breaking up your in-class lesson plans day-by-day into carefully sequenced content subtopics to cover throughout the course. Another way to look at it is to think of your overall course as a tree, the modules as branches on that tree, and the topics as leaves on each branch. A detailed explanation with examples follows. Each module and topic that you create as your lesson plan can be placed in a clickable Web page address inserted into online course reading material that takes students to supplementary learning materials on the Internet related to their main reading if they click on it; such **hyperlinks** should be accessible to students from your course home page.

Take a look at the breakdown of modules and topics in the following Algebra I online course: http://teachers.henrico.k12.va.us/math/hcpsalgebra1/modules .html. "Mr. Rabbit's Rock Soup" incorporates creative use of graphics and helpful hyperlinks, as well as eye-friendly placement of reading content, in its learning module: http://ocw.mit.edu/OcwWeb/hs/home/home/index.htm.

2. Begin with how to be a successful online student.

Before launching into your content discussion, it might be helpful to give your K–12 students a little coaching in how to be successful online students. The online classroom will be very different in some ways from the face-to-face classroom. You want to be sure they know what to expect and get started on the right foot. The following link from Oregon's online "Cool School" provides some helpful tips for success as an online student: http://coolschool .k12.or.us/courses/orientation/.

The following online self-quiz can be readily adapted for the K–12 level. It alerts students to the technology skills and personal work habits they will need to be successful in the online classroom: http://www.onlinelearning.net/ OLE/holwselfassess.html?s=725.40100993s.093m521k80. Check out the following topic outline for a seventh-grade math class online: http://www .sd01.k12.id.us/schools/west/teachers/kormys/Website/acc7.html. The following shows a subtopic outline breakdown for an eighth-grade math class: http://schools .cbe.ab.ca/b682/pdfs/CourseOutline_Math8.pdf.

3. Break up the text in each module and topic into short paragraphs and lists with spacing in between.

It's easier on the eyes than trying to run too many lines of text together in your online lectures. Take a look at the page layout and placement of information on the following high school English course Web page: http://grammar.ccc.commnet .edu/grammar/composition/tone.htm.

The following tutorials for seventh-grade math combine animation and fun, practical applications for specific math topics: http://www.theonestop.net/ tutorials.htm.

4. Add embedded hyperlinks throughout your online reading material.

They can point students to additional explanations or advanced reading on your current topic. Here are some links to additional practice problems for K–12 math students: http://www.theonestop.net/tutorials.htm and http:// mathforum.org/dr.math/.

5. Add Web-based games and other creative learning activities throughout your online lectures.

These add interest and make learning fun for your students because they are not just passively reading your lecture notes from a Web page. The following two links blend math and music, making it especially appealing to students with auditory as well as visual learning styles: http://www.geocities.com/Vienna/9349/ and http://www.escape.com/~paulg53/math/pi/music/.

Math students will enjoy applying their skills to the following puzzles and games: http://www.coolmath4kids.com/, http://www.funbrain.com/kidscenter.html, and http://www.mathplayground.com/.

6. Add graphics and animation to help break up the text and also add interest.

Think of it as how a good cook uses spices. Too little means the dish is too bland (i.e., straight reading of plain text by students). Too much is overwhelming and can blot out the taste of the main dish. You should aim for a creative sprinkling of such visuals throughout your online lectures. Note the creative, inviting animation that is also a clickable link to a "one-stop" Web page of information for a seventh-grade math class in Boise, Idaho: http://www.sd01.k12.id.us/schools/west/teachers/kormys/Website/acc7.html.

You can download lots of free clip art, graphics, and animation that will appeal to your online students at the following sites: http://www.freefever.com/graphics/, http://www.gifanimations.com/, and http://www.webweaver.nu/clipart/.

7. Add audio to your online class lessons.

As Draves (2000) has pointed out, audio takes your online course to the next level. In addition to traditional recorded lecture presentations, you can record and embed anything from individual comments on students' papers to short recorded announcements within most online classroom software. The following Web site lets you see examples of K–8 lessons in art, history, math, science, and music that contain audio narration: http://www.k12.com/get_a_taste_of_k12/k12_lessons/.

The following link contains a variety of learning materials to supplement a lesson on the Constitution: http://www.egusd.net/tor/constitution.html.

8. Add PowerPoint files to your text-based online lecture notes.

They combine the potential of both visuals (Point 6) and audio (Point 7) as enhancements to your text-based lecture notes. Check out the following collection of online PowerPoint files for math, science, social studies, English, and other subject areas in the elementary grades: http://www.graves.k12.ky.us/powerpoints/elementary/.

Pete's PowerPoint Station contains a creative collection of PowerPoint files and games to add to your online course content: http://www.pppst.com/.

You can also download templates to create your own PowerPoint files for your online courses at the following link: http://www.animationfactory.com.

Take a look at the lesson plans for an online "digital history" course in the link below: http://www.digitalhistory.uh.edu/historyonline/lesson_pl.cfm. The "teacher's toolbox" link below contains collections of lesson plans in every subject area: http://www.proquestk12.com/curr/teachers.shtml#general.

Putting It to the Test: Adding Assessments to Your Online Classes

In addition to your presentations, you'll want to build in some Web-based equivalents of tests and measurements. Of course, you still also have the option of requiring students to come to a physical location to take a closed-book timed test, such as a cumulative final exam. Indeed, many online courses still contain this option. However, its use seems to be on the wane. A typical online course may include students from different continents, not to mention countries, states, and cities. Adult professional learners who need the flexibility of such online courses may live and work at a distance from campus. They can include military personnel on active duty. All of these factors may make a traditional proctored, sit-down, timed, closed-book exam impractical as an assessment for an online course. Even locally based K–12 students may appreciate some additional flexibility when it comes to taking their course assessments. What other options exist for assessment of student learning in the online classroom? There are actually a number of such assessments you can conveniently build in. They include the following:

Ungraded Self-Quizzes

LERN's COI certification program highly recommends such ungraded quizzes as a best practice of online instruction. For one thing, they remove the fear of the dreaded "pop quiz" for students. Instead, students can conveniently access such quizzes to get a quick gauge of their understanding of the current topic of focus. With the pressure of the grade removed, students can use the results of these quizzes for informational purposes: to let them know which course concepts they have a good handle on and which ones they may need to restudy. Most online course software allows you to readily create such quick checkpoint quizzes for your students. The Moodle online course software, for instance, lets you draft such quizzes in a variety of response formats, including true or false, fixed choice, and even short answer. They can be embedded within your online course content as hyperlinks or at the end of the related lecture topic to which they refer. You can find a variety of quiz games for spelling, geography, current events, and other subject areas at the following link: http://quizhub.com/quiz/quizhub.cfm. The following is an example of a self-graded online quiz in computer vocabulary at a K–8 school: http://www.englishmedialab.com/Quizzes/intermediate/computer%20vocabulary %20quiz.htm. Note how the following Abraham Lincoln self-paced quiz for the primary grades combines appealing animation and graphics: http://www.siec.k12 .in.us/west/proj/lincoln/quiz.htm.

One-Minute Papers

These are intended as focused quick assessments that are graded. Students are invited to share any remaining questions they might have on this current focus area of the one-minute paper. The one-minute paper is a quick way to provide students with such feedback and an initial grade—in a way that is not as intimidating to them as a full-fledged exam. Examples of this are noted below. Take a look at the creative fairy-tale assignments on Ms. Effie's literature Web page: http://homepage.mac.com/mseffie/assignments/fairy_tales/fairytale.html. In the following link, elementary students are asked to read a description of Pandora's box and write a one-minute essay restating the main points of what they read and giving an example: http://www.dositey.com/2008/Topics/topic.php?&sub=58&subsub=1 &topicId=21. Students get a chance to be a book reviewer, summarizing the best features of a book they would recommend to others in the following link: http://www.dositey.com/2008/Topics/topic.php?&sub=58&subsub=1&topicId=3.

Web-Based Open-Book, Open-Notes Tests

This is an increasingly popular method of assessment in online courses. As noted earlier with regard to quizzes, most online classroom software will allow you to create online exams with starting and ending release dates. The open-book format once again removes some of the anxiety for students. At the same time, it allows you to assess more complex understanding than simple factual recall. Students can complete the exams online and submit them with several mouse clicks, according to the specific submission features in the particular online classroom software that you are using. The following link contains a collection of Web-based tests, including mock practice tests and other student review materials, for an online Algebra I course: http://teachers.henrico.k12.va.us/math/hcpsalgebra1/soltests.html.

Papers and Case Studies

Papers and case studies can be completed either individually or in groups. Such assessments are not much different from traditional face-to-face classes. You can post instructions for completion and submission in your online course materials. Take a look at this writing assignment on the American Revolution from an online course in U.S. history: http://www.montereyinstitute.org/courses/US%20History%20I/nroc%20prototype%20files/coursestartc.html. The Web link below would make a fun writing project on fairy tales from around the world for grades 7–12: http://homepage.mac.com/mseffie/assignments/fairy_tales/folk.html.

Let's Chat: Creating Discussion Posting Areas

Palloff and Pratt (2007) have written extensively regarding the value of **online learning**, or studying a topic area by interacting with teacher and students in an online classroom. Their research indicates how peer-to-peer interaction enhances the learning experience overall. In particular, a successful online learning community helps dispel the sense of isolation that an online student can sometimes feel. One way to encourage such peer-to-peer interaction is by the creation of discussion questions. Many online teachers create at least one discussion question per course topic. They require students to post their own thoughts on each question as well as provide a minimum number of responses to peers. Teachers should also engage in these discussions: More will be said on this topic in Chapter 11. The following link contains some helpful guidelines for teachers on how to plan and monitor online discussions for K–12 students: http://www.k12.com/our_approach/online_discussions/.

The following fun math discussion topics can be used in the elementary grades:

- "Gimme Five!" asks students to think of five examples where math is mentioned in the popular media—for example, TV, songs, book titles, or advertisements—and then share these examples with their classmates.

- "Meet an Alien" challenges K–3 students to think about what parts of their world, such as nature or human-made things, they would share with an alien who is visiting them from another planet (adapted from http://www.dositey.com/2008/Topics/topic.php?&sub=34&subsub=1&topicId=1).

Tell Me About It: Creating an Announcement Posting Area in Your Online Course

A typical face-to-face course may start with the teacher making some quick announcements before launching into the topic discussion of the day. These announcements may include late-breaking developments, as well as reminders of upcoming due dates for assignments and tests. You can create a similar announcement posting area in your online course. It serves as a convenient equivalent of a bulletin board for students. Some types of course room software such as Blackboard or WebTycho will place these announcements so that they are the first thing your online students see when they log into your online course. Or you can create a read-only **discussion forum**, a posting area inside an online course where students and teacher share ideas on an open-ended topic of focus, for this purpose. It can be titled "Announcements and Updates." Some teachers require students to check it at least every other working day to ensure that they are not missing important information that their classmates are receiving. You will especially want to have some necessary information waiting for your incoming students in this announcements area at the beginning of the term to help them get started on the right foot. Figure 8.1 shows a sample of such an announcement post letting students know how to contact tech support.

Figure 8.1	Sample Announcement Post

IMPORTANT TECH SUPPORT PHONE NUMBERS Welcome, everyone! I'm so glad you're here! ☺

Please make note of these important tech support phone numbers:

For our Flagstaff-based partners: 523-XXXX

Long-distance toll-free tech support number: 1-888-520-XXXX

Good to have handy just in case! ☺

Note the clever "scrolling-banner" use of animation on the following announcements page for an Algebra II online course: http://teachers.henrico.k12.va.us/math/hcpsalgebra2/.

Check out the warm, student-friendly conversational tone of Mrs. Kormylo's opening comments in her seventh-grade math class online Web page: http://www.theonestop.net/.

You can also use this announcement posting area to inform your students if you need to be offline for any length of time and if you know this in advance (e.g., a faculty meeting, travel to a conference). In it you can inform your students of the approximate duration of your absence offline. By doing so, your students won't worry if they've posted a question, an assignment, or another message for you and think that you may not have received it.

Inquiring Minds Want to Know: Creating a Question-and-Answer Discussion Forum

Have you ever sat in a live and in-person class where one student asks a question and not only do you realize you have the exact same question but you also benefit from hearing the teacher give an answer? It's the same principle with a question-and-answer discussion forum (posting area). Sure, you could respond to student questions via e-mail. But doing so can quickly become unwieldy and inefficient if you happen to get the same question by e-mail multiple times from different students, as Draves (2000) has pointed out. With the question-and-answer posting area, you can answer the question only one time for all students to see. Some teachers require their online students to use this question-and-answer discussion forum (posting area) for any and all nonconfidential questions related to the course syllabus, readings, assignments, or other learning activities. In this way they may be benefiting other students as well as themselves when they publicly share their course-related question. In addition, such a question-and-answer discussion forum can actually provide a collaborative learning opportunity for students. You may have sometimes overheard a student in a live and in-person class explain something in such a way to another student that you found yourself thinking: "Why didn't I say it like that?!" The online posting area offers a similar opportunity for peer coaching. In one graduate-level course introducing educational research, 5% of the students' final grade depends on their monitoring of this question-and-answer discussion forum and helping the teacher respond to posted questions by their peers. This does not, of course, excuse the teacher from keeping a close eye on questions and answers and providing his or her own replies to students' posted questions. At the same time, though, another student might happen to beat the teacher to it: log in before the teacher does, see a peer's posted question, and provide a helpful reply. One final benefit of requiring students to provide replies to posted questions is that it discreetly reinforces their own understanding. We've all heard the classic saying: "The best way to learn something yourself is to try to teach it to someone else." In this way, the question-and-answer discussion forum can serve as another outlet for the type of peer community building that Palloff and Pratt (2007) have espoused.

Adding Those Creative Personal Touches

The image of online instruction as a cold, impersonal correspondence school can be debunked with some creative thinking on your part. There are an infinite number of ways in which you can add your individual touches to your online classroom.

Bill Draves of LERN likes to post cartoons dealing with humorous aspects of technology in a link he calls "Cyber Snack." He posts a different one daily in his weeklong online courses. It serves as a fun diversion and laugh break for students while they learn new course material.

This author personalizes the learning environment by newsy news bulletins and the sharing of student information that is appropriate and timely.

The above are just a few ways to bring your own unique creative touches to your online classroom. Figure 8.2, an opening splash screen for an evaluation research

Figure 8.2	Splash Screen Example

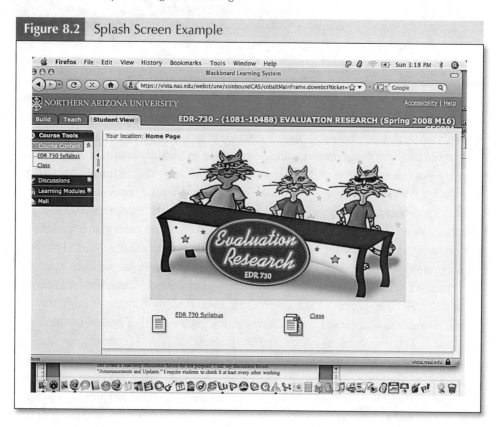

course, visually blends this author's passion for cats and connects the image of a popular current TV show to the idea of evaluation as judging.

You can find a collection of resources on how to use blogs and wikis in the following link: http://opencontent.org/wiki/index.php?title=Using_Blogs_and_Wikis_in_Education.

The Rules of the Road: Your Online Course

In a typical face-to-face course, the instructor may spend all or part of the first class meeting going over the class expectations. Attention to detail is even more important in the online classroom where you won't see your students' faces and be able to talk them through the parts of the syllabus in such a live and in-person class meeting.

Experts of best practices agree that the more detail, the better. You want to try to spell everything out to leave as little room for doubt or confusion as possible. Your contact information, accessibility, due dates for readings and assignments, and the grading and lateness policy are especially important. Many of us also include some links to online self-assessments (whether or not an online course is right for you), as well as links to study skills and time management skills resources. Note how the following online eighth-grade algebra syllabus contains essential information on the subtopics to be covered, related readings, assignments, and grading policy: http://www.chicousd.org/dna/marsh_jr/documents/CUSD_Course_Outline_Math_8_A.pdf.

You can download examples of K–12 online courses in a variety of subject areas at the following Web site: http://www.hoagiesgifted.org/online_hs.htm#collect.

The comparatively longer length of such a detailed online course may make it easy for students to miss important information in it. As a result, some teachers like to give students a quiz covering the essential information in the course outline to help draw their attention to it. The same design principles apply to the course as to the online instructional materials (e.g., attractive visual layout, prudent choice of font type and size, judicious use of borders and graphics, not running too much text together). While the course will usually be contained on a Web page in a clickable link, it's also helpful to provide students with access to a downloadable file version (e.g., a Microsoft Word or PDF file). Some teachers encourage students to print out a copy and keep it by their computer for convenient reference.

So How Do I Make This Happen? Converting Class Notes and Other Learning Activities Into Online Instructional Materials

Now that you have an idea of how to sketch out your online instructional materials, how do you turn it into an actual online course? There are a number of ways you can go about this conversion.

For example, online teachers need to make sure they know what the large conceptual knowledge is for learning. This means *beginning with the end in mind.* Lessons that introduce concepts should include activators with ways to build on prior/background knowledge and lesson reviews or summarizers at the end of the lesson to provide for some practice of key vocabulary and give the teacher formative conceptual assessment.

This author finds that the easiest way is to type lectures (module and topic content) into Microsoft Word files. Next, starting with this outline of modules and topic content topics, draft a separate Microsoft Word file for each topic within each module. Next, if you are able to write HTML coding you can proceed. If not, Bill Draves's (2000) sage advice is to "get a techie." Most schools will have a tech support department or a designated contact person who can do this for you. If not, Draves suggests you look into hiring a teenager or college student to convert your content into Web pages. He advises that many young people today are tech savvy and will welcome this opportunity to earn a little extra money. At the same time, it frees you up to concentrate on the course content rather than having to learn to become a programmer. In addition, you might ask your tech support person if the online classroom software your school is using offers an option of a blank course shell that you can fill with your course learning materials. The most popular ones such as WebCT Campus Edition and Vista offer such empty shells for course creation.

Finally, if you prefer the do-it-yourself approach, you can use Web page creation software such as Adobe Dreamweaver to do so. Microsoft Word will also allow you to save word-processed files as Web pages. The following link contains a collection of videos on how to create an online course: http://teachertube.com/searchList.php?search_type=video&tags=create%200nline%20course.

You can create a free online course learning space by registering with Nicenet at the following link: http://www.nicenet.org/.

Web 2.0 contains online course creation links and tools for the K–12 teacher: http://www.kn.att.com/wired/fil/pages/listweb20s.html. You can create an online gradebook and quiz maker using the following link: http://www.classbuilder.com/.

Conclusions

By careful attention to such course design principles, you can maximize for your teachers and students the flexibility of the learning experience along with conveying to your teachers their ability to use their own individual creative touches. As a result, students are likely to have a rewarding, high-quality learning experience that harnesses the efficiency of technology as a learning medium.

Key Principles for Leaders to Know

- It is possible to convey your creative individual touches in online course design.

- You do not have to be a computer programmer to design a successful online course.

- Online instructional materials should be visually appealing.

- Online instructional materials can be enhanced with graphic and audio elements.

- Online instructional materials should be divided into modules and topics.

- An announcements posting area creates a convenient visual bulletin board for students to find late-breaking developments and course reminders.

- A question-and-answer posting area is an efficient way to respond to student questions.

- An online course syllabus should be more detailed than a typical syllabus for a face-to-face course.

CASE STUDY 8.1 │ Transitioning Courses to Full Online Classes

You are a principal in a school that is experimenting with the idea of offering some classes online. As part of this initiative, you meet with your teachers to encourage them to consider designing and pilot-testing some online courses. At this initial meeting, several teachers fearfully admit: "Granted, this is the information age, where computer use is everywhere, it seems. It's one thing to add some computer enhancements to a traditional face-to-face course—for example, a Web search assignment for students to complete. But you're asking us to create all online courses completely from scratch! The thing is, I'm no computer techie! I can just about use a word processor, but that's about it. Wouldn't I need to know how to program in HTML and all that in order to create an online course?"

Discussion: Discuss the following questions: Can designing and teaching an online course be beneficial to your teachers' professional growth and development? If so, how? Decide as a group some specific ways that you would "sell" this idea to initially reluctant teachers, including specific identification of "what's in it for them."

Activity: Draft a response to these teachers to address their concerns. You are encouraged to be creative in the packaging of this response: For example, you might want to create a PowerPoint file or Web page. Ensure your teachers have supporting documents: Provide some additional supporting evidence from at least five other books, journal articles, or Web sites dealing with online instructional design.

CASE STUDY 8.2 │ Student Issues and Online Learning

One of the teachers in your school has accepted the challenge of designing an online course. She happens to teach in an area that is also a content specialty of yours. Shortly after agreeing to give it a try, this teacher shows up at your door one afternoon feeling frustrated. "I'm sorry, but I've got a real case of writer's block. It's hard to come up with learning activities and materials that are text-only . . . where I can't see their faces or hear their voices telling me where they might be feeling stuck!"

Discussion: Discuss the following to share with this teacher:

1. How would you explain one key concept in your field of study as an online Web page (instructor lecture)? Include any additional elements such as graphics, embedded hyperlinks, or audio files that you think would enhance this learning material.

2. Come up with an example of a related discussion question that would correspond to this concept and that could be shared with online students as a discussion forum.

(Continued)

(Continued)

Activity: Following your discussion points, help your teacher draft two fixed-choice and two open-ended questions that assess students' understanding of that concept and create a one-minute paper assignment covering this concept.

Web Resources

The **Certified Online Instructor (COI) Certification Program Requirements** (http://www.teachingonthenet.org/courses/certified_online_instructor/index.cfm) are detailed by the Learning Resources Network (LERN).

ClassBuilder (http://www.classbuilder.com/) provides an online gradebook and quiz maker.

A **collection of fun math games** can be found at http://www.netrox.net/~labush/math.htm.

A **collection of K–12 lesson plans for all content areas** is available from http://www.proquestk12.com/curr/teachers.shtml#general.

A **collection of online PowerPoint files for math, science, social studies, English, and other subject areas in the elementary grades** is available from http://www.graves.k12.ky.us/powerpoints/elementary/.

A **collection of resources on how to use blogs and wikis** is available from http://opencontent.org/wiki/index.php?title=Using_Blogs_and_Wikis_in_Education.

A **collection of videos on how to create an online course** are available from http://teachertube.com/searchList.php?search_type=video&tags=create%20online%20course.

Content Web pages (modules and topics) for an Algebra I online course are available from http://teachers.henrico.k12.va.us/math/hcpsalgebra1/modules.html.

Downloadable examples of syllabi for K–12 online courses in a variety of content areas are available from http://www.hoagiesgifted.org/online_hs.htm#collect.

Downloadable templates to create your own PowerPoint files to include in your online course are available from http://www.animationfactory.com.

Effective use of animation as a clickable link for a seventh-grade math class is demonstrated at http://www.sd01.k12.id.us/schools/west/teachers/kormys/Website/acc7.html.

An **example of a self-graded online quiz in vocabulary at the K–8 level** is available from http://quizhub.com/quiz/f-vocabulary.cfm.

An **example of an Abraham Lincoln self-paced quiz with graphics and animation for the primary (K–3) level** is available from http://www.siec.k12.in.us/west/proj/lincoln/quiz.htm.

An **example of Web page content for a high school English class grammar lesson** (http://grammar.ccc.commnet.edu/grammar/composition/tone.htm) is available from the Capital Community College Foundation.

Examples of K–12 lessons in art, history, math, science, and music that contain audio narration are available from http://www.k12.com/get_a_taste_of_k12/k12_lessons/.

General tips for effective online course design are available from http://74.125.113.132/search?q=cache:FKRn1NHaM7wJ:teaching.unr.edu/coursemakover/docs/instructionalDesignTips.pdf+online+instructional+design&cd=26&hl=en&ct=clnk&gl=us.

Guidelines for how to plan and monitor online discussions in grades K–12 are available from http://www.k12.com/our_approach/online_discussions/.

The **LERN Faculty Club** (http://www.teachingonthenet.org/faculty_club/index.htm) provides Web-based resources for online faculty.

The **lesson plan for a digital history course** is available from http://www.digitalhistory.uh.edu/historyonline/lesson_pl.cfm.

The **math discussion topic "An alien is here!"** is available from http://www.dositey.com/2008/Topics/topic.php?&sub=34&subsub=1&topicId=1.

Math puzzles and games are available from http://www.coolmath4kids.com/, http://www.funbrain.com/kidscenter.html, and http://www.mathplayground.com/.

The **"Mr. Rabbit's Rock Soup" online learning module** is available from http://ocw.mit.edu/OcwWeb/hs/home/home/index.htm.

Ms. Effie's fairy-tale short assignments in literature are available from http://homepage.mac.com/mseffie/assignments/fairy_tales/fairytale.html.

Nicenet (http://www.nicenet.org/) is a free resource for creating online courses.

One-minute paper assignments ask students to summarize and apply reading on Pandora's box (http://www.dositey.com/2008/Topics/topic.php?&sub=58&subsub=1&topicId=21)

and ask students in the elementary grades to review a book (http://www.dositey.com/2008/Topics/topic.php?&sub=58&subsub=1 &topicId=3).

OnlineLearning (http://www.onlinelearning.net/OLE/holwselfassess.html?s=725.40100993s.093m521k80) provides a self-quiz for readiness to be an online learner.

Pete's PowerPoint Station (http://www.pppst.com/) contains a creative collection of PowerPoint files and games to add to your online course content.

Practice problems for K–12 math students can be found at http://www.theonestop.net/tutorials.htm and http://mathforum.org/dr.math/.

Quiz Hub (http://quizhub.com/quiz/quizhub.cfm) is a source of online quizzes for spelling, geography, current events, and other subject areas.

Refereed proceedings for several years from the Technology, Colleges & Community Worldwide Online Conference (http://etec.hawaii.edu/proceedings/) contain valuable tips for effective leading-edge online course design.

A **sample announcement page for a seventh-grade math course** is available from http://www.theonestop.net/.

A **scrolling banner announcement post for an Algebra II online course** is available from http://teachers.henrico.k12.va.us/math/hcpsalgebra2/.

Seventh-grade math tutorials combining games and animation are available from http://www.theonestop.net/tutorials.htm.

Sources of free clip art and animation to include in your online course include http://www.freefever.com/graphics/, http://www.gifanimations.com/, and http://www.webweaver.nu/clipart/.

The **syllabus for an eighth-grade algebra course** is available from http://www.chicousd.org/dna/marsh_jr/documents/CUSD_Course_Outline_Math_8_A.pdf.

Tips for students on how to be successful in the online classroom are available from http://coolschool.k12.or.us/courses/orientation/.

Topic outlines are available for a seventh-grade math class (http://www.sd01.k12.id.us/schools/west/teachers/kormys/Website/acc7.html) and an eighth-grade math class (http://schools.cbe.ab.ca/b682/pdfs/CourseOutline_Math8.pdf).

Tutorials for applying online learning theories to instructional design are available from http://www.patsula.com/usefo/webbasedlearning.

Two collections of online instructional design resources are available from the University of Pittsburgh (http://www.pitt.edu/~poole/onlinelearning.html) and the Educational Technology Users Group (http://www.ibritt.com/resources/index.htm).

A **variety of learning materials to supplement a lesson on the Constitution** are available from http://www.egusd.net/tor/constitution.html.

Web 2.0 online course creation links and tools are available from http://www.kn.att.com/wired/fil/pages/listweb20s.html.

Web-based tests and review materials for an online Algebra I course are available from http://teachers.henrico.k12.va.us/math/hcpsalgebra1/soltests.html.

A **writing assignment on the American Revolution for an online history course** is available from the National Repository of Online Courses at http://www.monterey institute.org/courses/US%20History%20I/nroc%20prototype%20files/coursestartc.html.

A **writing project on fairy tales from around the world, for grades 7–12,** is available from http://homepage.mac.com/mseffie/assignments/fairy_tales/folk.html.

References

Draves, W. A. (2000). *Teaching online.* River Falls, WI: LERN Books.

Palloff, R. M., & Pratt, K. (2007). *Building online learning communities: Effective strategies for the virtual classroom* (2nd ed.). San Francisco: John Wiley & Sons, Inc.

PART III

Leadership
Social, Cultural, and Legal

Part III recognizes the social, cultural, and legal issues surrounding technology usage. **Chapter 9: School, Technology, and Society** discusses student and parental technology use and impact. **Chapter 10: Security, Internet Safety, Copyright, and Plagiarism** provides the basic information and challenges for school and student safety and security.

Chapter 9

SCHOOL, TECHNOLOGY, AND SOCIETY

Home-School Communications and Access

Laura Sujo-Montes and Lawrence Gallagher

Undoubtedly, our country needs to prepare citizens who are capable of taking on the challenges that a global society presents. Today's students need to be able to compete tomorrow within a multinational global workforce, perform jobs that may not exist, and work with people of different cultural and ethnic backgrounds. Technology can be a catalyst for this learning. However, many school leaders face societal challenges that take school administration to new levels. Some examples of those challenges are **achievement gaps**—the disparity in educational measures such as standardized tests, dropout rates, and graduation rates—between ethnic minority and ethnic majority students, between rich and poor students, between students with technology access and those without it (known as "digital divide"), and so on and so forth. Technology, a major social, educational, and economic catalyst, will provide the background to explore the role and impact of technology in schools from the school administrator's point of view.

The following questions are addressed in this chapter:

- How can leaders ensure they are proficient users and consumers of technology and supporters of a school vision that places technology as an essential part of the curriculum?

- What are the characteristics schools and universities need to educate a workforce that is capable of engaging in active learning and lifelong learning, higher cognitive skills, and collaboration and of using effective coping skills?

- What are the effective and efficient uses of technology for teaching and learning that enable faculty to feel comfortable using the technology to teach?

- How can leaders understand that different cultures use and perceive technology in different ways?

- What are the skills leaders need to help educators see assistive technology as a potential tool the student can use to improve his or her functioning or minimize the effects of his or her disability?

- How can leaders use the various models to help educational teams select the appropriate technology and understand that assistive technology is a highly integrated system, not just a device?

21st-Century Skills

The term *21st-century skills* has been in the education vocabulary for at least a decade. These are the skills that current pre-K–16 students need to master in order to be successful in a global economy. Although there are some different versions of these skills, such as the ones presented by the Partnership for 21st Century Skills (2008) and the slightly different skills presented by enGauge and the Metiri Group (Lemke, 2002), a constant in both sets is the ability to use knowledge to communicate, collaborate, analyze, create, innovate, and solve problems. More specifically, 21st-century skills are listed below (Partnership for 21st Century Skills, 2009).

- Core Subjects: English, reading, world languages, arts, mathematics, economics, science, geography, history, government, and civics, among others.

- Interdisciplinary Themes: global awareness; financial, economic, business, and entrepreneurial literacy; civic literacy; and health literacy. These should be woven through the core subjects.

- Learning and Innovation Skills: creativity and innovation, critical thinking and problem solving, and communication and collaboration. Skills in these areas will give students the ability to manage increasingly complex working environments.

- Information, Media, and Technology Skills: information literacy, media literacy, and ICT literacy—that is, being knowledgeable in **information and communication technologies (ICTs)**, which connect people and machines. These are must-have skills to be able to access, manage, and classify an abundance of information.

- Life and Career Skills: flexibility and adaptability, initiative and self-direction, social and cross-cultural skills, productivity and accountability, and leadership and responsibility. Such skills are necessary to remain competitive in the workforce.

In a few words, schools need to educate a workforce that is capable of engaging in active learning and lifelong learning, higher cognitive skills, and collaboration and of using effective coping skills (Kozleski, 2004).

The State Educational Technology Directors Association (SETDA) in its publication *Maximizing the Impact: The Pivotal Role of Technology in a 21st Century Education System* (2008) argues that technology is essential for any industry and organization to remain competitive and that education should be no different. According to Snyder (2009), the National Center for Education Statistics reported that 83.9 million people, or 1 in 4 people living in the United States, were either employed or enrolled in a public or private educational institution. However, the use of technology for teaching and learning is not widespread especially in schools with low-income students and high minority student enrollment. The educational system seems to be determined to keep the outdated agricultural and industrial models of education where the teacher's role and knowledge are pivotal for learning, as teachers are considered the holders and transmitters of knowledge, even when school-age children and young adults are more attuned to using technology for independent learning (Jackson & Crawford, 2008). Nevertheless, having knowledge is no longer enough to get ahead in a competitive global market, but having the ability to transform (more than hold) knowledge is the sought-after skill for today's and tomorrow's workers.

Digital Divide

Considering that the Internet is commonly used to do everyday things, such as shopping, completing bank transactions, and entertainment, and that its use will grow only bigger, it is important to know how ethnic minority populations are making use of it.

In other words, if culturally and linguistically diverse populations are far behind in the use of technologies, our society is at risk of lagging behind the rest of the developed countries because of the impact that having an ill-prepared citizenry will have on the United States. Unfortunately, research has already confirmed that these populations' use of technology is at much lower rates than that of the majority. Inequalities in the use of digital technologies have come to be known as the digital divide.

What is the digital divide? Why is it important to understand its consequences? Digital divide is the unequal access to ICTs dictated mainly by socioeconomic status (SES) or income. However, some (e.g., Besser, 2001) contend that the digital divide is more than access to the technology and that it also includes learning how to use information in an effective way, having access to relevant content, and being able to become an active, rather than a passive, user of ICTs. The digital divide may present itself in many different forms and have far-reaching consequences beyond being able to access the technology itself. Some forms of digital divide include the following.

- Connectivity at home. Households with high and moderate-to-high incomes represent more than 80% of connectivity. Consequently, only about 20% of low-income households have an Internet connection.

- Low **bandwidth**, or the speed of data transfer usually measured in bits per second. Many low- and medium-income households, if connected, have access mostly to low bandwidth (a very slow connection) preventing them from accessing media-intensive Web sites and from performing tasks that require a rapid server response.

- Disempowerment. In a time when most businesses and agencies have a Web presence to conduct government, money transactions, and education on the Web, being disconnected means being disempowered (Cooper, 2004).

- Better educational opportunities. A broadband connection (high-speed connectivity) may make the difference to be able to advance in a profession through distance learning. For schools, a broadband connection may give students access to advanced placement courses in rural and isolated high schools.

- Less civic participation. The latest presidential campaign demonstrated another use for the Internet: civic participation. Lack of connectivity may prevent people from becoming fully engaged in volunteerism or activism or even from knowing what the current political issues are that the nation is facing.

- Social inclusion. Social capital, in part, comes from social inclusion. ICTs can be used in ways that promote social inclusion for the disadvantaged when they are used to create, innovate, and transform knowledge (Warschauer, 2003).

Besides the digital divide, the economic divide is greatly affecting impoverished students and students of color because of the unequal distribution of funding. For instance, students in supported and well-funded schools perform at the levels that their international counterparts do, while low-income and ethnic minority students may have an achievement gap of several grade levels. DeVita, Colvin, Darling-Hammond, and Haycock (2007) state that in some schools with high minority student enrollment, 13-year-old Black and Hispanic students read at the level of White 9-year-olds. Unfortunately, the achievement gap continues to grow because low-income-serving schools have "lower budgets, larger class sizes, lower quality curriculum, and less-qualified teachers and school leaders in most states across the nation" (DeVita et al., 2007, p. 19). Besides having less state-of-the-art technology at their disposal, teachers in low-income schools assign technology use for low-level activities, such as drill and practice and word processing, and are less likely to use it to enhance their curriculum (Smerdon et al., 2000), as compared to their more wealthy counterparts who assign their students to use the technology for higher-level tasks, such as doing Internet research.

What to do? "The power of one" is not as crazy of a concept as it may seem. School administrator leaders have the opportunity to set the tone for special and curricular activities that can do more than teach students. For instance, an administrator can

- advocate to increase broadband penetration to low-income households by making it more affordable and by connecting rural areas;

- increase computer literacy by establishing community centers or opening schools to the community during after-school hours for computer access;

- promote technology infrastructure investments through partnerships between local governments and businesses;

- make it a school and district goal to provide broadband connection to schools; and

- make every effort to make available advanced placement courses through videoconferencing and distance learning technologies to high school students in rural, remote, or depressed economic areas.

The Administrator of Today

New times call for new attitudes, and the school administrator's role is no exception. In the past, the principal was seen as the authoritarian figure in the school, and in truth, many such principals had an authoritarian leadership style. However, the administrator of today is more expected to have a transformational leadership style where he or she will probably seek to form a community of learners, stimulate creativity among teachers, be a mentor or coach, and maybe even provide inspiration to teachers (Guthrie & Schuermann, 2010). The challenge for those administrators who are not very open to the use of technology is to find a way to incorporate it as part of their leadership style, if they want to truly create a 21st-century school.

The International Society for Technology in Education (ISTE) is the leader in setting technology standards for students, teachers, and administrators. As noted in detail in Chapter 2, the latest version of the National Educational Technology Standards for Administrators (NETS-A) contains five standards, three of which put special emphasis on the use of technology to foster 21st-century skills (i.e., to develop a digital society). The NETS-A (ISTE, 2009) are as follows:

1. Visionary Leadership

2. Digital-Age Learning Culture

3. Excellence in Professional Practice

4. Systemic Improvement

5. Digital Citizenship

Therefore, it is expected that school administrators are proficient users and consumers of technology and supporters of a school vision that places technology as an essential part of the curriculum. The importance of this expectation is based on the fact that the vision that the administrator sets for the school is one of the second most important influences (below teacher preparation) on student learning and achievement (DeVita et al., 2007). For instance, if the school administrator thinks that technology is important to use with students, it is very likely that his or her school would have technology available for teacher and student use, that faculty would be involved in technology professional development, and that he or she might even have a paper-free campus.

For example, Hess and Kelly (2007), in a study that examined hundreds of leadership preparation programs across the nation, found that in a "typical" program to prepare principals, less than 20% of instruction time was dedicated to learning how to use technology to make sense of data. If principals play a critical role in schools because they have the potential to impact all of a school's decision making and policy setting (Good, 2008), it becomes clear that an administrator with a strong technology vision has the best chance to lead a school that will fulfill the needs of the digital society. Technology can help create support systems that will make schools stronger; the key is having adequate professional development opportunities in technology use for teachers and administrators (SETDA, 2008).

In the same venue, comprehensive, district, and/or campus-wide use of technology will help create a robust learning environment by transforming data into a tool that helps make curricular decisions.

Professional Development in Schools

Schools are becoming a different place than they used to be. While baby boomer teachers attended schools that had chairs in rows and where the teachers were the holder of knowledge, learning was expected to be linear, and the most advanced technology was not interactive (e.g., the projector), current teachers have the task of educating a population of students who prefer to have control over their learning, who learn independently from the teacher, who prefer to learn using multitopic units, who use technology to access information through their social networks, and who are more producers of media than consumers of the same (Jackson & Crawford, 2008). The challenge becomes to staff a school that is in concert with the students' learning preferences and technology abilities.

Teachers and principals, as any adults, are not easily willing or able to move to attend courses for professional development or continuing education, especially if they live in remote rural areas. Fortunately, many universities and colleges offer online courses that provide meaningful and high-quality "just-in-time" professional development and ample opportunities to advance education. Unlike teachers, principals were not required to attend professional development for career advancement prior to the 1980s since they were believed to know everything they needed to know, from school finance to every curriculum subject, and thus they had no need for professional development (Harris-John & Ritter, 2007). Fortunately, it is now recognized that principals, as well as teachers, do need professional development opportunities to carry on school improvement and to create effective learning environments (Fenwick & Pierce, 2002).

Technology for Management

As discussed above, technology can be an ally in preparing the citizens of the global economy, and administrators play an important role in the use of technology in schools. In fact, Petrides and Guiney (2002) discuss that technology systems can help administrators rethink the school environment to make it a more innovative learning environment better suited for preparing learners for the digital global economy. Some of the applications that administrators can use to successfully manage a school are highlighted below.

Student Data Management Systems

These systems are Web based and provide districts and schools with several valuable features, such as being able to post grades for each student in a private way, serve as a gradebook for teachers, and generate custom reports for school administrators.

Personal Digital Assistants

Some years ago these handheld devices became very popular among administrators because they have the capability of holding data for each student and also of connecting to the school network to retrieve data. Teachers and administrators found the handheld very useful in tracking a student who, for instance, was in the hallways instead of being in class.

Project Management Software

Although this type of software was not developed with the school administrator in mind, it can be very helpful to track the different tasks and deadlines that are so abundant in the principal's job.

Web 2.0 and Social Networking Tools

Web 2.0 is a relatively recent term that refers to the use of applications and tools that run having the Internet as the interface. These tools can be useful to administrators if they are used wisely. For instance, a wiki can be set up to collect opinions from teachers (and parents, if desired) on specific changes that a school must overcome, such as rezoning or restructuring. Blogs can also be useful to administrators in that they allow them to keep a journal and become reflective practitioners. It should be noted that all or most of these applications can be controlled in terms of being private or public and in terms of membership.

Technologies for a Diverse Student Population

American schools may be the most diverse schools on the planet. The draw that this country has on individuals from all over the world results sometimes in more than 80 languages being represented in one school. Understandably, the school system faces a big challenge in trying to educate such a diverse population. On the other hand, it is precisely by educating and reaching this vastly diverse student population that the United States will remain competitive in the global economy. With that in mind, administrators and teachers need to realize that a shift must happen not only in *what* is taught but also in *how* it is taught. In other words, students need to be informed of the way learning environments are constructed; failing to do so will have dire consequences in educating a large population of students (Kozleski, 2004). The following section will bring into light some issues that our schools face in educating students from diverse ethnic, cultural, and ability backgrounds.

The Role of Culture in the Use of Technology

The educator of the 21st century needs to be armed with a plethora of resources, techniques, and strategies that are targeted to meet the needs of all students, including culturally and linguistically diverse students. Among those resources, technology stands out as an indispensable tool that reaches students from all ethnicities and cultures to prepare future citizens for a world that will be negotiated through technology.

Different cultures use technology in different ways. Many times, the use of technology illustrates and affirms the culture's worldview (Carlson, 2007). For example, as part of a thesis for a master's degree, a student invited the elders in an Apache village to come together and name the parts of a computer, something that did not exist in Apache language. Besides naming the computer, the elders came up with a graphic interface for the computer desktop. Each of the regular functions of the computer was represented by a symbol that was related to Apache traditions and culture. For instance, a folder was represented by a special pouch that Apache used to carry things when they traveled; turning on the computer would bring the sun, but turning it off would bring the moon and stars. Myths, religion, art, and philosophy of the culture will interface with the use of technology.

In the classroom, besides using sheltered English methods, teachers need to look at the differences in learning depending on culture. For instance, Armenian and Korean students prefer to work individually while Latino, Hmong, and Vietnamese students prefer to learn in cooperative groups (Park, 2002). Regardless of the learning preference, the same author reported that all English language learners learn better if a combination of visual objects; kinesthetic activities, including tactile learning; and auditory activities are used as part of instruction. An interactive multimedia Web site or presentation would be an excellent way of using technology for this group of students.

Administrators and teachers must know that there are two types of technology use in the classroom: traditional and authentic (Holum & Gahala, 2001). In the traditional type, technology is used to do old things with new tools. That is, technology is used to complete a crossword puzzle, read a linear document, reinforce skills, or perform any other activity that does not require technology. Examples of this technology include some integrated learning systems, computer-assisted instruction, and computer-based tutoring systems (Boethel & Dimock, 1999). The authentic type, on the other hand, gives the user control over the functions of the technology itself and uses technology to complete complex tasks, such as investigation reports where the student may use a word processor to write the text, format it, edit it, add hyperlinks to Web sites, and add pictures. It is pertinent to reiterate that both uses of technology have their niche in the classroom and that the best teacher is the one who is eclectic and knows when to apply the best use of technology.

Technology in Schools With High Ethnic Minority Enrollment

In schools where minority student enrollment is the highest (50% or more), 81% of instructional rooms are connected to the Internet, as compared with 88%–90% of rooms in schools with less minority enrollment. The differences are even bigger when schools are compared by SES. While only 79% of instructional rooms have access to the Internet in schools that have 75% or more of the population eligible to receive free or reduced-price lunch, 90% of instructional rooms enjoy the same access in schools with only 35% or less of their population with eligible status to receive free or reduced-price lunch (Kleiner & Farris, 2002). Within the same building, middle- and high-income students are more likely to have access to the Internet not only in their classroom but also in the lab and the library/media center. In comparison, low-income students are more likely to have access to the Internet only through a computer lab (Corporation for Public Broadcasting, 2003). Unfortunately, the disparities between minority and majority groups do not stop at access but continue in the classrooms.

Smerdon et al. (2000), in their report *Teachers' Tools for the 21st Century,* explained how pedagogy and school-related activities differ for teachers and students depending on the percentage of minority enrollment. For example, for *teacher-related activities,* teachers in schools with low minority enrollment (less than 6%) are more likely to (a) use computers or the Internet for instruction during class time—56% and 45% for high and low percentages of minority students; (b) create instructional materials—81% compared with 71% in schools with high minority enrollment; and (c) communicate with colleagues—62% against 41%, among other activities, but similar disparities between teachers in schools with low and high minority enrollment were found for the percentage of usage of the Internet to communicate with parents and to post homework. Furthermore, in terms of *pedagogical uses of computers,* marked differences were found depending on the percentage of minority enrollment. In schools with low minority enrollment (6% or less), teachers were more likely to (a) assign students to use these technologies for multimedia presentations—49% compared with 36% in schools with high minority enrollment; (b) assign CD-ROM research—55% compared with 38% in minority schools; and (c) use computers or the Internet for Internet research—57% in schools with low minority enrollment compared with 41% in schools with high minority enrollment, among other activities.

Technology for Students With Disabilities

Technology, for many of us, is a tool that makes our lives easier and more productive. As many of us can attest, computers and other electronic technologies are playing an increasingly larger role in all of our lives. For persons with disabilities, however, technology holds the promise of helping them function in integrated settings and accomplish their learning and career goals. The work of Kirkhart and Lau (2007) shows that most children with disabilities who receive adequate support (including technology) and education eventually become independent and productive members of society. Despite this finding, data collected about the technology use with students 15 years old or older indicate that children and adults with disabilities access and use technology significantly less often than their typical peers (Kirkhart & Lau, 2007). For example, surveyed children 15 years old or older indicate that (a) only 44% of people with disabilities have a computer at home (compared to 72% of those without disabilities), (b) only 38% of people with disabilities have access to the Internet at home (compared to 64% of those without disabilities), and (c) only 24.3% of people with disabilities use the Internet at home (compared to 50.5% of those without disabilities).

Yet, technology has been demonstrated to be an effective tool for developing academic skills such as basic literacy (Wilkins & Ratajczak, 2009) and for improving writing abilities (Barbetta & Spears-Bunton, 2007; Gardner, 2008), developing mobility skills for children with intellectual disabilities (Lancioni et al., 2009), helping children with vision impairments explore science content (Jones, Minogue, Oppewal, Cook, & Broadwell, 2006), and improving math abilities of children with hearing impairments (Liu, Chou, Liu, & Yang, 2006).

Technology for students with disabilities is often referred to as assistive technology (AT). These assistive technologies often adhere to the same principles and factors discussed both in this chapter and in other chapters in this volume. As such, they constitute another category in the continuum of technology. Yet, assistive technologies, due to the differences in design, appearance, and operation and by virtue of the populations that use the devices, are frequently seen as a different form of technology, invoking a different set of policies and procedures governing their use.

Recognizing the need to ensure access to assistive technology devices for children with disabilities, Congress included specific provisions for AT in the **Individuals with Disabilities Education Act (IDEA)**. IDEA regulations require that school personnel must consider the need for AT in the educational planning process for all students with disabilities. IDEA defines an assistive technology device as "any item, piece of equipment, or product system, whether acquired commercially off the shelf, modified, or customized, that is used to increase, maintain, or improve functional capabilities of a child with a disability" (IDEA 2004, Section 300.5). In addition, assistive technology must include both devices and services. AT services include any activity that directly helps the student acquire or use the device. These services might include helping the student identify the appropriate device (assessment), customizing or adapting the device to match the student's unique needs, providing training for the student or his or her family, and providing training for school personnel so that they can support the student using the device.

Assistive technologies come in many shapes, sizes, and configurations. For example, using a communication board composed of letters or numbers a student with a speech impairment can spell out words and phrases that communicate basic wants and needs and can engage in social interaction; or the same student can use a computerized, voice-output device that speaks the message after the student touches certain words or pictorial representations of phrases and sentences. A student with a spinal cord injury might use **voice recognition**, an assistive technology that converts spoken language into written text, to write a term paper or dictate a note to a friend. A child with a severe cognitive limitation may use a computer-based learning program to help him- or herself develop sight word skills or operate a tape recorder that speaks the words on flash cards by using a large button switch to turn the tape recorder on or off. A student with a vision impairment might use a handheld magnifier to enlarge the text on a page or use a closed-circuit television to read the same book. Assistive technology devices are available that help children communicate, control their environment, move about their settings, learn, recreate, live more independently, and compensate for sensory limitations. Within these broad categories of devices, there exists a range of possible options, from relatively simple, inexpensive, non-electronic devices (typically referred to as low tech or no tech) to relatively sophisticated, expensive, computer-based devices (high tech).

To help students with disabilities be successful with assistive technology, however, requires more than just providing the device. How educators think about AT is equally as important as access to the technology itself because the thinking process will ultimately govern the decisions that are made. If educators see AT as something that is simply acquired for someone or given to a student with a disability, then they may fall into a dangerous trap of considering the simple access to the device sufficient for success. If educators see AT as a potential tool the student can use to improve his or her functioning or minimize the effects of his or her disability, then they will be less likely to misapply the technology. In this latter case, educators must commit to thinking differently about AT.

Knowing about the person's disability helps somewhat but is of little use in selecting appropriate AT devices. Successful use of technology is a product of many interrelated factors (c.f., Edyburn, Higgins, & Boone, 2005), of which the disability is only one element. Therefore, we must come to understand the factors that interrelate and affect the student's performance to prevent us from employing potentially ineffective or unnecessary AT solutions. Various models have been proposed including the Human Activity Assistive Technology model (Cook & Hussey, 2007), the Bain Assistive Technology System (Bain & Leger, 1997), a human factors approach (King, 1999), and others. While each approach is slightly different, all of them generally involve three critical factors that must be considered when thinking about AT: the person (someone), who must complete a task (something), in a specific setting (somewhere). Taken together, these factors give educators a much better chance of selecting the appropriate AT solution. To understand a person's abilities it is important to gather information about his or her sensory, cognitive, motor, speech and language, and social skills, as well as other characteristics. It is also important to gain an understanding of the student's preferences. Preferences are rarely addressed in a typical AT decision-making process. Yet, as we all know, preferences often determine whether a device will be used effectively. The environment refers to a broad array of potential influences in the areas where the person lives, learns, and recreates. The physical arrangement of the classroom, whether power is readily available, the sophistication of the student's teachers or peers, and the attitudes of those individuals who will directly support the person with a disability all contribute significantly to the eventual effectiveness of the AT solution. Sadly, even when an AT device has all the appropriate features, the environment may restrict or prevent the student from effectively using a device. The tasks a person must perform when using an assistive device are the last critical area we must gather detailed information about. For example, knowing that a specific learning task requires that a person read a passage, take notes on the material, and then study his or her written notes for a quiz helps the educational team focus on technology that will allow the person to read, write, and study. This is much more helpful than simply knowing that the student must participate in a social studies lesson. All tasks can vary along several dimensions. When considering AT devices, however, it is useful to gather information about three important task properties: the types of tasks the person must perform, the variety of tasks he or she must perform in a given day, and attributes of each task (how it is done). Once we have gathered and analyzed the important information, our job is to match the unique set of abilities of the person, the requirements of the tasks he or she performs regularly, and existing environmental constraints to the characteristics of the available assistive technology devices.

While the various models may help educational teams select the appropriate technology, it is important that we understand that assistive technology is a highly integrated system, not just a device. Thinking back to the discussion of the public law, AT is composed of both devices and services. Thus, AT is a system. This AT system can be broadened to include three interlocking parts like those found in a puzzle, as shown in Figure 9.1. The AT puzzle pieces are the devices the student uses, the supports that surround the device use (a service), and the strategies that the person is taught to effectively use his or her device (also a service).

| **Figure 9.1** | The Assistive Technology Puzzle |

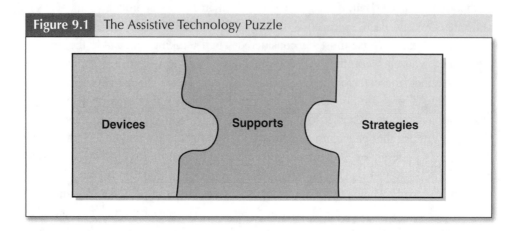

A host of AT devices is available to assist a student with a disability. AT devices may be low tech or high tech and vary across several categories. Training and technical assistance supports are needed by the student who is using the AT or those educators who are working with students who use AT devices. Supports can include modifications to the student's setting, educational interventions to increase the student's skills (either directly related to the technology or of a more general educational nature targeting improved skills across academic areas), and training for the student's service providers. Typically the group of persons who are in need of supports includes the student with a disability, family members, teachers or instructional assistants, therapists, and the student's peers. Strategies are the final essential element in any AT intervention. Students with disabilities (and their support network) need to learn how to operate the AT device(s) they own. Beukelman and Mirenda (2005) identify three levels of competency needed to effectively use AT: operational competence (the ability to operate the device), strategic competence (knowing how to use the device to accomplish a goal), and problem solving or coping (knowing what to do when the device fails or malfunctions). Without this type of support (training), AT devices are often underused or abandoned, an unfortunate but not-that-uncommon finding (Phillips & Zhao, 1993; Riemer-Reiss & Wacker, 2000; Scherer, 1993, 2000).

Even with the best of intentions, AT applications rest on a well-trained workforce that has the necessary knowledge and skills to assist the student with a disability in using the device effectively and appropriately. Assistive technology training in schools and school districts can be characterized as attempting to develop broad assistive technology knowledge and skills through a combination of workshops, coursework, and experiences. While sometimes these efforts produce the needed knowledge and skills, the process lacks cohesion and often produces fairly diffuse knowledge of AT that may or may not help the school district meet its AT service needs. Fifield and Fifield (1997) described the problem of and proposed a multitiered model for assistive technology training. For schools, however, a variation of this model provides a context for an overall training plan. A more cohesive and potentially more effective approach would be to develop training that produces AT capabilities using three distinct levels of knowledge/expertise. See Figure 9.2.

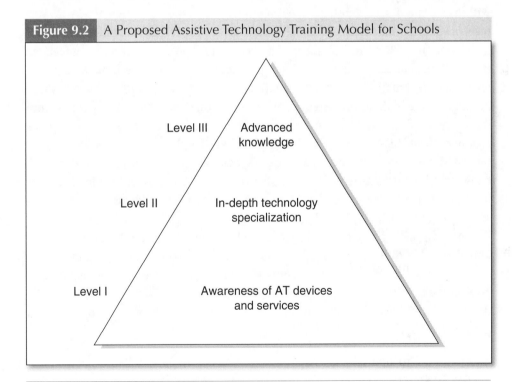

Figure 9.2   A Proposed Assistive Technology Training Model for Schools

Level III — Advanced knowledge

Level II — In-depth technology specialization

Level I — Awareness of AT devices and services

Source: Adapted from Fifield & Fifield, 1997.

At the most basic level, awareness, training efforts should involve a broad audience of school personnel including general education teachers, related service personnel, instructional assistants, and administrators. The emphasis of training efforts at this level is on creating a broad-based awareness of the benefits of AT devices, creating an understanding of the legal requirements for providing AT devices and services, developing awareness-level knowledge of the range of possibilities across AT device and service types, and helping the trainees identify AT resources they can call upon in the future when they work with students who use AT devices. Training should be broadly distributed throughout a school system, enabling that system to address up to 50% of its AT needs through simple solutions. The next highest level of training activities, in-depth knowledge, would seek to develop specific expertise in effective, evidenced-based AT practices and focus on developing specific in-depth knowledge and skills in the principles and practices of AT. Training efforts at this level target a smaller number of trainees, often persons within a classroom serving a student with a disability or a team of **related service providers**—any of a number of professionals who support the education of children with disabilities (e.g., physical therapy, speech pathology, audiology, occupational therapy, counseling)—and attempt to create expertise within a limited set of potential AT applications. When combined with lower-level awareness activities, training at this level can enable a school system to address up to 85% of its AT needs. The last and highest level requires advanced training, specialization, and significant practical experience in a limited set of AT areas. These practitioners often practice AT exclusively and master a small number of areas. School systems sometimes do not have the resources to hire these types of specialists, choosing to subcontract instead. If employed by the school district, these persons with high-level knowledge and skills may be used by districts as their "assistive technology specialist" or serve school systems as a consultant for instructional staff with their most difficult cases. Persons with this highest level of knowledge and skills can help districts address the remaining 15%–20% of their complex AT needs.

For the hope of AT to be fully realized in our schools, educators must be knowledgeable of the promise of AT, understand the range of possible options, be able to see AT as a complex system with many interrelated components, and possess the requisite knowledge and skills to appropriately identify and provide AT devices and services. While we have made great strides over the past several decades, much remains to be done.

Conclusions

It is important that administrators do not relegate the use of technology as an unimportant aspect of school life. As the old proverb advises, principals need to show how to use technology, not to tell others to use it. Universally designed instruction is adapted by astute practitioners and embraced by leadership practices that display effective leader use of technology. Administrators are vested with a big responsibility: to facilitate the effective participation of the entire student population, regardless of individual students' ability, in learning and becoming productive members of society. The use of AT is an involved process that includes more than simply identifying devices or providing funding for their purchase. AT is a system and, as such, will only function properly when all of its parts are in tune and fostered.

Key Principles for Leaders to Know

The effective use of technology for learning, discovery, and reaching the 21st-century skills will soon become a marker of a good administrator. Our nation cannot afford being left behind because of a citizenry that is not adequately prepared to face the new millennium challenges. The following principles are provided to focus the attention on key issues.

- It is expected that school administrators are proficient users and consumers of technology and supporters of a school vision that places technology as an essential part of the curriculum. The importance of this expectation is based on the fact that the vision that the administrator sets for the school is the second most important influence (below teacher preparation) on student learning and achievement.

- Schools need to educate a workforce that is capable of engaging in active and lifelong learning, higher cognitive skills, and collaboration and of using effective coping skills.

- Effective and efficient use of technology for teaching and learning will not happen until faculty feel comfortable using the technology to teach. As such, professional development of teachers is of utmost importance to achieve a 21st-century school.

- The digital divide is more than access to technology; it also includes learning how to use information in an effective way, having access to relevant content, and being able to become an active, rather than a passive, user of information and communication technologies.

- Administrators of today will benefit from having a transformational leadership style. This style will allow them to bring together the interest of all the school stakeholders: administrators, teachers, students, parents, and community.

- Different cultures use and perceive technology in different ways. The best pieces of technology are those that allow the user to create and discover from his or her own point of reference.

- Schools can be used during after-school hours to facilitate technology learning by parents. When parents and students are technology savvy, half of the schoolwork in terms of technology is already done.

- Assistive technology should be thought about in the same terms that other school technologies are thought about. How educators think about AT is equally as important as access to the technology itself because the thinking process will ultimately govern the decisions that are made.

- If educators see AT as a potential tool the student can use to improve his or her functioning or minimize the effects of his or her disability, then they will be less likely to misapply the technology.

- While the various models may help educational teams select the appropriate technology, it is important that we understand that assistive technology is a highly integrated system, not just a device.

- Training and technical assistance supports are needed by the student who is using the AT or those educators who are working with students who use AT devices.

- Three levels of competency are needed to effectively use AT: operational competence (the ability to operate the device), strategic competence (knowing how to use the device to accomplish a goal), and problem solving or coping (knowing what to do when the device fails or malfunctions). Without this type of support (training), AT devices are often underused or abandoned.

- Supports can include modifications to the student's setting, educational interventions to increase the student's skills (either directly related to the technology or of a more general educational nature targeting improved skills across academic areas), and training for the student's service providers. Typically the group of persons who are in need of supports includes the student with a disability, family members, teachers or instructional assistants, therapists, and the student's peers.

- AT training may be proposed as a multitiered model with three distinct levels of knowledge expertise: awareness of AT devices and services, in-depth technology specialization, and advanced knowledge of AT devices.

CASE STUDY 9.1	How Would You Use Technology?

You have just been hired to direct a school that has been put on an improvement plan because it has failed to achieve adequate yearly progress. Before going for an interview at that school, you did a search on the Web for the school Web site, but you did not find one. Once installed in your new job, you met with your faculty and administrators and determined "how things worked" in the school. For instance, you learned that teachers have access to technology only through a computer lab, which they can reserve for their classes only every 2 weeks. Teachers are not keen on technology, so they still report grades using paper sheets. Any communication that the past principal wanted to give to the staff was put in the teachers' mailboxes.

Discussion: Discuss how when you were hired you were given a specific responsibility to bring this school into the 21st-century: How will you do it? Gather in a group and determine the following:

What leadership style will better suit you?

Which 21st-century skills should you target for the first 3 years in the job?

What considerations should you take into account when determining what technology should be purchased?

Who should be trained to what level of expertise in assistive technology? Include in your consideration whether you as the principal should be involved in the training and at what level.

How should you communicate with parents: via mail, e-mail, an Internet-based system, or another method? What are the reasons for your decisions?

Activity: Do a search on the Internet for assistive technologies that can be helpful for the following: learning to read, helping a deaf student be part of the class, helping a blind student have the least restrictive environment, and providing help for dyslexic students. Give at least two names of devices (low tech and high tech) for each category. Provide some examples of technology software and hardware that you as the principal can use to improve school management.

Web Resources

Apple (http://www.apple.com/education/mobile-learning/) allows for mobile learning by providing free access to courses, lectures, articles, and so forth from universities around the nation and the world by using iTunes. Some examples of universities that offer this service are Carnegie Mellon University, the University of Cambridge, and Stanford University.

Assistive and adaptive technology resources are available from http://www.disabilityinfo .gov/digov-public/public/DisplayPage.do?parentFolderId=109 and http://www.emtech .net/assistive_technology.htm.

The **Children's Partnership** (http://www.childrenspartnership.org/) provides access to research reports on children placed in general and special education. Learn of new technology initiatives to help all students reach their potential.

The **EDUCAUSE Learning Initiative's "7 Things You Should Know About . . ." series** (http://www.educause.edu/7ThingsYouShouldKnowAboutSeries/7495) provides concise information on emerging learning technologies and related practices.

Marc Prensky Writing (http://www.marcprensky.com/writing/default.asp) provides access to a wealth of articles from the author of *Digital Natives, Digital Immigrants.*

The **National Educational Technology Standards for Administrators** (NETS-A; http://www.iste.org/Content/NavigationMenu/NETS/ForAdministrators/2009 Standards/NETS_for_Administrators_2009.htm) are the technology standards in which you should be proficient to be able to lead a 21st-century school.

The **State Educational Technology Directors Association** (SETDA; http://www .setda.org/) shares what technology directors across the nation are doing to improve student achievement. You will also have access to research reports.

The **Wallace Foundation** (http://www.wallacefoundation.org/Pages/default.aspx) provides free access to resources on different topics, especially those related to educational leadership.

References

Bain, B., & Leger, D. (1997). *Assistive technology: An interdisciplinary approach.* New York: Churchill Livingstone Inc.

Barbetta, P., & Spears-Bunton, L. (2007). Learning to write: Technology for students with disabilities in secondary inclusive classrooms. *English Journal, 96*(4), 8.

Besser, H. (2001, Spring). The next digital divides. *Teaching to Change LA, 1*(2). Retrieved April 30, 2009, from http://tcla.gseis.ucla.edu/divide/politics/besser.html

Boethel, M., & Dimock, K. V. (1999). *Knowledge with technology: A review of literature.* Retrieved February 18, 2009 from http://www.sedl.org/pubs/catalog/items/tec27.html

Beukelman, D., & Mirenda, P. (2005). *Augmentative and alternative communication: Supporting children and adults with complex communication needs.* Baltimore: Paul H. Brookes Publishing.

Carlson, W. B. (2007). Diversity and progress: How might we picture technology across global cultures? *Comparative Technology Transfer and Society, 5,* 128–155.

Cook, A., & Hussey, S. (2007). *Assistive technology: Principles and practices.* St. Louis, MO: Mosby.

Cooper, M. (2004). *Expanding the digital divide & falling behind on broadband: Why a telecommunications policy of neglect is not benign.* Consumers Union and Consumer Federation of America. Retrieved April 30, 2009, from http://www.consumersunion.org/pub/ddnewbook.pdf

Corporation for Public Broadcasting. (2003). *Connected to the future: A report on children's Internet use.* Retrieved December 2, 2008 from http://www.cpb.org/stations/reports/connected/

DeVita, M. C., Colvin, R. L., Darling-Hammond, L., & Haycock, K. (2007). *Education leadership: A bridge to school reform.* New York: The Wallace Foundation.

Edyburn, D., Higgins, K., & Boone, R. (2005). *Handbook of special education technology and practice.* Whitefish Bay, WI: Knowledge by Design.

Fenwick, L. T., & Pierce, M. C. (2002). *Professional development of principals.* Washington, DC: ERIC Clearinghouse on Teaching and Teacher Education. (ERIC Document Reproduction Service No. ED 477731)

Fifield, M. G., & Fifield, M. B. (1997). Education and training of individuals in delivery of assistive technology devices. *Technology and Disability, 6,* 77–88.

Gardner, T. (2008). Speech recognition for students with disabilities in writing. *Physical Disabilities: Education and Related Services, 26*(2), 43–53.

Good, T. L. (2008). In the midst of comprehensive school reform: Principals' perspectives. *Teachers College Record, 110,* 2341–2360.

Guthrie, J. W., & Schuermann, P. J. (2010). *Successful school leadership: Planning, politics, performance, and power.* Boston: Allyn & Bacon.

Harris-John, M., & Ritter, S. (2007). *E-based professional development (e-PD) for effective teaching and leadership.* The Connexions Project, Connexions module m15069. Retrieved March 19, 2009 from http://cnx.org/content/m15069/1.1/

Hess, F. M., & Kelly, A. P. (2007). Learning to lead: What gets taught in principal-preparation programs. *Teachers College Record, 109,* 244–274. Retrieved August 28, 2009, from http://www.tcrecord.org/content.asp?contentid=12742

Holum, A., & Gahala, J. (2001). *Critical issue: Using technology to enhance literacy instruction.* Naperville, IL: North Central Regional Educational Laboratory. Retrieved January 19, 2009, from http://www.ncrel.org/sdrs/areas/issues/content/cntareas/reading/li300.htm

Individuals with Disabilities Education Act (IDEA). Pub. L. No. 108–446, 20 U.S.C. § 1400 *et seq.* (2004).

International Society for Technology in Education (ISTE). (2009). *National educational technology standards for administrators.* Washington, DC: Author. Retrieved July 5, 2009, from http://www.iste.org/Content/NavigationMenu/NETS/ForAdministrators/2009Standards/NETS_for_Administrators_2009.htm

Jackson, S. H., & Crawford, D. (2008). *Digital learners: How are they expanding the horizons of learning?* The Connexions Project, Connexions module m17218. Retrieved March 19, 2009, from http://cnx.org/content/m17218/1.2

Jones, G., Minogue, J., Oppewal, T., Cook, M., & Broadwell, B. (2006). Visualizing without vision at the microscale: Students with visual impairments explore cells with touch. *Journal of Science Education and Technology, 15*(5/6), 345–351.

King, T. (1999). *Assistive technology: Essential human factors.* Boston: Allyn & Bacon.

Kirkhart, A., & Lau, J. (with W. Lazarus and L. Lipper). (2007, March). *Helping our children succeed: What's broadband got to do with it?* Retrieved August 28, 2009, from http://www.childrenspartnership.org/AM/Template.cfm?Section=Technology&Template=/CM/HTMLDisplay.cfm&ContentID=9734

Kleiner, A., & Farris, E. (2002). Internet access in U.S. public schools and classrooms: 1994–2001. *Education Statistics Quarterly 4*(4). Retrieved March 24, 2009, from http://nces.ed.gov/programs/quarterly/vol_4/4_4/q3_1.asp

Kozleski, E. B. (2004, August). Technology transfer and the field of education: The research to practice conundrum. *Comparative Technology Transfer and Society, 2,* 176–194.

Lancioni, G., Singh, N., O'Rielly, M., Sigafoos, J., Didden, R., Manfretti, F., et al. (2009). *Research in Developmental Disabilities: A Multidisciplinary Journal, 30*(2), 308–322.

Lemke, C. (2002). *enGauge 21st century skills: Digital literacies for a digital age.* Naperville, IL: North Central Regional Educational Laboratory. (ERIC Document Reproduction Service No. ED 463753).

Liu, C., Chou, C., Liu, B., & Yang, J. (2006). Improving mathematics teaching and learning experiences for hard of hearing students with wireless technology-enhanced classrooms. *American Annals of the Deaf, 151*(3), 345–355.

Park, C. C. (2002). Crosscultural differences in learning styles of secondary English learners. *Bilingual Research Journal, 26*(2), 213–229.

Partnership for 21st Century Skills. (2008). Teaching and learning for the 21st century: Report and recommendations of the Arizona summit on 21st century skills. In *Arizona summit on 21st century skills.* Tucson, AZ: Author. Retrieved September 2, 2009, from http://www.21stcenturyskills.org/documents/arizona_summit_on_21st_century_skills_report.pdf

Partnership for 21st Century Skills. (2009). Framework for 21st century learning. In *Arizona summit on 21st century skills* (p. 3). Tucson, AZ: Author.

Petrides, L. A., & Guiney, S. Z. (2002). Knowledge management for school leaders: An ecological framework for thinking schools. *Teachers College Record, 104,* 1702–1717.

Phillips, B., & Zhao, H. (1993). Predictors of assistive technology abandonment. *Assistive Technology, 5*(1), 36–45.

Riemer-Reiss, M. L., & Wacker, R. R. (2000). Factors associated with assistive technology discontinuance among individuals with disabilities. *Journal of Rehabilitation, 66*(3), 44–50.

Scherer, M. (1993). What we know about women's technology, use, avoidance, and abandonment. *Women and Therapy, 14*(3/4), 117–132.

Scherer, M. J. (2000). *Living in the state of stuck: How technology impacts the lives of people with disabilities* (3rd ed.). Cambridge, MA: Brookline Books.

Smerdon, B., Cronen, S., Lanahan, L., Anderson, J., Iannotti, N., & Angeles, J. (2000). *Teachers' tools for the 21st century: A report on teachers' use of technology.* Washington, DC: National Center for Education Statistics.

Snyder, T. C. (2009, March). *Mini-digest of education statistics 2008.* Washington, DC: National Center for Education Statistics.

State Educational Technology Directors Association (SETDA). (2008). *Maximizing the impact: The pivotal role of technology in a 21st century education system.* Glen Burnie, MD: Author.

Warschauer, M. (2003). *Technology and social inclusion: Rethinking the digital divide.* Cambridge, MA: MIT Press.

Wilkins, J., & Ratajczak, A. (2009). Developing literacy skills using high-tech speech-generating augmentative and alternative communication devices. *Intervention in the Schools, 44*(3), 167–172.

Chapter 10

SECURITY, INTERNET SAFETY, COPYRIGHT, AND PLAGIARISM

Janet Tareilo and Theodore Creighton

The amazing world of the Internet and the advances in technology have broadened and expanded our lives in such ways that former social, economic, political, and educational boundaries are rapidly disappearing from our current thinking. This phenomenon occurs daily in various perspectives but nowhere more than in the educational setting where technological advancements are opening new and adventurous avenues for teaching and learning. While technologies in and for education offer a wealth of valuable information, the use of said technologies also presents distinctive concerns for any school system and especially the people chosen to lead it.

School leaders must prepare themselves and their schools not only for the benefits technology can bring to their schools but also for the possibility of unseen dangers associated with the use of the Internet. Questions and concerns arise revolving around the use and misuse of computers, the legal issues associated with technology, and the shifting role and responsibilities of school personnel to provide a continuously safe environment for students as they investigate this somewhat new avenue for learning.

Presently, school leadership demands that principals focus on schools that are moving into the 21st century at an alarming pace. Preparing students for a successful future includes using modes of instruction that correlate with their already existing abilities. Many of today's students already come to school with more technological abilities than their instructors.

When compared to that of the other staff members of a school, the responsibility of the campus principal takes on a different perspective (Tucker & Codding, 2002). Furthermore, any proposed plan to enhance the educational process focuses directly on the effectiveness of the school leader. This responsibility does not change simply because new educational outlooks involve the impact of technologies or the expansiveness of the Internet. Seyfarth (1999) acknowledges that the school principal needed on campuses across the nation must be prepared to be a leader who is constantly aware of educational reforms and who possesses the ability to mobilize a campus and its people toward effective and lasting changes. If the use of various technologies enhances and supports a new wave of teaching, then the principal must accept yet another responsibility, that of **technology leader**, an administrator who possesses the knowledge and skills to address the technology needs that enhance student and staff learning.

As with any aspect of a school's instructional process, the principal serves as the leader who is ultimately responsible for ensuring that the Internet and the technologies provided are properly used and whose intent is to enhance teaching practices and the acquisition of student learning.

The following questions are addressed in this chapter:

- How can leaders plan for and develop their skills as technology leaders?

- How do leaders establish the necessary practices and procedures to safeguard their schools and students?

- How can leaders help others understand that using the Internet means policies and practices to protect students must be in place?

- What are the characteristics of the acceptable use policies of a school that should be considered nonnegotiable?

- How can a leader gather information regarding the **filtering system** used by the school, district, or university to provide protection from inappropriate Internet sources, usually referred to as a "firewall"?

Impact of Technology

The broad realm of the Internet and the various types of available technology provide an atmosphere for student learning that surpasses traditional textbooks, chalkboards, or paper-and-pencil activities. Instructional delivery; **digital learning**, or using various forms of technology for instructional purposes; and open-access communications bring students extensive models of teaching that enriches curricular standards, broadens the problem-solving process, and creates further possibilities for interactive learning. With the simple click of a button, a student has the ability to access a vast amount of information that was unavailable to students just a few years ago. Communication with the outside world becomes not only a possibility but a reality. Interactive learning no longer means group work at a table or having a study partner. Now that partnership happens across geographic borders, time zones, and economic strata. The benefits of technology in the world of education are endless when considering maximizing instruction, increasing teacher effectiveness, and preparing students for their futures (Valdez, 2004).

But as with any new and amazing adventure, using the Internet in a school setting also brings with it a set of distinctive and problematic concerns not only for a school system but also for campus administrators. Common practices associated with traditional leadership roles include creating a school vision, developing mission statements, planning for professional development, incorporating effective instructional measures, and supervising every aspect of the school (Maurer & Davidson, 1998). Because these responsibilities already exist in the realm of school leadership, taking these same duties into the technology arena should not present any additional worries or concerns.

Strong leaders use human resources (e.g., librarians and multimedia experts) for training opportunities for topics such as copyright, intellectual property, and cyberplagiarism. Effective leadership provides for professional learning in these areas.

Providing Safety for All

School leaders receive training and preparation in order to perform the duties of the principalship in a capable and successful manner. During that preparation, principals are constantly studying and reviewing practices and policies that involve instruction, managerial responsibilities, and supervising personnel. With the joining of leadership and managerial skills, school leaders are developing who are able to oversee the day-to-day functioning responsibilities of a school (Dunford, Fawcett, & Bennett, 2000). Now that the instructional possibilities are expanding beyond the classroom and looking to technology to provide additional learning experiences, school leadership takes on a new dimension.

Providing a safe and secure atmosphere at a school is not a new aspect of leadership that falls to the campus administrator. Keeping children safe at school requires constant action on the part of the principal and the staff. Crisis management plans are adopted, evacuation scenarios are regularly practiced, and campuses are maintained to ensure maximum protection for the students and the staff. While educators (Duke, 2002) are continually focused on the welfare and safety of their students during the school day, the spectrum of threats when students enter the Internet reaches beyond recognizable concerns such as assaults or gang-related activities to now include hidden **computer-based crimes**, which involve unauthorized use of the Internet or related technologies.

Not only are school leaders expected to accept this responsibility, but they are equally accountable for ensuring the safety of every child. Because the feeling of safety is a perception, "a safe school can be considered a place where students and staff not only are physically and psychologically safe, but where they believe themselves to be safe" (Duke, 2002, p. xvii).

Acceptable Use Policies

The newness of computer-based crimes does not permit an administrator to simply wait for something to happen on his or her campus to confirm that a problem may or may not exist. With discipline policies and codes of student conduct in place, principals have an established set of guidelines and rules that provide them with a means to protect students as well as the educational process. Most schools also adopt an **acceptable use policy** that requires a parent or guardian's permission before a child is allowed to use a computer or any school-related technological services (Criddle, 2008). These policies also govern how the Internet is to be used, rules and regulations associated with computer use, and the expected behaviors when a student is online (Scholastic Inc., n.d.). When students sign this contract, they are agreeing that their use on a computer or working with the Internet will be for educational purposes only. If students break this agreement, discipline consequences are clearly stated, and students may lose their right to use a computer while at school.

Acceptable use policies are in place to protect the child as well as the school. They are clearly established to help all school personnel and students of every age understand that using the Internet at school is a privilege, not a right, and that any behavior that prevents learning or disrupts the educational process will result in that privilege being taken away. These policies are simply in place to ensure that students will be protected from any unwanted or inappropriate material that has no educational importance or significance (Scholastic Inc., n.d.).

Government Involvement

Countless state and federal initiatives were enacted to ensure the development of policies and procedures that provided protection to anyone using the Internet, especially children. The Equal Educational Opportunity Act of 1974, the Safe and

Drug Free Schools and Communities Act of 1994, and the Goals 2000 program provided information, guidelines, and assistance to school systems in their attempts to establish policies that directly focused on the issue of school safety. But none was more effective in the attempt to protect children's safety while using the Internet or any other online service than the federal laws established in the Children's Online Privacy Protection Act of 1998 (COPPA) or the Children's Internet Protection Act (CIPA).

COPPA encompasses all the states, the District of Columbia, and any territory specifically under the guidelines of the Federal Trade Commission. The Nemours Foundation (2008) through KidsHealth offered the major points of this act:

- Protection is afforded at all times to any child (age 13 or under) when he or she uses the Internet.

- Personal information regarding a child may not be obtained without parental permission.

- Web sites are required to fully explain their privacy policies regarding their use and are not allowed to release any pertinent or personal information about a child without the direct consent of the parent.

- Web sites are prohibited from asking children to provide more personal information than is necessary in order to play an online game or enter a contest.

Even with this federal guideline in place, the best protection for a child at school when on the Internet is the personal involvement of the adults already given the responsibility of protecting and safeguarding a student: the teacher and the principal (Nemours Foundation, 2008).

In 2001, the Federal Communications Commission enacted CIPA. This act required schools and libraries to address any concerns about students' use of the Internet if they wanted to continue receiving federal funding for accessibility to the Internet and additional hardware (Federal Communications Commission, n.d.). An example of the major points of this federal law was clearly detailed by the Smyth County, Virginia, School Board (n.d.) when defining its Internet safety policy:

- Minors will have no contact with inappropriate material while on the Internet or when using the World Wide Web.

- Schools and libraries will provide for the safety and security of minors when using any electronic technology.

- Schools and libraries are to prevent any unauthorized access by minors to the Internet or World Wide Web.

- Schools and libraries are prohibited from disclosing any unauthorized information regarding a minor.

- Schools and libraries are required to establish measures that restrict any minor's access to potentially harmful or dangerous materials.

The Principal and Internet Safety

In order to expand a child's learning base, an effective administrator recognizes the various vehicles available to him or her that embrace the world of possibilities. No longer do school field trips require a bus. A piece of paper, a pen, and a stamp are no longer necessary in order to share an experience with a pen pal. And, most of all, teachers are recognizing that the expansion of a child's education has no boundaries when using the Internet. Through this medium, teachers can enhance instruction, study various cultures, and bring a world of knowledge into their classrooms. Because the principal's role as an instructional leader continues to grow and the use of the Internet and other technologies is quickly overtaking traditional instruction, administrators have no choice but to become as knowledgeable as their students. Valdez (2004) asserts that this new arena of technological awareness requires administrators to accept the additional responsibilities of understanding what technology can and cannot do and then be the catalyst in preparing and readying their campuses for its use.

Duke (2002) contends that effective learning occurs when a school system provides a sense of order and safety. While student codes of conduct are established to provide this, the use of technology presents a new dimension of safety with regard to students and how the Internet and various technologies are being used. This may require an administrator to rethink his or her involvement in how technology is applied at a school.

With new horizons for education developing with the use of the Internet and the World Wide Web, changes in leadership perspective are also vastly important. Valdez (2004) states, "The only way to prepare for the future is to create a capacity for change. A leader must help others develop their capacity to respond to changing conditions and then to support and guide them through the change process" (p. 4). He also purports that because use of the Internet and advanced technologies causes pedagogical shifts in instructional methodologies, principals become change agents to ensure and secure the proper intent of using said technologies.

Strategies for Campus Leaders

School administrators are ultimately responsible for every instructional program that exists on their campuses. From providing resources to establishing programmatic procedures, the principal's awareness and attention to the guidelines of any program are essential to the success of that program and the educational growth of any child who receives services from that program. Because technology often takes on the mantle of a program offered on a campus, the principal has a responsibility to know how the computers are being used, where they are housed, and what software applications are available (Kearsley, 1990).

Every time a student sits down at a computer and opens a portal to the Internet, he or she has in essence located needed information as well as brought his or her classroom and the school into a realm of unwanted possibilities. This silent threat is no different from an unwanted intruder to the campus, and most principals know how and are prepared to deal with that type of emergency. When considering safety measures that administrators can easily implement, Reksten (2000) provides several practices and strategies for administrators as they begin thinking about how they can protect their schools in an easy and efficient manner. She suggests that principals

- continuously manage the technological environment at school;

- prepare the staff through professional development activities for the challenges and potential threats that exist when students use the Internet;

- support teachers who are willing to use the Internet correctly with time and resources;

- collaborate with all stakeholders to acknowledge the appropriate way to use the Internet and the school's technology;

- be open-minded about the possibilities for the future of the educational process that the Internet can provide;

- learn about the various types of technologies that are offered and used on the campus; and

- accept the fact that technology and the use of the Internet do not have to be separate or independent from the other instructional disciplines offered at the school.

There is no doubt that technology and the Internet are improving our lives, and it did not take very long to learn that those improvements could also affect learning in a positive way. However, Maurer and Davidson (1998) recognize that "technology will continue to be instrumental in making possibilities a reality. There will always be a need for human guidance in making learning decisions" (p. 308). That human guidance comes in the form of a well-prepared, knowledgeable, and readied principal who accepts the good side of technology and plans for the uncertainties and unknowns that may occur. Maurer and Davidson (1998) also believe that principals serve as a force of protection for their schools when students explore with technology: "If our children are connected intimately to the net and that net represents our world, then children can be exposed to every negative aspect of our world" (p. 216). Students who use the Internet and associated technology must be monitored in such a way that safety assurances are not merely a thought but expected, initiated, and evaluated.

Salter (2001) proposes further actions and practices for school leaders as technology and Internet use intertwine themselves into the daily operational procedures for a school. He suggests school leaders

- need to stay aware of the positive and possibly negative aspects of technology on their campuses;

- should, with the help of all stakeholders, establish goals, practices, and policies associated with the proper use of the Internet and computers;

- need to be willing to share the leadership responsibilities with others to ensure a safe school environment for all children all the time;

- be an ever-present participant in the use of technology on the campus by visiting classrooms and lab settings that are regularly using technology and the Internet for instructional purposes;

- ensure that the software programs used in the classrooms for instructional purposes support the educational focus of the school;

- develop a systematic plan to monitor the use of computers by the students and the staff; and

- ensure that all children receive and return an acceptable use form that permits them to use computers and the Internet.

From the very first day of school, teachers and students should learn that while the Internet will open several doors and has the potential to exponentially increase their learning, there are several safety issues and concerns directly connected to the use of the Internet. Criddle (2008) identifies at least three definite actions that principals can employ to prepare their students and staff as they become responsible users of campus technologies:

1. The entire population of the school should be constantly aware of the appropriate use of computers, software, and available technology. This information should correlate with district standards regarding the use of the Internet.

2. Impress upon the entire student population and staff members that they should always protect themselves, respect the rights of others, and be responsible enough to follow existing rules and guidelines when using the Internet.

3. Address every infraction of the school's Internet use policy when and if any misuse of the Internet or the school's technology occurs.

Duke (2002) supports this line of practice when he writes, "The ultimate goal where school safety is concerned is to teach what will prevent threats to safety from occurring in the first place" (p. 30). One of the best tools available to administrators is the development of their proactive thinking abilities especially in the realm of Internet use.

Security Issues

Students arrive at schools every day with more technological knowledge than many of their teachers or their principals. Regardless of their age, children have ready access to many forms of computers, regularly talk or text on cell phones with lightning speed, share their innermost feelings on blogs or in chat rooms, and are always on the cutting edge of finding new and innovative tools to help them communicate and connect with the world around them (Sloan, 2009). These abilities do not stop when they enter the school doors. This evolution of connectedness to the information highway provided by the Internet and their extensive use of this technology substantiate the way learning communities are occurring in the 21st century.

Not only does the safety for students using the Internet fall in the hands of the administrator, but so does providing the security system that ensures the school is safe and protected at all times. Long (2000) suggests that without "adequate security" measures in place a school's network system that provides the availability of technology is subject to many forms of disruption and unpredictable intervention of unwanted use (p. 56). He also suggests that principals become aware of how rapidly technology changes and what this means for network planning. Therefore, safety as well as security measures are another aspect of technology leadership that must be assumed by the campus administrator. Providing security measures for a networking system does not happen accidentally. It occurs through the purposeful and intentional actions of a savvy and proactive principal.

Preparedness and Protection

With measures in place to ensure a student's safety at school while he or she is using the Internet or exposed to the various forms of technology offered on a campus, the issue of providing secure sites is of equal importance to the administrator. Because of the cost of the hardware, the monetary investments for software programs, and the wealth of educational resources that support a school's technological direction, securing these features of the technology system is of the utmost importance. Once again, the principal in his or her role as protector and servant of the campus and its inhabitants leads the initiative to keep the school secure as well as safe from unwanted outside forces.

The Nemours Foundation in its 2008 KidsHealth report on Internet safety provides several online protection tools that may prevent the misuse of technology. They encourage the school to

- provide a means of control for access to unwanted sites;
- teach students to recognize online predators;
- incorporate Internet service providers to stand guard when adults cannot be present; and
- continually protect the identity of students when using the Internet at school.

All of the above suggestions are very doable to ensure that impressionable students and eager teachers are kept safe while using the Internet as an interactive learning device.

Picciano (2002) addresses the importance of security when dealing with the issue of technology. He contends that technological leaders acquaint themselves with the following concepts:

- The protection of the school's software regarding the management of school records is vital to ensure students' records remain confidential.
- Students' records must be protected at all costs and only used for educational purposes.
- Policies must be in place to detail how computers are used and the degree of access.
- The purchase of antivirus software prevents extensive damage to the existing computer system in place.
- Procedures at the school should mirror district procedure for protecting all the components of technology afforded to students and teachers.

These are not mere suggestions. An administrator who cannot protect or shield his or her school from unwanted access, viruses, or threats of theft increases the chance that the school will fall prey to technology-related crimes, and the loss to the educational process will be monumental. Proactive leaders are responsive to the intent and purpose of technology usage on their campuses and refuse to compromise when confronted with the security needs that should be in place to provide constant protection of student information, intranet services, and instructional programs. Just as an administrator is committed to the safety of every child on his or her campus, he or she should equally be adamant about the security measures that protect any aspect of the learning process afforded to his or her students.

Securing the School

No one person on a school campus has more responsibility than the principal. Whether determining a lunch schedule or learning how to program a computer, the principal carries the daunting obligation to protect every student, teacher, and staff member. This responsibility also means that every child will be safe and secure during the school day in order to maximize the learning process. The use of technology and the Internet, while expanding learning and teaching, is not free from bringing to school unwanted, unnecessary, or inappropriate information. Protecting students from this kind of threat is no different from protecting students from a fire or an uninvited intruder.

The principal is the key to developing security guidelines that protect students at all times, especially when they use the Internet. Administrators can use the following tasks to help them protect their schools:

- Become familiar with the technology support system provided by the district.

- Secure students' confidential information by using an alternative means (a backup system) to save it.

- Know and enforce the acceptable use policy.

- Employ filtering software.

- Constantly reinforce procedure for using computers and the Internet.

- Establish and enforce disciplinary policies for any infractions that occur.

- Strategically place computers on the campus to avoid possible theft and ensure those rooms are always kept locked and secured.

On the most basic level, the principal is considered the custodian of security when it comes to keeping the school a safe place to learn and work.

Knowing this, administrators face security issues regarding technology that create an ever-present need to protect their schools from current or future attempts to ruin or sabotage existing software, hardware, or students' records. Kearsley (1990) offers several potential considerations for school leaders:

- Piracy of existing software programs
- Maintenance of private and personal student records
- Prevention of incoming viruses
- Protection of the school site from theft
- Prohibiting access to illegal Web sites

First and foremost, Valdez (2004) calls on principals to take proactive measures to consider all issues regarding the interconnectedness among technology, its use, and the development of clear and creative responses that protect their students and their schools.

Copyright and Open Educational Resources

The technology for information organization, communication, storage, and use has for hundreds of years been the book (Burrus, 2007). The book and the classroom have been the main technologies used by teachers in education. As recently as during the last 10 years, a movement has been surfacing that will impact not only teaching and learning but also how we view author roles and copyright issues. The book, and its 500-year history, has tied the author directly to the written work, and copyright has been a relatively straightforward issue.

Open Educational Resources

The term *open educational resources (OER)* was first adopted at the United Nations Educational, Scientific, and Cultural Organization's 2008 forum on the impact of open courseware in higher education for developing countries. The purpose was to help equalize the access to knowledge and educational opportunities throughout the world (Breck, 2007). Open educational resources include full courses, course material, modules, textbooks, streaming videos, tests, software, and other tools and materials used to support access to knowledge.

The feature of the OER initiative that will greatly change—and actually has already begun to change—our traditional view of copyright is the granting of freedoms to share, reprint, translate, combine, or adjust that makes these published works educationally different from our traditional publications and access via a printed text (Breck, 2007).

Advances in computer hardware and software now provide us with many different and better systems for the "generation, organization, storage, and use of information" (Burrus, 2007, p. 19). The most powerful and significant new system is the Connexions project, started at Rice University in 1999 (http://cnx.org/). There are three parts of the Connexions system:

1. The information itself is organized in the form of small modules that can be linked and searched. These modules use the XML protocol and are located in an open **repository** or data storage center accessible globally over the Internet.

2. Tools that help create, maintain, share, and use these modules are built into a Web- and browser-accessible service specialized for this application.

3. A community develops and uses these modules, which are modeled around the ideas of the open software projects but operate in a somewhat different environment.

For educational purposes, there are several participants:

1. The author creates the modules. This is done by writing a new module or by modifying an existing one that may have been written by the modifier or by a completely different author. There are software tools to write, edit, and collaborate. This is strongly aided by the open Creative Commons copyright.

2. The instructor creates courses or plans of study by creating a "road map" through the modules in the repository. The instructor may write all, some, or none of the modules for a particular course. The resulting course may be used by a class in a school, by an individual doing self-study or distance education, or by a business for documentation. The course material may be used from a screen or be printed out as a paper book.

3. The learner or student uses Connexions to learn not only the factual information but also the contextual "connections" to the piece of information. This allows the traditional instructor to lead teaching but also allows a learner to actively participate in a controlled discovery experience.

4. The community, which consists of all three participants and especially the first two, allows all individuals to gain maximum benefit from this new technology. It also includes legal, commercial, and educational infrastructure. (Burrus, 2007, p. 21)

The Open Creative Commons Copyright

The Creative Commons open-access license (http://creativecommons.org/licenses/) makes it easy for authors to share their work—allowing others to use and reuse it legally—while still getting recognition for their efforts. All materials are stored in XML (extendible markup language), ensuring the material works on multiple computer platforms now and in the future. Authors are encouraged to write and upload modules that can stand on their own so that others can use them in different courses and contexts. Connexions also allows instructors to *customize* content by overlapping their own set of links and annotations.

Cyberplagiarism

In an age when students gravitate to online resources for research—and when tremendous amounts of both reputable and questionable information are available online—many have come to regard the Internet as a culprit in students' plagiarism (Moore-Howard & Davies, 2009). Some teachers do not allow students to use the Internet for research—others issue a strict warning with accompanying consequences and move on.

Moore-Howard and Davies (2009) believe that this "getting tough" approach with severe punishments (e.g., using automated plagiarism-detection devices such as Turnitin.com) as an attempt to legislate the wired world is an approach that does not work. The authors offer the following as a guide to preventing **cyberplagiarism**, downloading or copying material from an Internet source without providing proper acknowledgment:

1. Discuss intellectual property and what it means to "own" a piece of writing.

2. Discuss how to evaluate both online and print-based sources (for example, comparing the quality of a Web site created by an amateur with the reliability of a peer-reviewed scholarly article).

3. Guide students through the hard work of engaging with and understanding their sources, so students don't conclude that writing a technically perfect bibliography is good enough.

4. Acknowledge that teaching students how to write from sources involves more than telling students that copying is a crime and handing them a pile of source citation cards. (Moore-Howard & Davies, 2009, p. 65)

They conclude by stating:

Students don't need threats; students need pedagogy. That pedagogy should teach both source-reading skills and take into consideration our increasingly wired world.

And it should communicate that plagiarism is wrong in terms of what society values about schools and learning, not just in terms of arbitrary rules. (p. 65)

Conclusions

The Internet and associated technologies that students are exposed to every day open doors to uncharted learning opportunities, connect them to cultures from around the world, and allow them to become explorers in their own learning process. The physical boundaries that still exist in the real world no longer hinder students when they enter the World Wide Web. The 21st century promises to only push forward with the evolution of new and faster technology that makes life as well as learning uncomplicated and within their reach by simply clicking a button on a small mouse. Yet with all the positive and potential aspects of what technology offers students and teachers, there still exists the threat that every time a child uses the Internet he or she leaves a part of him- or herself behind: a fingerprint, an address, a way for unwanted and undesirable people or information to enter his or her world.

For this reason, school administrators must remain on constant watch to ensure their school communities are kept safe and free from any impending harm. Maurer and Davidson (1998) recognize this when they write, "The unfortunate reality is that nothing as powerful as telecommunication can come to us without unique problems" (p. 214). However, they also include that these problems should not be enough to warrant the nonuse or abandonment of the Internet or related technologies. Kearsley (1990) concludes:

Computer technology is transforming our world. There can be no doubt this technology will eventually transform our school system, for better or worse. To ensure that it is for the better, we need strong leadership in the educational computing domain. (p. ix)

Key Principles for Leaders to Know

The issues of school safety and security are not new to campus administrators, but as they face their new responsibilities as technology leaders these concepts take on a new meaning and purpose. From planning to proactive thinking, principals need to be aware of some common core assumptions that will assist them as they plan to keep their schools safe.

- The use of the Internet and varying technologies is not a solitary action.

- Students are to be kept safe at all times.

- The responsibility for keeping a school safe lies in the hands of the principal.

- There are several ways to provide safety for the students.

- Using the Internet means policies and practices to protect students must be in place.

- Planning for computer use and constant communication about acceptable use policies of a school should be considered nonnegotiable.

- Gather information regarding the filtering system used by the school or district.

- Securing the school means providing safety for the children.

CASE STUDY 10.1 | Acceptable Use Policy

State and federal guidelines require that parental permission be given before a student is allowed to use computers or the Internet at school. By signing an acceptable use policy, students are held to contractual standards that must be adhered to if they want to take part in the technologies offered on their campuses. Without this permission, students are denied the right to use a computer and most assuredly the Internet. Your district has initiated several new safety mandates to prevent the use of outside software and the possibility of losing secured information. A new use policy is needed to reflect these changes. You are to investigate your district's existing acceptable use policy and how to implement the new changes.

Discussion: Using your district's acceptable use policy, discuss the expectations for students and parents. Are there aspects needed to change the acceptable use policy? What would an optimal acceptable use policy include?

Activity: Interview a district technology supervisor to determine how the use of outside software affects the network system and the safeguards that are in place to protect student records.

CASE STUDY 10.2	Planning to Safeguard Student Access

You have recently been hired as the principal of a middle school. The school district is a small one in a city experiencing economic difficulties. The paper mill and local metal foundry are failing and about to close their doors. In the midst of the economic decline, the school just received a $500,000 grant to implement a new technology center on the campus. In order to receive the money, you are required to submit a proposal on how part of the funds will be used to safeguard the students' use of the computers.

Discussion: Discuss a plan of action for developing a safety plan to protect the students.

Activity: Outline a speech for your school board on how the plan was developed, what legal issues were considered, and how the safety plan will be implemented on the campus.

Web Resources

Childnet International (http://www.childnet-int.org) provides safety guidelines, publications, and current information for parents and schools on how to keep the Internet a safe place for children.

Connexions (http://cnx.org) is a place to view and share educational material made of small knowledge chunks called modules that can be organized as courses, books, reports, and so forth. Anyone may view or contribute.

CyberSmart! (http://www.cybersmart.org/home) fosters 21st-century skills to increase student engagement and prepare students to achieve in today's digital society.

EDUCAUSE (http://www.educause.edu/) promotes the use of technology as a means to further one's intelligence and personal learning. This site is a wealth of resources that effectively uses various technologies.

The **Federal Communications Commission** (http://www.fcc.gov) Web site allows parents and educators to investigate and examine information regarding the many bureaus and agencies associated with keeping children safe while they use the Internet.

The **Federal Trade Commission** (http://www.ftc.gov/bcp/edu/pubs/business/idtheft/bus45.shtm) provides an extensive amount of information that is valuable to businesses, agencies, and organizations. This site details how a student's privacy while working online must be protected and kept confidential.

GetNetWise from the Internet Education Foundation (http://www.security.getnetwise.org) provides tips, tools, and actions for keeping the Internet safe and secure. Information is also provided on the ways to keep personal computers free from unwanted or inappropriate materials found on the Internet.

The **International Journal of Educational Leadership Preparation** (http://ijelp .expressacademic.org) is the official publication of all peer-reviewed Connexions modules of the National Council of Professors of Educational Administration.

The **NetSafeKids** site from the National Academy of Sciences (http://www.nap.edu/net safekids) allows parents and educators the opportunity to study and research the many ways children can be kept safe as they explore the Internet for educational purposes and entertainment.

WiredSafety (http://www.wiredsafety.org) is the world's largest Internet safety, help, and education resource.

References

Breck, J. (2007). Introduction to special issue on opening educational resources. *Educational Technology, 47*(6), 3–5.

Burrus, C. (2007). Connexions: An open educational resource for the 21st century. *Educational Technology, 47*(6), 19–22.

Criddle, L. C. (2008, September). *Back to school and Internet safety.* CyperPatrol: Protecting people online. Retrieved February 26, 2009, from http://blog.cyberpatrol.com/?p=22

Duke, D. L. (2002). *Creating safe schools for all children.* Boston: Allyn & Bacon.

Dunford, J., Fawcett, R., & Bennett, D. (Eds.). (2000). *School leadership: National and international perspectives.* London: Kogan Page.

Federal Communications Commission. (n.d). *2001 Children's Internet Protection Act.* Retrieved February 26, 2009, from http://www.fcc.gov/cgb/consumerfacts/cipa.html

Kearsley, G. (1990). *Computers for educational administrators: Leadership in the information age.* Norwood, NJ: Ablex.

Long, P. E. (2000). Planning, designing, and growing a campus network for the future. In M. A. Luker (Ed.), *Preparing your campus for a networked future* (pp. 41–58). San Francisco: Jossey-Bass.

Maurer, M. M., & Davidson, G. S. (1998). *Leadership in instructional technology.* Upper Saddle River, NJ: Prentice Hall.

Moore-Howard, R., & Davies, L. (2009). Plagiarism in the Internet age. *Educational Leadership, 66*(6), 64–67.

Nemours Foundation. (2008). *KidsHealth: Internet safety.* Retrieved February 23, 2009, from http://kidshealth.org/PageManager.jsp?dn=KidsHealth&lic=1&ps=107&cat_id=150&article_ set=22145

Picciano, A. G. (2002). *Educational leadership for planning technology* (3rd ed.). Upper Saddle River, NJ: Merrill Prentice Hall.

Reksten, L. E. (2000). *Using technology to increase student learning.* Thousand Oaks, CA: Corwin.

Salter, D. (2001). *Leadership and technology: Ten thoughts.* Retrieved December 9, 2008, from http://www.studentaffairs.com/ejournal/Winter_2001/thoughts.html

Scholastic Inc. (n.d.). *Internet safety for schools: A quick guide to finding the solution that's right for your school.* Retrieved February 26, 2009, from http://www2.scholastic.com/browse/article.jsp?id=4395&print=2

Seyfarth, J. T. (1999). *The principal: New leadership for new challenges.* Upper Saddle River, NJ: Prentice Hall.

Sloan, W. M. (2009, January). Creating global classrooms. *Education Update, 51*(1), 1, 4–7. Alexandria, VA: ASCD.

Smith County School Board. (n.d.). *Internet safety: Technology usage policy.* Retrieved February 26, 2009, from http://www.scsb.org/internetsafetypolicy.htm

Tucker, M. S., & Codding, J. B. (Eds.). (2002). *The principal challenge: Leading and managing schools in an era of accountability.* San Francisco: Jossey-Bass.

Valdez, G. (2004, July). *Critical issue: Technology leadership: Enhancing positive educational change.* North Central Regional Educational Laboratory. Retrieved December 9, 2008, from http://www.ncrel.org/sdrs/areas/issues/educatrs/leadrshp/le700.htm

PART IV

Leadership Digital Assessments and Evaluation

To conclude, Part IV embraces issues concerning assessment and evaluation. **Chapter 11: Online Evaluation** addresses issues of evaluation for online teaching and learning. **Chapter 12: Using Technology for Assessing and Evaluating Student Learning and Instructional Practices** examines student learning assessment. And finally, **Chapter 13: Program Evaluation and Technology Integration Strategies** describes the process for overall program evaluation.

Chapter 11

ONLINE EVALUATION

Mary I. Dereshiwsky

Consistent policies at the school level help prevent cyberbullying. Assessing instructional performance in the online classroom focuses on many of the same overall qualities as in the traditional face-to-face classroom. They include effective communication with students, quality of instructional delivery, provision of feedback on assignments, and fostering a positive classroom climate. At the same time, the principal will need to look for different evidence of each of these qualities in the online classroom. They will be discussed in this chapter. One subsection will deal with **cyberbullying**—that is, harassing or threatening other students using such technology as instant message, e-mail, or posting in public areas such as Facebook or MySpace—and what teachers can do to help prevent it.

The following questions are addressed in this chapter:

- What are the components of quality instruction, such as effective communication with students, quality of instructional delivery, provision of feedback on assignments, and fostering a positive classroom climate, that are the same regardless of classroom format (e.g., face to face, online)?

- How can leaders spot-check the online course area for effective practice at the start of the term, while the course is underway, and toward the end of the course?

- What are the key assessment criteria that leaders can look for in teacher postings, discussion interactions, and input into course assignments?

- How can leaders ensure teachers are providing *substantive* comments to students in response to questions, during discussions, and on assignments?

Curtain Up: Getting the Online Course Set Up and Ready to Go

First impressions of anything are all-important. With some students taking their first online course and maybe feeling a bit jittery about it, it's especially important to do some preliminary housekeeping to ensure that the course is accessible and inviting.

The first thing you should do is to request a course designer or teacher login so that you can periodically visit your teachers' online courses throughout the term. This will allow you to view what the teacher sees, including all group posting areas. Student access alone will not give you the big picture. For example, it will not allow you to see all group online work spaces, which will likely be set up as restricted access so that students can access only their own group's posting areas but not those of other groups.

Table 11.1 displays a preliminary checklist of what you might want to check for in the online courses in your department that are ready to launch in the upcoming term. It contains many of the features used in the Certified Online Instructor (COI) course evaluation certification program offered by the Learning Resources Network (LERN; http://www.teachingonthenet.org/courses/certified_online_instructor/index.cfm). Many of them are discussed in greater detail in Chapter 8.

Table 11.1	Principal's Prelaunch Checklist
Course Feature	*What Principal Should Check For*
Syllabus	• Ability to access visually and ideally in downloadable printout format
	• Teacher contact information (e-mail, fax, telephone, other means of communication; office hours, virtual or real-time)
	• Readings and assignments displayed by due dates
	• Grading policy
	• Lateness policy
	• Other institution-specific required information (e.g., codes of conduct, disability accommodation, hyperlink to student handbook)
Login information to course	• Login user name and password (does it work?)
	• Relative speed of access to course home page
Instructional materials	• Sorted by module and topic hyperlinks (see Chapter 8 for more information)
	• Accessibility of external embedded hyperlinks (check a random sample of such external hyperlinks to make sure they work)
	• Accessibility of embedded audio files and PowerPoint files cross-linked to course materials (check a random sample of such external hyperlinks to make sure they work)

Course Feature	What Principal Should Check For
Assignments	• Sorted by module/topic (check a random sample using the syllabus information to be sure that they are placed in the correct module and topic)
	• Accessibility of assignment submission area (check a random sample to be sure that a submission area/link or posting area exists for students to upload or post each assignment if relevant)
Online gradebook	• Set up per individual assignment; ready to enter points per student and assignment
	• Accessible by student and teacher hyperlinks
Welcome post	• Welcomes students to the course
	• Reminder of course name and number
	• Brief instructions on how to get started (e.g., link to syllabus, location of additional posted announcements)
Other startup announcement posts	• Information on how students can contact tech support (e.g., toll-free telephone number, hours of accessibility, e-mail address)
	• Location of campus-based computer labs and staffing by lab aides, including office hours if relevant
Discussion forums/posting areas	• Posting area set up for introducing oneself or other icebreaker activities
	• Discussion forum set up for announcements and updates (see Chapter 8 for more information)
	• Discussion forum set up for questions and answers (see Chapter 8 for more information)
	• Discussion forum set up and accessible to students for first week's learning activity (e.g., group topic discussions and work spaces)

Source: Copyright © LERN. Reprinted with permission.

The above checklist, while detailed, should also give you a list of items to look for as you do a quick sweep through the online classes that are imminently set to launch. As indicated in Table 11.1, you do not have to check each hyperlink or gradebook entry individually, although you should share with your teachers the advisability of doing so as they get ready to teach their courses. You can spot-check a random sample of these items as you do this quick prelaunch check. It's vitally important to verify that such external links are functional. This is so students won't worry that there's something wrong at their end when they can't access something inside the course.

There are two distinct benefits of applying such a checklist. For one thing, it allows you to bring a valuable outside pair of eyes to the prelaunch review process. In addition, it gives you an idea of what to look for in the preinstructional readiness phase of your course and teacher evaluation.

Table 11.2 contains a checklist for evaluating K–12 online products. It can be readily adapted to the evaluation of a K–12 online course.

Table 11.2	Checklist for Evaluation of K–12 Online Products

First Look: Evaluation Form for K–12 Online Products

Name of Company _____

Product Reviewed _____

Web site Address _____

Login _____

Password _____

This product meets the needs of the student populations that I have marked below:

❏ Home school	❏ Supplement to existing course	❏ Correctional education
❏ Credit recovery	❏ School-to-work	❏ Dropout retrieval
❏ GED completion	❏ Accelerated credits	❏ Gifted and talented
❏ Remediation	❏ Alternative education	❏ Teenage parents
❏ Advanced placement	❏ Migrant education	❏ Basic skills
❏ Course otherwise not available	❏ SAT/ACT preparation	❏ Other _____

Comments:

This product provides evidence of the following elements in its instructional design:

❏ Complete course syllabus	❏ Offline tasks complement online activities	❏ Student-to-student interaction
❏ Supplemental resources/tools, such as data sets, images, simulations, animation, video	❏ Strong organization	❏ Group interaction
	❏ Clear course and unit goals	❏ Feedback and formative assessment
❏ Self-paced	❏ Realistic course and unit goals	❏ Accommodates varied learning styles
❏ Instructor's role focuses on student learning	❏ Project-based learning	
	❏ Student-to-teacher interaction	

Comments:

This product provides evidence of the following elements in its curriculum content:

❏ Aligned to WA's EALRs [Washington's Essential Academic Learning Requirements]	❏ Critical reasoning/abstract thinking	
	❏ Customized content	
❏ Extensive introductory level	❏ Flexible sequence of units/ modules	
❏ In-depth coverage of material		

Comments:

This product provides evidence of the following elements in its course delivery:		
❐ Appropriate course structure for intended student population ❐ Customized course length	❐ Involvement in online learning community ❐ Availability of remedial help for struggling students	❐ Availability of enhancing resources ❐ Accommodation of course for student disabilities

Comments:

This product provides evidence of the following elements in its evaluation and assessment:		
❐ Alignment of course objectives and assessment strategies ❐ Multiple means of assessment ❐ Procedures for proctoring/ monitoring student testing ❐ Process for retaking a test ❐ Extra credit work	❐ Regular monitoring of student participation and performance by instructor ❐ Clear assessment systems and evaluation criteria ❐ Timely and informative feedback to students on their progress	❐ Timely and informative feedback to school and/or parents on student progress ❐ Student self-assessment ❐ Student peer assessment ❐ Customized assessments by instructor

This product provides evidence of the following elements in its management:		
❐ Clear procedures for fees and payment ❐ Clear policy for early withdrawal ❐ Credit is granted upon course completion ❐ Self-contained course; additional resources such as textbooks are not required ❐ Student work is secure from access by unauthorized users ❐ Monitored chat sessions or other student interactions ❐ Availability of offline options (CDs) if Web access is interrupted		

Comments:

Now that you have learned about the product itself . . .

What questions do you still have about this product?

Please mark all of the following that apply to your school's readiness to use this product:

(Continued)

Table 11.2	(Continued)

❏ Teachers in our school are open to implementing this delivery model in their classrooms.

❏ This product's technical requirements are within the limitations of the current equipment in our school.

❏ The price point of this product is within our school's (or district's or program's) budget capacity.

Please mark all of the following that apply to the successful implementation of this product:

❏ This product is a good solution for the intended student population; it is a good match.

❏ This product utilizes an approach that will capture and maintain the interest of students.

❏ Minimal teacher training is required, *or* this company provides training to ensure teachers are prepared to use this product.

❏ This product calls for minimal technical support from our district.

Overall thoughts and reflections about how this product meets the needs of the intended student population you have in mind: _____

Source: www.k12.wa.us/edtech/pubdocs/Eval_Form.doc

Following are some preliminary things you can do as a principal to prepare your K–12 teachers to teach their first online course: http://home.sprynet.com/ ~gkearsley/TeachingOnline.htm.

The following link describes what a K–12 online course should look like: http://www.netc.org/digitalbridges/online/essentials/#B.

You can use the following guidelines on how to write a K–12 online course to develop a checklist for review: http://www.netc.org/digitalbridges/online/ community/teachers2.php.

Getting Students Started on the Right Foot: What to Look for in Your Classroom Visits

As the first week or so gets underway, you should be especially alert to how the courses are starting out. Dereshiwsky (2008) notes the importance of *continual engagement* by the teacher throughout the term. In addition, Draves (2000) recommends more frequent teacher check-in during those all-important first couple of weeks or so, when things are brand new to students and they may need a little extra help getting started comfortably. Such continual engagement should receive particular weight in your evaluation of instructors. It should drive what you look for as you drop in on their courses to have a look at how things are going during this crucial startup time.

Online classroom software programs such as WebCT Campus Edition and Vista will allow you to monitor the frequency and duration of instructor login. In addition, you can spot-check the items shown in Table 11.3 as you log into the actual course to take a peek at how things are going.

Table 11.3	Principal's Startup Checklist
Course Feature	*What Principal Should Look For*
Introduction or icebreaker activity posting area	• Has teacher introduced him- or herself to students to get things started (short biography, photo optional)? • Has teacher individually welcomed each student (responded to students' self-introduction posts or other icebreaker activities being posted by students)?
Announcements and updates	• Posting of any changes or late-breaking developments • Optional but recommended: posting of a quick announcement to acknowledge how well students are getting started in the course
Questions and answers	• Is the teacher logging in regularly (ideally every working day) to check for posted questions by students? • Is the teacher providing prompt and substantive help to answer students' posted questions?

During this critical startup time, students will want the reassurance that their teacher is present in the classroom. Because you can't see the instructor walk into the classroom and talk with students, you will be looking for these other text-based cues of teacher engagement in helping his or her students get started comfortably.

Responding to Students' Initial Postings

The self-introduction activity gives students a valuable chance to road test some key technology navigational skills that they will need throughout the course. These skills include locating a posting area, making their own discussion posting, and responding to other students' posts. In this regard, your teachers have a prime opportunity to set the tone with their own self-introduction post. You can check whether they have provided a readable, relevant summary of their professional backgrounds and activities. In addition, they may convey the personal touch—so particularly important in the text-based online classroom where we don't have the visual and body language cues. Some ways to do this in the teacher's self-introduction are sharing about family, travel experiences, pets, and hobbies. Students will then have a model to emulate when drafting their own self-introduction posts. Here is a list of best practices with examples of self-introductions from the Quality Matters online course evaluation rubric: http://www.cvtc.edu/pages/277.asp.

Your teachers may choose to create alternative fun icebreaker activities for their incoming online students. They help warm students up, dispel those invariable course startup jitters (which may be exacerbated by the online classroom setting), and also allow students to practice some important navigational skills. For specific examples of such icebreaker activities, see Ko and Rossen (2008) and Palloff and Pratt (2007). Take a look at the following collection of creative icebreaker activities for online courses: http://twt .wikispaces.com/Ice-Breaker+Ideas.

In both of the above cases, you should be looking for evidence of active engagement by your online teachers. Is there evidence that teachers are logging in to read students' postings? Are they welcoming students by perhaps mentioning something they have in common in response to a student's self-introduction post (e.g., having visited that geographic area, a hobby that they share) or otherwise actively engaging with students in the icebreaker activity?

Updating the Announcement Posting Area as Needed

We all know the feeling of starting a live and in-person class by the teacher making some preliminary announcements before launching into the instructional activity of the day. In like manner, the first week or so of the term is bound to have some late-breaking developments. They could include information on policy for course adds and drops or a last-minute change in tech support telephone access or computer lab hours, for example. You can check to be sure that your online teachers are posting information on late-breaking developments, as well as other helpful startup information, in this announcements and updates area.

In addition, while perhaps not as crucial, it's a nice plus for teachers to post an affirming announcement several days into the term to let students know they're coming aboard well. This lets students know that their teacher is watching and aware of what they're doing. It also helps dispel students' fears about their own evaluation to see their teacher starting out by catching them doing something right, not just correcting them for what's wrong. In both cases this serves to motivate students to keep checking the announcements and updates posting area as the course unfolds. This will ensure that they are receiving the same all-important updates that their classmates are receiving. They will also learn not to assume that all posted announcements are corrective or punitive in nature, particularly when seeing such an affirming glad-you're-here announcement post so early in the term.

Being Responsive to Posted Questions and Answers

We are all familiar with the stereotype of the online classroom as "just a cold, impersonal correspondence school." Coupled with this is the sense of abandonment an online student may feel when he or she has a question or when something is confusing or doesn't work as it should. This student may truly feel lost in cyberspace, as if he or she is dealing with only an inanimate computer screen rather than a real live human being.

For this reason, Draves (2000) and others have reiterated the importance of frequent teacher monitoring of the posting area for questions and answers. By doing so, once again your teachers are modeling the importance of making their presence felt according to Dereshiwsky's (2008) continual engagement best-practice concept. Students who receive prompt, helpful responses to posted questions are more likely to feel connected. They realize that someone is keeping an eye on things and alert to when they might need some extra help. You should therefore be alert for such continual engagement and substantive instructor help to students as you make your early-semester sweep of your teachers' online classrooms.

There is one caution to keep in mind, however. You may want to coach your teachers to not cross the line into "playing technology help desk," as Draves (2000) and Schweizer (1999) have cautioned. It is fine for your teachers to walk a student through a particular focused navigational question, such as how to access a particular assignment or reading. But for more complex technology-related concerns, it is not only *OK* but also advisable for teachers to point students to the technology help desk contact information. The tech support staff can resolve the hardware or software problem for students most efficiently. This frees up your teachers to focus on the content-related instructional interaction with their students, as Schweizer has pointed out. Send your online students to the tech support contact information and add a closing line to the post: "Please let me know what happens and what tech support advises."

You may want to share these tips with your teachers so that they can most efficiently concentrate on handling course-content-related questions while at the same time being maximally responsive to students' questions.

As the Semester Progresses: What to Look for in Your Classroom Visits

Continued teacher engagement in announcement and question-and-answer postings remains important as the instructional session continues. In addition, in your periodic classroom drop-ins, you will want to look at instructor interaction in two areas: course discussions and course assignments. Table 11.4 outlines these evaluation criteria.

Table 11.4	Principal's Checklist for Duration of Semester
Course Feature	*What Principal Should Look For*
Announcements and updates	• Weekly wrap-up and preview post by instructor • Reminders of upcoming due dates as relevant (e.g., discussion participation, quizzes, assignments) • Other late-breaking developments shared with class as posted announcements
Questions and answers	• Continued periodic monitoring by instructor • Prompt posting of substantive responses to student questions (24–48 hours usual standard)
Course discussions	• Posting of discussion topics before the scheduled start of the group discussion (e.g., weekly) • Continued teacher engagement in current discussions (e.g., sharing additional information on the topic, reiterating what other students have said, asking follow-up questions to keep the discussion going)
Assignments, quizzes, and tests	• Prompt return of individual and group assignments (one week usual standard) • Manual scoring of any test or quiz items that are not auto-scored • Manual entry of grades in the gradebook if they are not auto-entered • Provision of substantive feedback on assignments

Adding to Announcements: The Weekly Wrap-up and Preview

As the semester progresses, you'll want to be sure that your online teachers are continuing to post announcements for students. In addition to late-breaking developments, it's considered best practice to post a periodic update of "here's where we've been and here's where we're going." This author refers to them as "Taking the Pulse: Week X," where Week X refers to the upcoming week. The weekly time interval corresponds nicely to the typical one-week duration of a course topic, as discussed in Chapter 8.

There are several benefits to such a periodic posting. It helps students see the big picture of the concepts they are learning about. It is natural for them to take the "micro" view at first—that is, to focus in depth on only the current week's learning material. At the same time, you want to help students make the connections of how earlier concepts relate to upcoming concepts. Your teachers can do this by recapping the prior week's learning material and showing how the upcoming week's material will build upon it. In addition, such a periodic announcement posting is another way that your teachers can make their presence and visibility to students known. It therefore becomes an additional way that you can evaluate their continual engagement in their online course.

Questions and Answers: Keep It Covered

As discussed earlier, prompt teacher responsiveness to questions is vitally important throughout the course so that students do not feel isolated, lost, or overwhelmed. You can do a quick check of the posting activity in your teachers' discussion forum for questions and answers to ensure that they are engaging regularly with timely, substantive responses to students' posted questions. See the following posted answer to an all-too-typical student question ("What can I do to be more interested in math?"): http://mathforum .org/library/drmath/view/52283.html.

Can We Talk? Engagement in Discussions

LERN's COI certification process recommends at least one discussion per course topic. This means that your teachers should have at least one weekly discussion for students to participate in.

In your visits to ongoing discussion forums, watch for the optimal balance of teacher input. As Draves (2000, 2001) has cautioned, if the teacher weighs in too soon on a given discussion topic, it may accidentally shut down the flow of student interaction as a result. This is because some students, mindful of the old top-down, authority-figure-standing-in-front-of-the-room model of the class-room, may feel that the teacher has spoken the last word on the subject. On the other hand, if teachers take a hands-off approach to such discussions, students may get the idea that no one is listening to what they have to say. Therefore, they may also assume that the discussion activity simply isn't as important as assignments and tests. In addition, the discussion may hit a dead end, go off on an unintended tangent, or, even worse, spiral into a flame war (inappropriate posts of attack).

Once again, you want your teachers to make their presence known to students as they engage in discussions. At the same time, you want them to do it in such a way that the discussion progresses on topic without getting derailed or prematurely fizzling out.

Draves (2000, 2001) and Palloff and Pratt (2007) have written extensively on how teachers can keep online discussions rolling at such an optimal balancing point. In general, you should look for periodic teacher engagement in such activities. Online teachers can recap what another student has shared, build upon it in a follow-up comment to the discussion forum, or ask a question that moves the discussion forward, particularly if it seems to be lagging. They should also be on the lookout for inappropriate postings or flame wars and be quick to take action. According to a number of online instructional experts (Ko & Rossen, 2008; Palloff & Pratt, 2007), such inappropriate posts may need to be promptly removed. The teacher may use this opportunity as a "teachable moment" to post a friendly reminder announcement to the entire class, without identifying any individuals, indicating why the post represented a particular violation of code of conduct. All of these best practices of effective online discussion facilitation should be on your evaluation checklist as you periodically observe the interaction in these discussion forums.

Testing, Testing, 1-2-3: Quizzes, Assignments, and Tests

Online classrooms offer a number of ways to assess student performance that are comparable to traditional live and in-person assessments. A number of them are discussed in Chapter 8. They include quizzes, one-minute papers, case studies, traditional term papers, other written assignments, and examinations. Students can be asked to complete assignments individually or in groups.

Many types of online classroom software such as WebCT Vista and Moodle can be set up to auto-grade quizzes and examinations that contain fixed-choice questions. The auto-graded scores are also automatically posted to the online gradebook. In addition, it is possible for teachers to preprogram in an explanation for why each response choice is either correct or incorrect. After students submit their completed quiz or test, they are able to access this answer key to see how they did and get an explanation for any items they may have missed. It is also possible to add short-answer and open-ended questions to such quizzes and tests. Such items would need to be manually scored. The teacher can specify start and end dates and times for such quizzes and exams similar to those in a live and in-person setting. The quiz or test opens and closes to student access accordingly.

As with the question-and-answer posting area, *timeliness* in responding to student assessment submissions of quizzes, tests, and assignments is key. If the test is fixed-choice and auto-graded by the online classroom software, the instructor simply needs to verify that the points and grades are being entered in the gradebook so that students can view them.

In the case of open-ended test items or written assignments such as case studies, teachers should plan to review, annotate, and return them to students. Usually there is an assignment drop box submission area inside the online course room where teachers receive and return such assignments.

As a general rule of thumb, one week is considered standard to grade and return quizzes, tests, and short papers. In the case of a more writing-intensive student assessment such as an end-of-course term paper, one to two weeks would be more realistic. You will be able to view the dates of student submissions and teacher returns as you check the assignment submission area.

In addition to timeliness, *substantive teacher feedback* on student submissions is vitally important. This is particularly true for any open-ended types of assessments such as essay questions, papers, and case studies. Teachers should be telling students what they did right as well as offering corrective feedback. The corrective comments should help students understand as specifically as possible why their original response was either incorrect or not the best choice. This feedback should empower them to apply it and do better in the future.

A number of models exist for how to provide this optimal blend of affirming and corrective feedback. Please see especially the 2 + 2 model of Allen and LeBlanc (2004). And, for how to use mark-up tools for papers and assignments online, see Dereshiwsky (2006). You can review a sample of such assessments as the term progresses to see if they meet these criteria of timeliness and substantive teacher feedback.

The following link discusses traits that you should look for in your online teachers: http://www.eschoolnews.com/news/top-news/?i=55930.

Winding Down the Course

As the instructional session draws to a close, you will want to be sure that some essential housekeeping tasks are taken care of. Table 11.5 shows you what to look for.

Table 11.5	Principal's Checklist for End of the Course
Course Feature	*What Principal Should Look For*
Final posted announcement	• When/how final papers or exams will be returned to students • When/how students may expect to receive their final course grades • Reminders about policy regarding incompletes, if relevant • Last day that teacher will be in the course room • Contact information on how to reach instructor after that date
Submission of grades to Registrar's Office	• Completed on time and correctly
Teacher retrospectives about the instructional session	• What worked • What didn't work • What might be done differently or better in the future

Students will naturally be concerned about their final course grade. You will want your online teachers to inform their students about when and how they should expect to receive their final course grade. Due to the privacy and confidentiality provisions of the Family Educational Rights and Privacy Act, teachers are not allowed to post final grades in any public-access places in the course room. They are allowed to send students their grades via the e-mail feature inside the course room area.

In like manner, your teachers will also want to inform their own students about how they can expect to receive notice of their course grade. It would also be helpful for teachers to remind students of any existing district/school policies for requesting or completing an incomplete to allow them extra time to finish the course.

In addition to notifying students of their course grade, your teachers should also let them know if, when, and how they can expect any final course papers or projects to be returned to them. In the case of a final exam that is fixed-choice, is auto-scored, and has an answer key as discussed earlier in this chapter, this will not be necessary. But in the case of a course paper or project, students may want to have their teacher's annotated comments.

Some other desirable elements of a final wrap-up announcement posting include informing students of the last day that their teacher will be in the course room. Otherwise, students may continue to post questions and wonder why they don't receive any responses. Along these lines, the teacher should also provide students with his or her contact information after the course has ended, in case they have a follow-up question or concern. You can easily spot-check the final posted announcement for these items in your wrap-up visit to the course room.

Finally, some schools/districts ask their online teachers to provide their immediate supervisor with an overall course retrospective. Regardless of the form it takes, such a retrospective invariably asks teachers to reflect on their immediate past instructional experience. They are then asked to share any successes (what worked well), challenges (what didn't work as well), and recommendations to improve things in the future. By asking your online teachers to provide you with such end-of-course retrospectives, you will have valuable information to supplement your own summative evaluation.

Cyberbullying: What Teachers Should Be Doing

In your role as evaluator of K–12 courses, you also want to assess what teachers are doing to ensure safe learning environments for their students. A discussion of online classrooms therefore must include mention of cyberbullying.

According to www.safe2tell.org, "cyberbullying is the use of technology to harass, threaten, embarrass, or target another person. Online threats or 'flames' (rude texts, IMs, or messages) count. So does posting personal information or videos designed to hurt or embarrass someone else."

What should your teachers be doing to help prevent cyberbullying? The Seattle Public Schools have developed a comprehensive cyberbullying prevention curriculum. It is available online (http://www.seattleschools.org/area/prevention/cbms.html) and includes student learning activities and teacher manuals. The Deer Valley Unified School District in Arizona has recently adopted this cyberbullying prevention program (http://www.azcentral.com/arizonarepublic/local/articles/2008/12/21/20081221gl-cyberbully1222-ON.html).

In addition to the above curriculum, teachers can address the problem of cyberbullying in a number of ways. They can advise students to keep passwords and real last names confidential. They can also show students how to block messages from sources who have harassed them. Students should be advised to delete suspect e-mail messages. In addition, teachers should be alert to signs of students who appear to be in emotional distress or quieter than usual, as this may be a sign that they have been the targets of cyberbullying. Targets should be advised to confide in trusted adults about the problem (http://www.hotchalk.com/mydesk/index.php/back-to-school-tips/312-ten-ways-to-prevent-cyberbullying).

The National Crime Prevention Council (2009) recommends a number of strategies that young people can use if they are victimized by cyberbullying. These include safeguarding personal information such as personal and school addresses, keeping passwords confidential, and keeping parents closely informed of their online activities.

What can you do in your role as administrator to help prevent cyberbullying? The experts agree that a clear, consistent school policy is key. You can find a sample policy at http://www.bullypolice.org/bullying_policy.html. Take a look at how one middle school created an antibullying program spearheaded by the students themselves at http://www.hotchalk.com/mydesk/index.php/editorial/121-classroom-best-practices/488-kids-stopping-kids-from-bullying-a-middle-school-intervention-. You can also find additional resources on stopping cyberbullying at http://www.cyberbully411.org. CyberSmart (http://cybersmartcurriculum.org/cyberbullying/prevention/) has an online CyberSmart Curriculum with links to learning activities for grades 2–12. The Indiana Department of Education (http://www.doe.in.gov/isssa/bullyingprevention_pg2.html) has a number of downloadable materials with tips for teachers, administrators, and parents on how to respond to cyberbullying.

Conclusions

Evaluating instruction is an important responsibility of educational administrators. The growth in popularity of the online classroom requires administrators to be aware of what to look for in assessing instructional performance in a Web-based classroom. This chapter has highlighted key things to look for in assessing instructional quality.

Key Principles for Leaders to Know

- Components of quality instruction such as effective communication with students, quality of instructional delivery, provision of feedback on assignments, and fostering a positive classroom climate are the same regardless of classroom format (e.g., face to face, online). The methods of their assessment, how they are observed or measured, will differ.

- You can spot-check the online course area for effective practice at the start of the term, while the course is underway, and toward the end of the course.

- *Continual teacher engagement* and *timeliness* are key assessment criteria that you can look for in teacher postings, discussion interactions, and input into course assignments.

- Teachers should provide *substantive* comments to students in response to questions, during discussions, and on assignments.

- Teachers can share valuable feedback with you at the end of the course to supplement your own summative evaluation.

- Consistent policies at the school level help prevent cyberbullying.

CASE STUDY 11.1 | Teacher Responsibilities for Online Learning

During the middle of the semester, you begin to receive an increasing number of complaints from students regarding one particular online teacher. According to the complaints, this teacher does not post anything in the weekly discussions beyond the discussion topic itself. In addition, this teacher does not make any comments on students' papers beyond "Good job" or "Needs improvement."

Discussion: Discuss a sample topic in your area of interest. Then, taking the role of an online teacher, draft two sample teacher discussion postings: one on the topic itself and one that is intended to jump-start a discussion that has apparently stalled (where the students are no longer posting).

Activity: Using the topics you created for the discussion above, devise and share a specific plan for coaching this teacher on how to improve his or her performance in the online course.

Web Resources

An **article on growth in popularity of online K–12 schools** is available from http://www.foxbusiness.com/story/markets/industries/finance/k-leads-way-school/.

Best practices for administrators to use in evaluating online teaching (http://www.westga.edu/~distance/ojdla/summer72/tobin72.html) are provided by the State University of West Georgia.

Best practices for online courses, including examples of self-introductions, are available from the Quality Matters online course evaluation rubric (http://www.cvtc.edu/pages/277.asp).

The **Certified Online Instructor (COI) certification program requirements** (http://www.teachingonthenet.org/courses/certified_online_instructor/index.cfm) are available from the Learning Resources Network (LERN).

A **checklist for evaluating online courses** (http://74.125.95.132/search?q=cache:6G6GKeVknwYJ:www.opi.state.mt.us/pdf/advplacement/OLC_Checklist.pdf+teacher+interaction+%2B+online+course&cd=13&hl=en&ct=clnk&gl=us) was adapted from guidelines developed by the National Education Association.

Criteria for evaluating online courses are available from http://74.125.95.132/search?q=cache:A4SqZRwqewEJ:www.cde.state.co.us/edtech/download/online-evaluating-courses.pdf+teacher+interaction+%2B+online+course&cd=5&hl=en&ct=clnk&gl=us.

The **Cyberbullying Research Center** (http://www.cyberbullying.us/) is a repository of case studies, publications, and other helpful resources on cyberbullying.

CyberSmart (http://cybersmartcurriculum.org/cyberbullying/prevention/) provides learning activities to prevent cyberbullying for grades 2–12.

The **Deer Valley Unified School District in Arizona adopted the Seattle Public Schools anticyberbullying curriculum** (http://www.azcentral.com/arizonarepublic/local/articles/2008/12/21/20081221gl-cyberbully1222-ON.html).

For an **example of a posted student question and the instructor's response,** see http://mathforum.org/library/drmath/view/52283.html.

Examples of creative icebreaker activities for online courses are available from http://twt.wikispaces.com/Ice-Breaker+Ideas.

Flash presentations on cyberbullying—what it is and what schools can do to stop it—are available from http://www.stopcyberbullying.org/.

General tips for effective online course design are available from http://74.125.113
.132/search?q=cache:FKRn1NHaM7wJ:teaching.unr.edu/coursemakover/docs/instruc
tionalDesignTips.pdf+online+instructional+design&cd=26&hl=en&ct=clnk&gl=us.

Guidelines for the content of a K–12 online course are available from http://www.netc.org/
digitalbridges/online/community/teachers2.php.

The **Illinois Virtual High School Web site** (http://www.ivhs.org/index.learn?action=other)
contains links to program evaluations of online high schools.

iSafe (http://www.isafe.org/channels/sub.php?ch=op&sub_id=media_cyber_bullying)
provides statistics on cyberbullying, as well as helpful resources.

Learn how to prepare your teachers to teach their first online course at http://home
.sprynet.com/~gkearsley/TeachingOnline.htm.

A **middle school program in which kids stopped kids from cyberbullying** is described at
http://www.hotchalk.com/mydesk/index.php/editorial/121-classroom-best-practices/488-
kids-stopping-kids-from-bullying-a-middle-school-intervention-.

Ms. Parry's rules of netiquette to help prevent cyberbullying are available from
http://www.stopcyberbullying.org/take_action/msparrysguidetonetiquette.html.

The **National Crime Prevention Council** (http://www.ncpc.org/cyberbullying) provides a
variety of online safety and bullying prevention tips.

**Refereed proceedings for several years from the Technology, Colleges & Community
Worldwide Online Conference** (http://etec.hawaii.edu/proceedings/) contain
valuable tips for effective leading-edge online course design.

Resources for Internet safety and prevention of cyberbullying are available from
http://www.cyberbully411.org/.

A **rubric for evaluating online instruction** (http://www.csuchico.edu/celt/roi/) is
available from California State University, Chico.

Another **rubric for evaluating online instruction** (http://www.sloan-c.org/node/367) is
available from the Sloan Consortium.

A **sample cyberbullying policy** is available from http://www.bullypolice.org/bullying_
policy.html.

The **Seattle Public Schools cyberbullying prevention curriculum** (http://www
.seattleschools.org/area/prevention/cbms.html) includes teacher guides and
student learning activities.

Suggested elements for review of online teaching are available from http://74.125.95 .132/search?q=cache:RtV_RhELiuYJ:ecampus.oregonstate.edu/faculty/manual/sug gestedelementreviewofonlineinstruction.pdf+evaluation+online+instruction&cd=28& hl=en&ct=clnk&gl=us.

Ten ways schools can prevent cyberbullying are detailed at http://www.hotchalk .com/mydesk/index.php/back-to-school-tips/312-ten-ways-to-prevent-cyberbullying.

Traits to look for in your online teachers as part of your evaluation are available from http://www.eschoolnews.com/news/top-news/?i=55930.

Tutorials for applying online learning theories to instructional design are available from http://www.patsula.com/usefo/webbasedlearning.

Two collections of online instructional design resources are available from the University of Pittsburgh (http://www.pitt.edu/~poole/onlinelearning.html) and the Educational Technology Users Group (http://www.ibritt.com/resources/index.htm).

Web-based resources for online faculty (http://www.teachingonthenet.org/faculty_club/ index.htm) are available from the LERN (Learning Resources Network) Faculty Club.

What a K–12 online course should contain is detailed at http://www.netc.org/digitalbridges/ online/essentials/#B.

What schools can do to prevent cyberbullying is described at http://www .cyberbullyingprevention.com/prevention.shtml.

In terms of **what to look for in K–12 program evaluation,** principals may find the following article (http://www.irrodl.org/index.php/irrodl/article/view/607/1182) helpful.

WiredSafety (https://www.wiredsafety.org/forms/stalking.html) is a site for reporting incidents of cyberbullying and cyberstalking.

References

Allen, D. W., & LeBlanc, A. C. (2004). *Collaborative peer coaching that improves instruction: The 2 + 2 performance appraisal model.* Thousand Oaks, CA: Corwin.

Dereshiwsky, M. I. (2006, June). *Grading papers and homework online.* Presented at the Learning Resource Network "Saving Faculty Time" Conference, online.

Dereshiwsky, M. I. (2008, February). *Continual engagement: Why it's important to effective online instruction.* Presented at the Learning Resource Network Annual Conference, Savannah, Georgia.

Draves, W.A. (2000). *Teaching online.* River Falls, WI: LERN Books.

Draves, W. A. (2001). *Learning on the net.* River Falls, WI: LERN Books.

Hanna, D. E., Glowacki-Dudka, M., & Conceicao-Runlee, S. (2000). *147 practical tips for teaching online groups: Essentials of web-based education.* Madison, WI: Atwood Publishing.

Hinduja, S., & Patchin, J. W. (2009). *Bullying beyond the schoolyard: Preventing and responding to cyberbullying.* Thousand Oaks, CA: Corwin.

Ko, S., & Rossen, S. (2008). *Teaching online: A practical guide* (2nd ed.). New York and London: Taylor & Francis Group.

National Crime Prevention Council. (2009). *Cyberbullying.* Retrieved September 14, 2009, from http://www.ncpc.org/cyberbullying

Palloff, R. M., & Pratt, K. (2001). *Lessons from the cyberspace classroom: The realities of online teaching.* San Francisco: John Wiley & Sons, Inc.

Palloff, R. M., & Pratt, K. (2003). *The virtual student: A profile and guide to working with online learners.* San Francisco: John Wiley & Sons, Inc.

Palloff, R. M., & Pratt, K. (2007). *Building online learning communities: Effective strategies for the virtual classroom* (2nd ed.). San Francisco: John Wiley & Sons, Inc.

Schweizer, H. (1999). *Designing and teaching an online course: Spinning your web classroom.* New York: Allyn & Bacon.

Shank, P. (Ed.) (2007). *The online learning idea book: 95 proven ways to enhance technology-based and blended learning.* San Francisco: John Wiley & Sons, Inc.

Shariff, S. (2009). *Confronting cyber-bullying: What schools need to know to control misconduct and avoid legal consequences.* New York: Cambridge University Press.

Chapter 12

Using Technology for Assessing and Evaluating Student Learning and Instructional Practices

Cynthia Conn

Evaluation, or assessing teaching performance for its effectiveness, is a fundamental aspect of instructional design and the education process. Although viewed negatively by some, especially in light of the heavy emphasis on standardized testing implemented through the passage of No Child Left Behind, evaluation is key to **student learning**—instructional practices focused on student-based acquisition—and teachers' reflective practice. **Formative** assessments help students and teachers alike evaluate progress and mastery of content and principles throughout a lesson and tend to be informal in nature. **Summative** assessments help teachers evaluate comprehensive, integrated knowledge of students typically at the conclusion of a lesson or unit of study and are often formally documented. School administrators need to understand formative and summative assessments and how to leverage technology for collecting assessment data for locally developed instruments.

Evaluation of student learning and instructional practices occurs at multiple levels. A teacher tends to focus on lesson- or unit-level assessments: "How are my students doing in relation to objectives outlined for the lesson I am teaching in relation to addition and subtraction?" A school- or district-level educational leader asks, "How are all first graders at my school or in my district doing in relation to grade-level state math standards?" Teachers focus maybe on specific state standards and related objectives for one or multiple content areas for their class, whereas school or district leaders are interested in seeing academic progress in relation to state standards for an entire grade level.

The following questions are addressed in this chapter:

- What does a leader need to emphasize for curriculum mapping to serve as the foundation for developing a comprehensive assessment system?

- What are the professional development opportunities a leader should use to enhance and support knowledge and skills in relation to the curriculum mapping process and a locally developed assessment system?

- How can leaders help others understand that rubrics are explicitly tied to academic standards and objectives and can be used to provide individual as well as aggregate feedback regarding knowledge and skills?

- How can leaders help others seek out commercial as well as freely available tools for use in managing and implementing curriculum mapping and assessment processes?

- What are the skills leaders need to leverage technology for collecting, aggregating, and reporting assessment data for locally developed assessment systems?

NETS for Administrators (International Society for Technology in Education [ISTE], 2009) Standard 4, Systemic Improvement, emphasizes the importance of educational leaders "to continuously improve the organization through the effective use of information and technology resources." One method for ensuring improvement is to "establish metrics, collect and analyze data, interpret results, and share findings to improve staff performance and student learning." To monitor and evidence continuous improvement requires data, qualitative and/or quantitative. However, in order for an **assessment system**—the process by which metrics are established, data are collected and analyzed, and results are interpreted for students, teachers, and staff—to be successful, it must be **manageable**, or able to be organized, and **feasible**, or realistic, to implement. At a class, school, or district level, technology should be leveraged to help make assessing **instructional strategies**—well-defined and replicable activities used to guide those of the future—and student performance on **project-based** or discreet and other **authentic** or performance-based activities both manageable and feasible. This chapter will look at Web-based and other software applications that can be powerful tools for assessing student learning. These tools can assist school administrators and teachers in providing individual, detailed feedback to students and parents.

Additionally, these tools provide an efficient mechanism for aggregating student responses or proficiency levels in order to gain a data-based view of student achievement related to specific academic standards and objectives at a class or grade level. Using these data, teachers can provide evidence of their own reflective practice in relation to modifying the curricula to address gaps or successes in student learning. Some of these tools include **electronic portfolios**, which serve as a repository of student work; **rubric generation software**, which allows for computer-based assessment; **quiz or survey tools**, which are also assessment based; and spreadsheet software.

Three key questions form the framework for this chapter: What are the primary challenges school administrators face in using technology for assessment purposes? What influence do changing technology practices have on expectations for the learner and assessment of academic standards or objectives? Why are multimedia applications that connect to the visual, auditory, verbal, and kinesthetic important to the learner and to **demonstration** of academic standards or objectives, an active learning strategy?

Authentic Assessment of Student Learning Outcomes

Although largely ignored by state departments of education due to the overwhelming emphasis on standardized testing requirements, No Child Left Behind does call for multiple assessment measures, "including **classroom-based assessments** [which are explicitly aligned to academic standards and constitute the second part of the assessment system process, as part of a state assessment system]" (Neill, Guisbond, & Schaeffer, 2004, p. 146). Neill and colleagues (2004) state that schools and districts should be responsible for assessing the extent to which students learn agreed-upon knowledge (i.e., academic standards) at both a conceptual and an application level. Standardized tests offer one means of assessment. However, a more complete picture of student learning can be seen when a combination of qualitative and quantitative methods that directly align to academic standards is included in a school, district, and/or state assessment system.

Several formal, classroom-based, authentic assessments that should be considered are "teacher evaluations of student achievement, portfolios as evidence of student work, final projects presented to a panel of community members," and so forth (Neill et al., 2004, p. 152). Cole, Ryan, Kick, and Mathies (2000) describe several methods for evaluating authentic assessments such as "kidwatching/anecdotal records," "checklists," "interviews/conferences," "performance assessments," and "classroom tests" (p. 9). In order to assess student learning and report achievement levels on an aggregate level, a manageable and feasible assessment system or plan is needed that includes collection of data through **standards-based scoring guides or rubrics**, tools for both the student and teacher that provide explicit grading expectations.

Developing a District- or School-Level Assessment System

Assessment planning starts with a fundamental question: What do I want my students (i.e., first graders, second graders, English language learners, etc.) to "know or be able to do" (Marzano, Pickering, & McTighe, 1993, p. 13) at the conclusion of the academic year? As educators, we look to state or national grade-level standards to guide our efforts in **curriculum mapping**—the first part of the assessment system process—and assessment planning. Developing a school- or district-level assessment system starts with curriculum mapping. Once the curriculum mapping process is complete, the teacher (or team of teachers) should identify or develop classroom-based assessments that are explicitly aligned to the academic standards for the content areas he or she teaches. These classroom-based assessments or "benchmark tasks" (Jacobs, 2004, p. 112) form the basis for the assessment system. Each classroom-based assessment should include a scoring guide or "scoring rubric" (Marzano et al., 1993, p. 29), again explicitly aligned to academic standards. The following sections discuss each of these topics: curriculum mapping, developing an assessment system, and scoring guides (rubrics).

Curriculum Mapping

Curriculum mapping is the process of documenting and aligning the operational or actual curriculum to the academic calendar (Jacobs, 1997, 2004).

> Data are gathered in a format that allows each teacher to present an overview of his or her students' actual learning experience . . . Mapping is not presented as what *ought* to happen but what *is* happening during the course of a school year. (Jacobs, 1997, p. 61)

English and Steffy (2001) use the term *curriculum alignment* and define it as the "process in which the curriculum in use is matched to the test in use" (p. 17).

Jacobs (1997) offers a guide for the curriculum mapping process. She outlines seven phases:

Phase 1: Collecting the Data

Phase 2: The First Read-Through

Phase 3: Mixed Group Review Session

Phase 4: Large Group Review

Phase 5: Determine Those Points That Can Be Revised Immediately

Phase 6: Determine Those Points That Will Require Long-Term Research and Development

Phase 7: The Review Cycle Continues (pp. 8–16)

Jacobs (1997, 2004) should be consulted for an in-depth description of each of these phases. However, following is a brief summary of the phases. Phase 1: Collecting the Data is the key to the curriculum mapping process. This first step should be completed by the teacher and provide a high-level view of what is occurring in the classroom each month in relation to content standards (knowledge and skills), "essential questions" (Jacobs, 1997, p. 8), and any performance assessments implemented. This process is the teacher, school, and district's "window" to seeing what, where, when, and how academic standards are addressed.

During Phases 2, 3, and 4, Jacobs (1997) outlines six tasks for readers/teachers to consider as they review a curriculum map. Two of the tasks are to "Identify Gaps" and "Identify Repetitions" (pp. 18–20). Through these tasks, teachers identify content standards that are not addressed—that is, **instructional gaps**—as well as document if particular standards are emphasized or possibly overemphasized (i.e., repetitions). How to address gaps or overemphasized standards is determined during Phases 5 and 6. In Phase 7, the review cycle continues.

The initial results of the mapping work should be documented in a curriculum map. The sample curriculum map described by Jacobs (2004) includes teacher name, class/course/content topic, grade, and year as heading information. The curriculum map is a table or grid that asks teachers to list essential questions, content, skills, and assessment type by month.

Sophisticated software is available from a variety of vendors. Curriculum Designers, Inc. (2007–2008), Jacobs's company, provides a comprehensive list of available products via its Web site (http://www.curriculumdesigners.com/index .php?Path=Public/Resources/Mapping%20Software). These products should be considered and evaluated especially for school- or district-wide curriculum mapping projects. They provide a collaborative space for documenting how standards align to the curriculum as well as advanced reporting features. In Jacobs's *Getting Results with Curriculum Mapping,* Kallick and Wilson (2004) offer recommendations for reviewing and evaluating products. However, if the cost of these programs is prohibitive, the curriculum mapping process is still possible with the use of a spreadsheet or database program, and collaboration features can be included by using easily accessible Web 2.0 technologies like Google for Educators, Google Docs, or Wikispaces (see Chapter 7 for more information on Web 2.0 technologies).

For school leaders, the overarching challenges of curriculum mapping are demonstrating the benefit to teachers and students, providing the necessary time to complete the mapping process and maintain the curriculum map, and using professional development opportunities to assist teachers in understanding and implementing the curriculum mapping process.

To summarize, the curriculum mapping process includes the following three components:

- Creating the curriculum map by asking teachers to document month by month the overarching elements of the actual curriculum being taught

- Reviewing the curriculum map to identify instructional gaps and overemphasized academic standards

- Determining immediate and long-term solutions to addressing instructional gaps and overemphasized academic standards

Developing an Assessment System

"It is in the classroom that the student and standard meet . . . Without evidence through student assessment, the standard is a shell" (Jacobs, 1997, p. 23). Yet, as mentioned in the introduction to this chapter, the only or primary method for collecting student assessment data currently is through standardized testing. Using the curriculum mapping process with notations related to state standards and assessment or benchmark tasks, an assessment system or plan (Maki, 2004; Suskie, 2004; Walvoord, 2004) can be developed to create a systematic process for collecting multiple forms of assessment data. Jacobs (2004) describes "the development of internally generated assessments of benchmarks" as "the natural outgrowth of curriculum mapping" (p. 114). One example of work in the area of using locally developed instruments for public accountability is PROPEL, a cooperative research project involving the Pittsburgh Public Schools, Harvard Project Zero, and Educational Testing Service (LeMahieu, Eresh, & Wallace, 1992).

An assessment system benefits students and teachers by using multiple measures, including qualitative measures, to view student achievement levels both individually and at aggregate levels (i.e., class, school, or district, depending on which levels are included in the assessment system). These comprehensive data, which can include standardized test results, allow teachers to identify student and class strengths and weaknesses and adapt instruction accordingly. One qualitative measure that can be used is authentic assessments. Cole et al. (2000) describe authentic assessments as allowing "students [to] demonstrate, rather than be required to tell or be questioned about, what they know and can do. Hence authentic assessment usually is classified as performance based" (p. 5).

The books by Maki (2004), Suskie (2004), and Walvoord (2004) all define, describe, and outline strategies and provide sample matrices for developing assessment plans. These texts are written from a higher-education perspective but still serve as a useful resource for K–12 leaders. In addition, the National Forum on Assessment (2008) has produced a listing of seven principles and indicators school administrators can use as a framework for developing a school-, district-, or statewide assessment system.

The curriculum mapping process serves as the first step in developing a comprehensive assessment system (or assessment plan). One of the most straightforward frameworks is produced by the National Council for Accreditation of Teacher Education (2008) and includes "Name of Assessment," "Type or Form of Assessment," and "When Assessment Is Administered" as the headers for the table. A data reporting guide, using information collected through the curriculum mapping process, becomes the basis for the assessment system. The content and skills sections of the curriculum map should explicitly specify the state academic standards being addressed. This information is used to create the data reporting guide, which should list the teacher, the grade, the academic standard, the standard's code, the unit and lesson the standard is aligned to, the assessment or benchmark task, and when the standard is addressed (see Table 12.1). This information is best developed in a spreadsheet or database application so it can be easily sorted and searched.

Initial planning time, as well as ongoing maintenance of the assessment system, needs to be appropriately assigned and integrated into the teacher's and administrator's professional practice, and the work should be rewarded. The data

Table 12.1	Data Reporting Guide (Example)						
Teacher	Grade	Code	Academic Standard	Unit	Lesson	Assessment Instrument	Month

reports should be shared in a routine manner, and use of the data for decision-making purposes should be documented. Initial and ongoing assistance and professional development regarding implementing the curriculum mapping process and assessment system should be provided. School leaders should take a role in monitoring progress for the main purpose of providing guidance and answering questions to ensure the time and effort put forth by teachers results in a comprehensive curriculum map; to encourage, when possible, the creation of common assessments that can be used by multiple teachers of the same grade level within a school or district; and to guide the formation of a comprehensive assessment system.

The data reporting guide is a means for documenting the alignment among standards, instruction, and assessment instruments that forms the basis for the assessment system. General guidelines for a grade-level assessment system include the following:

- Alignment between assessments and standards should be explicit.

- Number of assessments should be manageable.

- Assessments should be feasible to implement; when possible, common assessments should be created that can be used by multiple teachers of the same grade level within a school or district.

- Data collection should be streamlined using scoring guides or rubrics and electronic means for storing, aggregating, and reporting data.

- Multiple methods including both qualitative and quantitative assessments should be included.

Scoring Guides (Rubrics)

Stevens and Levi (2005) define a rubric as "a scoring tool that lays out the specific expectations for an assignment. Rubrics divide an assignment into its component parts and provide a detailed description of what constitutes acceptable or unacceptable levels of performance for each of those parts" (p. 3). Marzano et al. (1993) go on to define rubrics as providing "important information to teachers, parents, and others interested in what students know and can do. Rubrics also promote learning by offering clear performance targets to students for agreed-upon standards" (p. 29).

Stevens and Levi (2005) offer a detailed description of the components of a rubric as well as stages for developing a rubric. The stages for developing a rubric include "Reflecting, Listing, Grouping and Labeling, and Application" (pp. 29–30). For K–12 educators, Reflecting is a component of the curriculum mapping process where teachers look for instructional gaps and repetitions and how the benchmark task or assignment relates overall to the academic standards and unit of instruction.

Once a teacher is confident that the assignment is a good fit for measuring the specified academic standards, he or she moves into the Listing stage and notes the standards and objectives aligned to the assignment. Since the intention is to share the rubric with students to help clarify assignment expectations, the objectives should be written for students, student-friendly in terms of language, and written at an appropriate grade level. As part of the Listing stage, descriptions regarding the levels of performance should be developed. It is easiest to write the highest level of performance and unacceptable performance descriptions first before writing the middle performance level(s). As an alternative, students can be asked to assist with developing these performance level descriptions, creating a deeper understanding of the expectations of the assignment.

In the Grouping and Labeling stage, the authors suggest organizing or grouping the assignment objectives in a logical sequence, placing similar items together. Finally, in the Application stage, the information generated above is transferred to a grid or table.

The key to using a rubric as an assessment tool for a broader purpose such as a grade-level, school, or district assessment system is tying the criteria or dimensions (i.e., left column) to academic standards. By doing so, the rubric becomes an assessment instrument that is explicitly assessing academic standards and can be used as a means for documenting student learning at an individual and aggregate (e.g., class, grade, or school) level. The individual and aggregate data provide teachers and administrators with valuable information related to achievement and gaps in learning. For teachers, this type of information is a necessary component of reflective practice. It provides data for determining how to best improve instruction and student learning. For school administrators, the standards-based scoring guides provide a means for collecting evidence related to performance-based assessments of student learning.

One issue that often arises is the importance of documenting that assessment systems and instruments are fair, accurate, consistent, and free of bias. Accreditation agencies such as the National Council for Accreditation of Teacher Education (2007) require information from institutions of higher education that evidence these qualities. Suskie (2004) discusses the importance of evaluating the quality of assessment instruments to determine if they are effective in yielding "information about what students have *truly* learned" (p. 272). Throughout her book she recommends addressing several questions:

- *Is your assessment system fair?* As we know from Gardner's (1993) work, students bring a wide variety of learning styles to our classes. Thus, assessment systems should consist of a variety of instruments such as internally developed exams, papers, projects, concept maps, oral presentations, community-based projects, and portfolios.

- *Is your assessment instrument accurate? Is it working the way you intended?* Just as objective test questions can be reviewed for difficulty and discrimination, so can rubric criteria. Discrimination, or comparing assignments "with the highest overall scores against the assignments with the lowest overall scores in terms of ratings they earned on each criterion" (Suskie, 2004, p. 276), is another option for evaluating the accuracy of rubrics.

- *Does your assessment instrument produce consistent results?* A key element of assessment systems is the use of rubrics aligned explicitly to academic standards and objectives. The use of rubrics improves the consistency of grading. Stevens and Levi (2005) state "with rubrics . . . we know what we want from the very beginning when we tell the students about the assignment . . . we focus our attention on what we expect in the best and worst papers, and we do it the same way—in the same order—for each and every paper" (p. 74).

- *How well do your data reflect the characteristics of all your students (free of bias)?* Using key, summative classroom-based assessments that would normally require evaluation is one method for ensuring data reflect the characteristics of all students in your population.

Developing rubrics can be a challenging task for teachers. The initial investment of time can be significant. Additionally, the criteria or "dimensions" (Stevens & Levi, 2005, p. 6) of teacher-created rubrics often focus on following assignment directions or tasks (i.e., a research paper contains five pages, or a PowerPoint presentation contains 10 slides) rather than assessing student learning in relation to academic standards or objectives. Table 12.2 provides an example of criteria and performance levels aligned to an academic standard written to assess student learning, whereas Table 12.3 provides an example of rubric criteria written to assess a student's ability to follow directions. In Table 12.4, an example of assignment instructions and a rubric written for fifth-grade students and aligned to state technology standards is provided.

Table 12.2	Assessment of Student Learning		
Assessment of Student Learning			
Academic Standard/Objective	*Progressing*	*Acceptable*	*Excellent*
Demonstrate the 5 Ws to evaluate the quality of information/Web pages located on the Internet (NETS for Students [ISTE, 2007], Standard 4).	Some responses regarding the 5 Ws are documented.	Responses regarding each of the 5 Ws are documented.	Detailed, clear responses regarding each of the 5 Ws are documented.

Note: For the five Ws of Web site evaluation see Schrock (2001–2009).

Table 12.3	Assessment of Student Ability to Follow Directions

Assessment of Student Ability to Follow Directions			
Academic Standard/ Objective	*Progressing*	*Acceptable*	*Excellent*
Complete the 5 Ws Web site evaluation form for the three Web sites selected from the Google search.	One or two of the 5 Ws Web site evaluation forms are not complete or completed.	A separate 5 Ws Web site evaluation form has been completed for each of the three Web sites.	A separate 5 Ws Web site evaluation form has been completed and well written for each of the three Web sites.

Note: For the five Ws of Web site evaluation see Schrock (2001–2009).

Table 12.4	Favorite Book Presentation Assignment Instruction and Rubric (Fifth Grade)

Learning Activity: Favorite Book Presentation

Assessment Strategy: Hands-on Project

Instructions: For this project, you will use a template with four slides to develop a presentation about your favorite book. Your presentation should include

- the title of the book, author's name, and student's name;
- an image of the book cover with a favorite quote;
- a personal statement about the best part of the book; and
- reference information for the book.

Please make sure to choose a design, color, and animation scheme for your presentation.

Objectives (Arizona State Technology Standards):

- Gather research from a variety of electronic sources (5T-E2. PO 2.)
- Design and create a multimedia presentation (3T-E3. PO 1.)
- Save file to student work space on server (1T-E2. PO 2.)

Rubric:

Criteria	*Needs Improvement*	*Acceptable*	*Exceptional*
Gather research from a variety of electronic sources, including an image of the book cover or author or a related picture (5T-E2. PO 2.)	It was difficult to remember and complete the steps for searching and downloading an image of the book cover or author or a related picture	I (the student) was able to complete the steps for searching and downloading an image of the book cover or author or a related picture independently or with limited assistance from a classmate or teacher.	I (the student) was able to complete the steps for searching and downloading an image of the book cover or author or a related picture independently and also assisted classmates with the process.

(Continued)

Table 12.4	(Continued)		
Criteria	*Needs Improvement*	*Acceptable*	*Exceptional*
Design and create a multimedia presentation (3T-E3. PO 1.)	It was difficult for me (the student) to access the presentation template, type in the requested information, and place the reference information in MLA format.	I (the student) was able to access the presentation template, type in the requested information, and place the reference information in MLA format independently or with limited assistance from a classmate or teacher.	I (the student) was able to access the presentation template, type in the requested information, and place the reference information in MLA format independently and also assisted classmates with the process.
Apply design template and color and animation scheme (3T-E3. PO 1.)	The PowerPoint presentation does not include a design, color, and/or animation scheme.	The PowerPoint presentation includes a design, color, and/or animation scheme.	The PowerPoint presentation includes a design, color, and/or animation scheme that relates well to the book selected.
Save file to student work space on server (1T-E2. PO 2.)	The PowerPoint presentation was not saved to the proper folder on the student server.	The PowerPoint presentation was saved to the proper folder on the student server, and I (the student) was able to access the file with limited directions.	The PowerPoint presentation was saved to the proper folder on the student server, and I (the student) remembered how to access the file independently.

Learners are experiencing changing expectations. Memorizing information for a test is no longer sufficient or considered the best means for assessing what students know and *are able to do* (i.e., performance).

What we know about learning indicates that assessment and learning are closely and intimately tied. The importance of changing assessment practices so they mirror the learning process becomes clearer when one realizes that students in American schools learn what they know they will be tested on. (Marzano et al., 1993, p. 11)

The underlying premise for building a rubric is to improve student learning. By clarifying objectives via a rubric, teachers are providing students with a "road map" to where they are going in relation to academic standards or learning objectives. This is good practice for all students but is especially helpful for English language learners or other learners who are struggling with comprehending class materials and instructions. However, new instructional strategies often need to be taught, so it is important to provide rubrics to students consistently over the course of an academic year so they become more aware of the type of information the rubric is communicating and how to best use the assignment rubric as a tool for meeting expectations and self-evaluating their own work.

Stevens and Levi (2005) document a variety of benefits to developing and using rubrics:

- Improving students' end products and increasing learning

- Assisting with clearly communicating assignment expectations to students, student teachers, and classroom aides

- Improving consistency of grading

- Speeding up the grading process

- Adapting quality rubrics that have already been developed to new situations or assignments

Based on Stevens and Levi's (2005) research and work in the area of rubrics, a useful sequence of steps for developing and implementing standards-based rubrics includes the following:

Step 1: What are the academic standards or learning objectives your assignment/ assessment is addressing?

Step 2: Choose the number of levels or a scale for your rubric such as Progressing, Acceptable, and Excellent.

Step 3: Pilot the rubric by using it to evaluate a previously graded set of assignments or requesting feedback from another similar grade-level teacher.

Step 4: Distribute the rubric to students before they begin the assignment.

Step 5: Evaluate student work with the rubric to determine level of achievement in relation to academic standards and objectives. Note issues related to use of the rubric such as additional items that should be included in the achievement-level descriptions.

Step 6: Review and revise the rubric based on the results of use.

Step 7: Update the assessment system and data reporting guide documents if any changes were made to the academic standards aligned to the assignment.

Standards-Based Scoring Guides

Online Rubric Generation Tools

Various online rubric generation tools are available and will likely continue to be developed as stand-alone tools as well as tools integrated in other products such as electronic portfolio and course management information systems. Table 12.5 contains a listing of some of the tools currently available.

Table 12.5	Online Rubric Generation Tools	
Software Application	*Vendor*	*Link to Product*
ClassMon (Fee)	Folios International	http://www.foliosinternational.com/content2.php?contentid=21
Project Based Learning Checklists (Free)	4Teachers.org	http://pblchecklist.4teachers.org/checklist.shtml
Rubric Machine (Free)	David Warlick & The Landmark Project	http://landmark-project.com/rubric_builder/
Rubric Maker (Free)	Recipes4Success	http://myt41.com/index.php?v=pl&page_ac=view&type=tools&tool=rubricmaker
Rubric Maker (Free)	Scholastic	http://teacher.scholastic.com/tools/rubric.htm
Rubric Makers (Fee)	teAchnology	http://www.teach-nology.com/web_tools/rubrics/
Rubric Template (Microsoft Word) (Free)	Kennesaw State University, Educational Technology Center	http://edtech.kennesaw.edu/intech/docs/rubrictemplate.doc
RubiStar (Free)	4Teachers.org	http://rubistar.4teachers.org/index.php
The Rubric Builder (Fee)	Gateway Software Productions	http://www.rubricbuilder.on.ca/

Tools for Implementing Authentic Assessments

Locally developed assessments tied to academic standards provide a means for collecting assessment data that can provide individual feedback to a student as well as aggregate (e.g., class or grade-level) data to teachers and school administrators. The key to developing an assessment system is that it must be manageable and assessment instruments must be feasible to implement. Leveraging technology for collecting, aggregating, and reporting assessment data creates a more manageable and feasible approach to a locally developed assessment system.

Some curriculum mapping tools are listed earlier in this chapter. In addition, electronic portfolios, quiz or survey tools, and spreadsheets can be used for management, collection, and reporting needs related to curriculum mapping and assessment monitoring. The following sections discuss each of these types of tools in greater detail.

Electronic Portfolios

> One of the most exciting developments in the school reform movement is the use of alternative forms of assessment to evaluate student learning, and one of the most popular forms of authentic assessment is the use of portfolios. The point of the portfolio is to provide a "richer picture" of a student's abilities, and to show growth over time. (Barrett, 2002, p. 7)

As discussed by Barrett (2002), the use of electronic portfolios for assessment purposes brings together the work of Ivers and Barron (1998) and Danielson and Abrutyn (1997). "Multimedia projects [like electronic portfolios] allow students to exhibit their understanding of a topic in a variety of ways, and they provide students with the opportunity to explain their work and ideas to others" (Ivers & Barron, 1998, p. 2). Ivers and Barron (1998) provide a model, DDD-E, for developing multimedia projects: "The DDD-E model consists of three main phases (DECIDE, DESIGN, DEVELOP), surrounded by and ending with EVALUATE" (p. 19). Danielson and Abrutyn (1997) offer a framework for developing portfolios that consists of collection, selection, reflection, and projection.

The authors describe the importance of portfolios as a method for assessing student learning.

> Educators have long recognized the gulf separating daily practice in the classroom and the types of tests to which their students have been subjected . . . Standardized, norm-referenced, machine-scorable multiple-choice tests are a quick, efficient, and inexpensive way to evaluate certain limited goals of schools—primarily, [students'] acquisition of bits of knowledge . . . They are of little value in evaluating any *generative* goals in which students must *produce* a response, such as skill in writing a persuasive essay, solving a nonroutine problem, or designing an experiment to test a hypothesis. (Danielson & Abrutyn, 1997, pp. 20–21)

Thus, one benefit of using electronic portfolios is that all types of work, including multimedia products, can be used to demonstrate student learning and levels of achievement in relation to academic standards and objectives.

A challenge of using electronic portfolios with K–12 students is finding a tool that is affordable, is secure, and can also be easily accessed by students and teachers. To truly leverage technology, the tool (or collection of tools) chosen needs to be simple enough to use and implement but sophisticated enough to allow for assessing student work and, if possible, generating reports.

Issues school leaders need to address when considering implementing electronic portfolios and evaluating products are as follows:

- Mechanisms for financing, managing, and implementing the selected tool(s)

- Privacy issues related to student identity and work

- Professional development opportunities for teachers

- Potential interface of tools with existing grading systems, school Web sites, and/or course management systems

- Ability to develop scoring rubrics that reference academic standards

- Capacity to generate useful reports aggregating data from common assessments at a class, grade, school, and/or district level

- Ability for students to maintain, expand, and enhance an electronic portfolio over time to demonstrate growth as well as use for purposes such as seeking employment, support for scholarship or other leadership opportunities, and admissions to college

A key aspect of using an electronic portfolio as a means for demonstrating student learning at a grade, school, and/or district level is the development of an overarching assessment system. The assessment system provides a guide to the academic standards and objectives that a grade level, school, or district desires to assess. The assessment system incorporates classroom-based or summative assessments that best assess the stated academic standards. Electronic portfolios might be selected as the best instrument for assessing one or more academic standards or might be used as a mechanism for collecting all assessments outlined in the assessment system. An electronic portfolio tool that allows for the creation of standards-based scoring guides and the reporting of data at the individual, class, or grade level is ideal in making the assessment system feasible to implement. Barrett (2007–2008) provides a list of available Web 2.0 products that can be used to create electronic portfolios via her Web site (http://electronicportfolios.org/web20portfolios.html). In addition, Table 12.6 contains links to commercial products specifically designed for K–12 students.

Table 12.6	Electronic Portfolio Tools	
Software Application	*Vendor*	*Link to Product*
FolioMaker (Fee)	Folios International	http://www.foliosinternational.com/content2.php?contentid=14
Grady Profile & Toot! (Fee)	Aurbach & Associates, Inc.	http://www.aurbach.com/
Roger Wagner's HyperStudio 5 (Fee)	The Software MacKiev Company	http://www.mackiev.com/hyperstudio/index.html

Quiz or Survey Tools

Web-based quiz or survey tools can be used in multiple ways to collect assessment data. In a traditional sense, they can be used to administer locally developed classroom tests. Quiz tools often have the option to automatically grade multiple-choice, multiple-answer, true-or-false, and fill-in-the-blank items. More sophisticated tools provide the option for immediate feedback to learners. Data are exported in a spreadsheet format for easy review of individual as well as overall class results.

Online survey tools can be used to collect self-evaluation data from students. Again, data can be exported in a spreadsheet format for easy review of individual as well as overall class responses.

These tools can also be used by teachers to enter data for scoring rubrics or checklists. This would be useful if your school is unable to purchase a commercial product that can be used to collect and report assessment data. It is especially useful if data are being collected for multiple classes using the same instrument, because data will be stored and exported from a central location. Table 12.7 contains a listing of some of the Web-based quiz and survey tools currently available.

Table 12.7	Web-Based Quiz and Survey Tools	
Software Application	*Vendor*	*Link to Product*
ClassMarker (Free)	ClassMarker	http://www.classmarker.com/
EasyTestMaker (Free/Fee)	EasyTestMaker	http://www.easytestmaker.com/default.aspx
ExamBuilder (Fee)	ExamBuilder	http://www.exambuilder.com/
Kwik Surveys (Free)	Kwik Surveys	http://www.kwiksurveys.com/index.php
MyStudiyo (Free)	MyStudiyo	http://www.mystudiyo.com/
Quia (Fee)	Quia Corporation	http://www.quia.com/web
Quiz Center (Free)	Discovery Channel	http://school.discoveryeducation.com/quizcenter/quizcenter.html
Smile (Free)	Michigan State University	http://clear.msu.edu/teaching/online/mimea/smile/v2/index.php
YacaPaca (Free)	Chalkface Project	http://yacapaca.com/

Spreadsheets

Spreadsheets remain a simple-to-use software application that allows for sorting of data by columns, calculations, and reporting of aggregate assessment results from scoring guides. The use of a spreadsheet was recommended earlier for creating a data reporting guide, a necessary component for tracking academic standards and alignment to a lesson and an assignment/assessment. As noted above, data from online quiz and survey tools are typically exported in spreadsheet format to allow for more advanced calculations, reporting, and storage purposes. In Table 12.8, a list of spreadsheet applications is provided.

Table 12.8	Spreadsheet Applications	
Software Application	*Vendor*	*Link to Product*
Google Docs	Google	http://docs.google.com
Excel	Microsoft	http://office.microsoft.com/en-us/excel/default.aspx
OpenOffice	OpenOffice.org	http://www.openoffice.org/

Conclusions

Implementing multiple methods of assessment rather than focusing entirely on standardized testing results creates a more complete picture of student learning and is integral to the learning process. Curriculum mapping is a reflective process engaged in by teachers to document the actual curriculum, and the results form the foundation for developing an assessment system. Scoring guides or rubrics explicitly aligned to academic standards provide one mechanism for collecting assessment data for authentic or performance-based assessments. Technology can provide an efficient mechanism for aggregating assessment data to gain an aggregate view of student achievement levels. Using these data, teachers can provide evidence of student success as well as document their own data-based decisions related to modifying the curricula to address instructional gaps. The tools reviewed in this chapter include curriculum mapping software, rubric generation software, electronic portfolios, quiz or survey tools, and spreadsheet software.

Key Principles for Leaders to Know

Evaluation is a fundamental aspect of the learning process and teachers' reflective practice. Standardized tests offer one means of assessment. However, a more complete picture of student learning can be seen when a combination of qualitative and quantitative methods that directly align to academic standards is used as part of a comprehensive assessment system.

- Curriculum mapping serves as the foundation for developing a comprehensive assessment system.

- Professional development opportunities should be used to enhance and support knowledge and skills in relation to the curriculum mapping process and a locally developed assessment system.

- Rubrics that are explicitly tied to academic standards and objectives can be used to provide individual as well as aggregate feedback regarding knowledge and skills.

- Seek out commercial as well as freely available tools for use in managing and implementing curriculum mapping and assessment processes.

- Leverage technology for collecting, aggregating, and reporting assessment data for locally developed assessment systems.

CASE STUDY 12.1 | Student Learning Outcomes in Technology

As the principal of a magnet school with a specialized curriculum (e.g., art, music, technology, science, bilingual, etc.), you are seeking assessment data on student learning outcomes for your school's specialty area that is not addressed by your state's mandated, standardized test. At your opening faculty meeting, you request one grade-level professional learning community to volunteer to work with you during the school year to develop a curriculum map and one to two common, summative assessments for the particular set of standards emphasized by the school.

Discussion: Discuss in groups one to two grade-level standards in a particular specialty area, and map those standards to the existing curriculum. How might one use spreadsheet software (available free through Google for Educators, http://www.google.com/educators/, or OpenOffice, http://www.openoffice.org) to create a data reporting guide?

Where and how is each standard addressed through the curriculum?

What standards are not currently addressed by the curriculum? If standards are addressed multiple times, discuss whether the repetition is appropriate or if the standard is being overemphasized.

Activity: Creating a curriculum map for the one to two grade-level standards in the particular specialty area of your school, identify an existing project or performance-based assignment or create one that could be used to collect summative assessment data related to three to five components of the standard(s) selected.

(Continued)

(Continued)

Using RubiStar (http://rubistar.4teachers.org/) or another rubric generation tool, develop a rubric aligned to the selected standards. Once you have developed a rubric for collecting data related to the standards you selected, reflect on how the data might be used by and/or communicated to teachers, students, parents, and school administrators.

CASE STUDY 12.2 | Student Learning Using Electronic Portfolios

As a school or district leader, you would like to see the development of electronic portfolios as a means of assessing and demonstrating student learning. However, funding is not available to purchase a commercial product.

Discussion: In a group discuss how one might conduct a keyword search in Google or another search engine using the following terms: Web 2.0 tools for electronic portfolios and assessment reporting and K–12 education.

Activity: Review one to two free products and describe the benefits and challenges of using the tool for electronic portfolios and how assessment data regarding student learning might be collected, communicated, and aggregated.

Web Resources

ClassMarker (http://www.classmarker.com/) is a free, easy-to-use online quiz maker that marks your tests and quizzes for you. Quizzes are both created and taken by learners online.

ClassMon (http://www.foliosinternational.com/content2.php?contentid=21) is a rubric-based observation portfolio product for observing students within a specific curriculum framework. It allows teachers to collect work samples to be used alongside rubrics to assess students.

ExamBuilder (http://www.exambuilder.com/) allows users to easily create and administer exams over the Internet.

FolioMaker (http://www.foliosinternational.com/content2.php?contentid=14) is a template-based application that creates digital portfolios, enabling users to integrate images, text documents, animation, and video and audio files.

Google Docs (http://docs.google.com) is a free Web-based word processor and spreadsheet that allows users to share and collaborate online.

The **Grady Profile** (http://www.aurbach.com/) engages students in learning by showcasing their performances, encouraging them to reflect, and providing them with feedback, as well as gives teachers a framework for managing alternative assessment. Also available from this site is *Toot!* software for making portfolios.

KwikSurveys (http://www.kwiksurveys.com/index.php) is a free and simple online survey service. Use it to create Web forms and e-mail surveys and collect and download results.

Microsoft Excel (http://office.microsoft.com/en-us/excel/default.aspx) is an application for creating and formatting spreadsheets.

OpenOffice (http://www.openoffice.org/) is a free online software package including word processing, spreadsheet, graphics, and database access applications.

Project Based Learning (http://pblchecklist.4teachers.org/checklist.shtml) provides free checklists to support project-based learning and evaluation. To make a project checklist for their students, teachers can choose the grade level for the type of project they want their students to do; choose from writing, presentation, multimedia, or science projects; choose from a list of project guidelines; and even add their own criteria to personalize their checklist.

Roger Wagner's HyperStudio 5 (http://www.mackiev.com/hyperstudio/index.html) is an electronic portfolio tool that includes podcasting support, a Webcam workshop, "live" object mode, the ability to import from iTunes and other sources, and a card index.

Scholastic's free rubric maker is a tool for evaluating whether students' skills (up to 10) are improving or whether students need additional support or instruction.

See also Tables 12.5, 12.6, 12.7, and 12.8.

References

Barrett, H. C. (2002). *Electronic portfolio handbook.* Retrieved March 18, 2009, from http://electronicportfolios.com/handbook/handbook.pdf

Barrett, H. (2007–2008). *Creating e-portfolios with Web 2.0 tools.* Retrieved September 14, 2009, from http://electronicportfolios.org/web20portfolios.html

Cole, D. J., Ryan, C. W., Kick, F., & Mathies, B. K. (2000). *Portfolios across the curriculum and beyond* (2nd ed.). Thousand Oaks, CA: Corwin.

Curriculum Designers, Inc. (2007–2008). *Mapping software.* Retrieved September 14, 2009, from http://www.curriculumdesigners.com/index.php?Path=Public/Resources/Mapping%20Software

Danielson, C., & Abrutyn, L. (1997). *An introduction to using portfolios in the classroom.* Alexandria, VA: ASCD.

English, F. W., & Steffy, B. E. (2001). *Deep curriculum alignment: Creating a level playing field for all children on high-stakes tests of educational accountability.* Lanham, MD: The Scarecrow Press, Inc.

Gardner, H. (1993). *Frames of mind: The theory of multiple intelligences.* New York: Basic Books.

International Society for Technology in Education (ISTE). (2007). *National educational technology standards for students* (2nd ed.). Washington, DC: Author.

International Society for Technology in Education (ISTE). (2009, March). *National educational technology standards for administrators.* Retrieved March 18, 2009, from http://www.iste.org/Content/NavigationMenu/NETS/ForAdministrators/2009Standards/NETS_for_Administrators_2009.htm

Ivers, K. S., & Barron, A. E. (1998). *Multimedia projects in education: Designing, producing, and assessing.* Englewood, CO: Libraries Unlimited, Inc., and Its Division Teacher Ideas Press.

Jacobs, H. H. (1997). *Mapping the big picture: Integrating curriculum & assessment K–12.* Alexandria, VA: ASCD.

Jacobs, H. H. (Ed.). (2004). *Getting results with curriculum mapping.* Alexandria, VA: ASCD.

Kallick, B., & Wilson, J. M., III (2004). Curriculum mapping and software: Creating an information system for a learning community. In H. H. Jacobs (Ed.), *Getting results with curriculum mapping* (pp. 83–96). Alexandria, VA: ASCD.

LeMahieu, F. G., Eresh, J. T., & Wallace, R. C., Jr. (1992). Using student portfolios for a public accounting. *The School Administrator, 49*(11), 8–15.

Maki, P. L. (2004). *Assessing for learning: Building a sustainable commitment across the institution.* Sterling, VA: Stylus Publishing, LLC.

Marzano, R. J., Pickering, D., & McTighe, J. (1993). *Assessing student outcomes: Performance assessment using the dimensions of learning model.* Alexandria, VA: ASCD.

National Council for Accreditation of Teacher Education. (2007). *NCATE unit standards: Standard 2 assessment system and unit evaluation.* Retrieved March 18, 2009, from http://www.ncate.org/public/unitStandardsRubrics.asp?ch=4#stnd2

National Council for Accreditation of Teacher Education. (2008). *Program report for the preparation of educational leaders (School building leadership level)* (p. 5). Retrieved March 18, 2009, from http://www.ncate.org/public/programStandards.asp?ch=4#ELCC

National Forum on Assessment. (2008). *Principles and indicators for student assessment systems.* Retrieved March 18, 2009, from http://www.fairtest.org/principles-and-indicators-student-assessment-syste

Neill, M., Guisbond, L., & Schaeffer, B. (2004). *Failing our children: How "No Child Left Behind" undermines quality and equity in education.* Cambridge, MA: Fairtest: The National Center for Fair & Open Testing.

Schrock, K. (2001–2009). *The five W's of Web site evaluation.* Retrieved September 17, 2009, from http://kathyschrock.net/abceval/5ws.pdf

Stevens, D. D., & Levi, A. J. (2005). *Introduction to rubrics: An assessment tool to save grading time, convey effective feedback, and promote student learning.* Sterling, VA: Stylus Publishing, LLC.

Suskie, L. (2004). *Assessing student learning: A common sense guide.* Bolton, MA: Anker Publishing Company, Inc.

Walvoord, B. E. (2004). *Assessment clear and simple: A practical guide for institutions, departments, and general education.* San Francisco: Jossey-Bass.

Chapter 13

PROGRAM EVALUATION AND TECHNOLOGY INTEGRATION STRATEGIES

Rosemary Papa

How we lead the adult learner is greatly impacted by knowledge of both the context and the learner him- or herself. Contextual understanding by the educational leader is as critical as the transfer of knowledge and how it is transferred through strategies and activities. One's skill and ability as an educational leader is tested now by both knowledge of how adults learn and the tools available today that were not available even 10 years ago.

—Papa & Papa, Chapter 5 (p. 98)

This chapter instructs school leaders in overall **program evaluation**, or the assessment of objectives followed by decisions based on data, and the effectiveness of technology integration strategies for student learning. The Interstate School Leaders Licensure Consortium (ISLLC) standards (Council of Chief State School Officers, 2008) and the International Society for Technology in Education (ISTE, 2009) National Educational Technology Standards for Administrators (NETS-A) are, as noted in Chapter 2, central in this discussion.

The following questions are addressed in this chapter:

- What are the primary challenges administrators face in optimally managing, utilizing, and evaluating technology use and tools?

- What are the technology integration strategies for teachers teaching today that educational leaders need to know?

- How can leaders ensure serendipitous data are explored?

- How can leaders choose the learning/technology strategies that are most effective for a building/district/university?

Program Evaluation

As shown in Figure 13.1, one mode of program evaluation starts with the mission and goals and then develops objectives, activities to meet these objectives, data collection, and discussions that loop to refinement. How school and district administrators meet the challenges in managing, using, and evaluating technology to improve student learning and teacher professional development is critical to their becoming great leaders.

Mission and Goals

Change among learning tools is rapid today and is clearly going to continue growing exponentially. This can be daunting as your mind must keep up with the ubiquitous growth of technology as it impacts the personal and professional lives we lead. Keeping pace is difficult. Ensuring that the policies and regulations remain useful is critical. Of equal concern are the continual assessments and evaluation procedures that assess curricular effectiveness for all learners. Always keep clear, hold dear, and remember the core mission of your school or district. This is easier said than done but is essential to what you need to assess, evaluate, and change.

Objectives to Implement Goals

It can be argued that the writing of objectives is both a boon and a bane to effective program evaluation. On the positive side, the writing of objectives allows both program developers and evaluators to ensure focus as programs are developed, implemented, and subsequently evaluated. On the negative side, objectives can be too numerous and/or overspecified and thus become a useless checklist of compliance. The extremes of a program without focus or an overspecified compliance model serves no one. As programs are developed and evaluation systems are put in place, it

| Figure 13.1 | Program Evaluation |

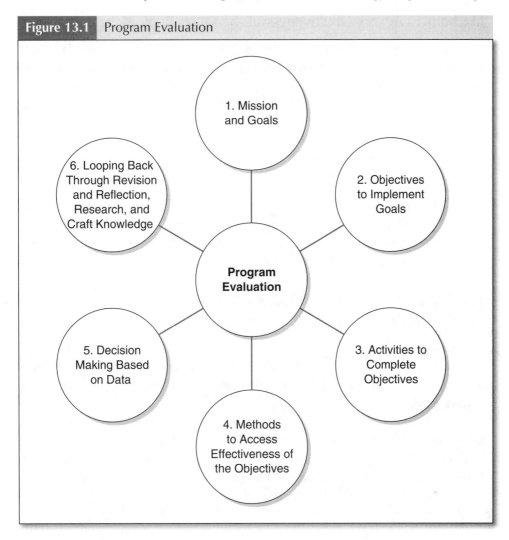

is essential that objectives are reasonable and focused, but with enough flexibility to cover a wide range of potential outcomes.

Activities to Complete Objectives

As effective objectives are developed (some broad, some specific), activities can be written to ensure that the objectives are implemented. It is within these activities that learning occurs. As with the objectives, the activities need to be reasonable and aligned with the authentic occurrences in the classroom, school, and district setting.

Methods to Access Effectiveness of the Objectives

If the objective is to learn a particular skill and the activities are the step-by-step process to provide that skill, then the method of assessment is the demonstration of that skill. If the objective is cognitive, what essential questions identify such learning? And, if the outcome is affective, what behaviors might exemplify particular attitudes or actions?

Decision Making Based on Data

Once data (scores, skill assessments, attitudinal changes, etc.) have been collected, then decisions regarding program effectiveness can be made. If you have gone to the actions and expense to collect data, then use of those data is essential. If data reveal findings that are either unintended or not originally expected, then subsequent objectives can be specified.

Looping Back Through Revision and Reflection, Research, and Craft Knowledge

If the program or program components are to be continued, then decisions that occur regarding effectiveness must be used to make program changes. What worked best? What was minimally effective? What changes need to occur for greater success?

Technology audits are discussed in Chapter 3. Williamson and Redish (2009) know that, "in the current age of accountability, educational leaders are required to be more skilled in assessment and evaluation than their predecessors were" (p. 77). Likewise, according to Anderson and Dexter (2005),

> technology leadership illustrates that technology leaders must be actively involved with technology—crafting policies, using e-mail, and generally spending time on it . . . our results suggest that a school's technology efforts are seriously threatened unless key administrators become active technology leaders in a school. Administrators who have not previously assumed these responsibilities might begin with a school technology audit to determine the degree to which the school has adequate technology goals, policies, budgets, committees, and supporting elements in place and where they should begin. (p. 74)

The full integration of program evaluation results in continuous program improvement. As noted by Spivack and Sienkiewicz (2008), Wholey, Hatry, and Newcomer stated, "The simple act of measuring and reporting on results will itself promote improvements" (p. 102) and "Too much monitoring can cripple efforts in the early stage; too little and the value will be lost" (p. 110).

Similar to the model in Figure 13.1, the Northwest Educational Technology Consortium (NETC, 2005) describes program evaluation as the use of research, and best practices indicate that a typical process for evaluation of technology efforts involves giving attention to the following steps:

- Identify basic issues/problems that need attention
- Determine data necessary for making informed decisions
- Determine the usefulness of existing data
- Determine new data that must be collected
- Identify evaluation design
- Determine tools and data acquisition strategies
- Determine timelines and assign staff roles
- Conduct evaluations
- Analyze data and develop conclusions
- Report data to address various audience(s) needs

In addition to the program evaluation noted, to ensure that we do not limit and narrow just to what we evaluate, it is recommended that the school leader consider the Scriven Goal-Free Evaluation process (Kaufman & Thomas, 1980). Goals we set determine the information we are seeking and thus the decisions we make. Serendipity has its place in school reform. The unintended consequences may be more fruitful to the larger picture.

> The premise of goal-free evaluation is that by not limiting oneself to, or biasing the evaluation with [the] stated goals, the evaluator can be more open to the total impact—positive and negative, intended or unintended—of the program . . . In fact, the only means of identifying serendipitous results is with goal-free evaluation. (Kaufman & Thomas, 1980, p. 129)

We all know about tunnel vision. Keep the Scriven model in mind. Remember, codes and standards are critical to school reform. Just remember to step back and see the surprises along the way.

Integration Strategies

As Papa and Papa stated in Chapter 5, "Great teaching is defined by the ability to inspire learners. Motivate the learner and you will grab his or her attention. Keeping a learner's attention is more difficult. Educational leaders need many strategies at their fingertips to keep others' attention" (p. 101). The chapters in this book are divided into four main parts: Part I: Leadership Policy and Innovative Practice; Part II: Leadership Teaching and Learning; Part III: Leadership: Social, Cultural, and Legal; and Part IV: Leadership Digital Assessments and Evaluation. Most chapter authors recommend **explicit learning strategies**, or well-defined and replicable activities used to guide future activities, and explicit **technology strategies**, or well-defined multimedia tools and replicable activities used to guide future activities. These are presented next as a recap of this textbook.

Part I: Leadership Policy and Innovative Practice

Chapter 1

A principal's mission must now include designing and implementing new strategies to help teachers and students recognize, understand, and integrate technology with teaching and learning in the classroom. The mere presence of hardware and software in the classroom does not ensure meaningful learning for students. We are beyond the point of deciding whether or not we will accept technology in our schools. The crucial task at hand is to decide how to implement this technology effectively into instruction (p. 5).

- Explicit technology strategy: If change in curriculum and instructional strategies is implemented, realign technology plans (p. 16).

Chapter 2

ISLLC 2008 Standard 6: An education leader promotes the success of every student by understanding, responding to, and influencing the political, social, economic, legal, and cultural context.
Functions:

a. Advocate for children, families, and caregivers
b. Act to influence local, district, state, and national decisions affecting student learning

- Explicit learning strategy: c. Assess, analyze, and anticipate emerging trends and initiatives in order to adapt leadership strategies (p. 26).

NETS for Teachers (ISTE, 2008) Standard 2: Design and Develop Digital-Age Learning Experiences and Assessments: Teachers design, develop, and evaluate authentic learning experiences and assessments incorporating contemporary tools and resources to maximize content learning in context and to develop the knowledge, skills, and attitudes identified in the NETS-S [NETS for Students; ISTE, 2007]. Teachers:

- Explicit technology strategy: a. design or adapt relevant learning experiences that incorporate digital tools and resources to promote student learning and creativity

- Explicit technology strategy: b. develop technology-enriched learning environments that enable all students to pursue their individual curiosities and become active participants in setting their own educational goals, managing their own learning, and assessing their own progress

- Explicit technology strategy: c. customize and personalize learning activities to address students' diverse learning styles, working strategies, and abilities using digital tools and resources

- Explicit technology strategy: d. provide students with multiple and varied formative and summative assessments aligned with content and technology standards and use resulting data to inform learning and teaching (Table 2.5, pp. 31–32)

NETS for Teachers (ISTE, 2008) Standard 4: Promote and Model Digital Citizenship and Responsibility: Teachers understand local and global societal issues and responsibilities in an evolving digital culture and exhibit legal and ethical behavior in their professional practices. Teachers:

- Explicit technology strategy: a. advocate, model, and teach safe, legal, and ethical use of digital information and technology, including respect for copyright, intellectual property, and the appropriate documentation of sources

- Explicit learning strategy: b. address the diverse needs of all learners by using learner-centered strategies and providing equitable access to appropriate digital tools and resources (Table 2.5, pp. 31–32)

That is, teachers should be encouraged to use different teaching strategies using tools that make sense for the learner. A teacher's tool kit needs to include strategies for facilitating student learning within an active learning environment from introduction to mastery of topics.

- Explicit technology strategy: The creation of rubrics for measuring some of the standards/functions makes sense. Other features of a tool kit are not easily measured. ISTE rubrics help teachers develop strategies and methods that will guide a student from an introductory stage to mastery. ISTE (2008) defines this rubric scale as moving from Beginning level to Developing level to Proficient level and finally to Transformative level (pp. 36–37).

- Explicit technology strategy: Tool kit leadership strategies include finding the courage to stay the course; using your voice in a plan; creating thought and actions in exploring the barriers and possible solutions; conducting formative assessments that allow for play activity learning; communicating with all stakeholders seeking transparency through blogs, wikis, podcasts, tweets, and so forth; and committing your artful leadership skills to your teachers in ways that foster their teaching experimentation in a safe environment to optimize student learning strategies for all learners (pp. 37–38).

- Explicit technology strategy: Encouraging teachers to work in collaborative teams that review student data, curriculum strategies, and activities will enhance the curriculum mapping that ensures a coherent implementation of both NETS standards and practices for all students (p. 38).

Chapter 3

Now, walk into your district office or school site. For example: Is it as up-to-date as society? Are your teachers and students taking full advantage of technology to teach and learn? Are your bus schedules, ordering processes, and payment processes efficient and effective? If you have to think more than 5 seconds about these questions, you need to reconsider your technology plan and strategies. To use some old clichés, you must walk the talk, practice what you preach, and model behavior you want.

- Explicit technology strategy: It is no longer enough to have a few zealous teachers who know technology or the one techspert business office employee. Schools of the 21st century need leaders with a comprehensive technology plan and a strategy to implement such a plan. Issues of instructional strategies, classroom materials professional development, hardware and software acquisition, data-based decision tools, and security require a knowledgeable leader/manager and an institutionalized commitment to appropriate and cutting-edge technology usage (p. 55).

- Explicit learning strategy: Administration will need to be problem centered and use all available tools and strategies. As well, to the maximum extent, include as many individuals in program development as possible (p. 56).

Chapter 4

A reader's response to the question "What's your Achilles' heel?" appeared in the online publication *School CIO: Strategies for K–12 Technology Leaders* (see http://www.schoolcio.com/shared/printableArticle.php?articleID=192203398):

- Explicit learning strategy: assisting educators as they struggle to understand and implement a vision of data-driven decision making (p. 81).

Part II: Leadership Teaching and Learning

Chapter 5

Attention and motivation and how we use these are critical to understanding how we approach classroom experiences for our learners. If we know how a learner approaches the acquisition of knowledge, then we can arrange classroom strategies that will enhance his or her learning. Various theories focus on the motivations of the learner: Are they internal or external in their locus of control? What motivates a person to want to learn? External motivation in the early years of schooling requires children in most countries to attend school, so the motivation to be there is one of first family approval and expectation and then legal requirement (p. 92).

- Explicit learning strategy: With no clear road map of acceptance by research and theory, we hope to persuade the reader that strategies from a variety of learning perspectives should be of benefit to the educational leader who seeks to be the best he or she can be (p. 92).

- An **explicit learning theory strategy** is a well-defined activity using explicit learning theory: The best educational leader is one with a focus on managing, leading, and teaching the adult learner as an individual (p. 93).

1. *Cronbach and Snow Attitude Treatment Interaction (1970+):* Learning is best achieved when strategies are geared directly to the learner's specific abilities (Table 5.1, p. 93).

2. Gardner's (1983, 1999a, 1999b, 2006) work continues to redefine the learner and what attributes he has identified have led to specific learner strategies. Influences from Bruner and Piaget are found in Gardner's work (p. 97).

3. Cronbach and Snow (1977) identified attitude at the heart of their theory. Learning, they said, is best achieved when strategies are geared directly to the learner's specific abilities. Their theory is called Attitude Treatment Interaction (p. 97).

4. How we lead the adult learner is greatly impacted by knowledge of both the context and the learner him- or herself. Contextual understanding by the educational leader is as critical as the transfer of knowledge and how it is transferred through strategies and activities (p. 98).

Chapter 6

Through the implementation of a community of practice, an administrator's role changes in the structure of the system. He or she is no longer deferred to for the final decision. Instead, he or she is a collaborator helping set long-range and overarching goals, innovation, and guidance. The administrator begins to develop the community by bringing faculty into the decision-making process (pp. 111–112).

- Explicit learning strategy: Communities of practice must provide a supportive environment where there is an openness and appreciation for new and unique ideas, where the individual is free to speak without worry of disparagement, and where the individual has time for reflection on individual and collective information (p. 112).

- Explicit learning strategy: The challenge for administrators is to begin to move teachers to understand that technology is part of the solution in meeting the needs of 21st-century learners. They must work to develop overarching goals that can then be fleshed out by the community of practice (p. 113).

- Explicit technology strategy: Finally, regardless of where individuals are in their abilities to integrate technologies into the classroom, they will benefit from personal, peer, and community reflection (p. 116).

- Explicit technology strategy: Discussing the content to be taught, the way it will be taught, and how technology will be integrated so that the students may develop deeper understanding gives the individual a way to reflect before proceeding to the implementation. This reflection also gives the community of practice the opportunity to share and gather ideas (p. 120).

Chapter 7

Many educational institutions perceive that course management systems (CMSs), also known as learning management systems, or LMSs (see Chapter 4), include most or many of the learning tools for online learning and online communication (i.e., e-mail, discussion boards, chats, grading systems, student grouping systems) as part of their core provision and strategic plans, rather than instructional designs and strategies that focus school policy on the use of personalized, student-centered tools. In fact, most educational institutions' current CMS or LMS has been through several versions, such as Blackboard and WebCT; however, it has remained the same or lacked innovated improvement for distance learning. Even where the pedagogy is student centered, CMSs/LMSs are not—administrative processes and assessment practice remain firmly bound to hierarchical, differentiated educational structures (p. 132).

- Explicit learning strategy: Collaboration could range from involving one's selves to involving others in meaningful and authentic/situated activities. How schools collaborate with their community and the district is critical. Meaningful and authentic activities bond students and teachers collectively to catalyze social interaction into skills and knowledge acquisition.

- Explicit learning strategy: Learning is conceived as a property of the group (social and cultural) and is built up from the individual participants.

- Explicit technology strategy: Online sociocultural learning that emphasizes collaborative, meaningful, and authentic learning activities could provide effective strategies to improve learning. Situated cognition theory (Lave, 1988) states that the environment is an integral part of cognitive activity and not merely a set of circumstances in which context-independent cognitive processes/activities are performed (p. 135).

Sometimes each individual collaborates with him- or herself to manage his or her multiple identities to engage in more constructive (articulate/reflective) acts. Sometimes individuals collaborate with other students' multiple identities to engage in more active (manipulative/observant) acts.

- Explicit technology strategy: Ideal, meaningful, and authentic online activities should allow students to acquire ownership in negotiating, planning, and managing processes in collaborative and authentic project-based learning activities in a learning community (p. 136).

A key characteristic of Web 2.0 is user participation—the "wisdom of the crowds," the "architecture of participation"—mashups, remixing, and co-construction are fundamental and widespread practices in Web 2.0. In contrast, despite the general increase in group collaboration in recent years, educational systems fundamentally revolve around individual testing—evidencing of attainment of a level of knowledge and understanding against a set of predefined criteria. Even where group work is encouraged, more often than not there are strategies to ensure recognition of individual contribution to some extent (p. 137).

- Explicit technology strategy: Online students have been using and managing Web 2.0 tools based on their own learning preferences, communication styles, and so forth. The plethora of free and often functionally better tools now available is challenging the notion of an institutionally developed and controlled CMS or LMS (p. 138).

- Explicit technology strategy: Harnessing collective intelligence, or aggregate intelligence that develops via social networking and connecting within a learning community: Integrate various Web 2.0 tools to create and foster a healthy social learning community for teachers to learn from each other and exchange effective online technology strategies (p. 142).

Chapter 8

What are the components of effective, creative online course design (p. 147)? One way to encourage peer-to-peer interaction is by the creation of discussion questions.

- Explicit technology strategy: Many online teachers create at least one discussion question per course topic. They require students to post their own thoughts on each question as well as provide a minimum number of responses to peers (p. 153).

- Explicit technology strategy: In addition, such a question-and-answer discussion forum can actually provide a collaborative learning opportunity for students. You may have sometimes overheard a student in a live and in-person class explain something in such a way to another student that you found yourself thinking: "Why didn't I say it like that?!" The online posting area offers a similar opportunity for peer coaching.

- Explicit technology strategy: One final benefit of requiring students to provide replies to posted questions is that it discreetly reinforces their own understanding. We've all heard the classic saying: "The best way to learn something yourself is to try to teach it to someone else" (p. 155).

- Explicit technology strategy: Experts of best practices agree that the more detail, the better [in the online syllabus] (p. 156).

Part III: Leadership: Social, Cultural, and Legal

Chapter 9

School administrator leaders have the opportunity to set the tone for special and curricular activities that can do more than teach students. For instance, an administrator can

- Explicit technology strategy: advocate to increase broadband penetration to low-income households by making it more affordable and by connecting rural areas;

- Explicit technology strategy: increase computer literacy by establishing community centers or opening schools to the community during after-school hours for computer access;

- Explicit technology strategy: promote technology infrastructure investments through partnerships between local governments and businesses;

- Explicit technology strategy: make it a school and district goal to provide broadband connection to schools; and

- Explicit technology strategy: make every effort to make available advanced placement courses through videoconferencing and distance learning technologies (p. 169).

The educator of the 21st century needs to be armed with a plethora of resources, techniques, and strategies that are targeted to meet the needs of all students, including culturally and linguistically diverse students. . . .

- Explicit technology strategy: Different cultures use technology in different ways. Many times, the use of technology illustrates and affirms the culture's worldview (Carlson, 2007). For example, as part of a thesis for a master's degree, a student invited the elders in an Apache village to come together and name the parts of a computer, something that did not exist in Apache language. Besides naming the computer, the elders came up with a graphic interface for the computer desktop. Each of the regular functions of the computer was represented by a symbol that was related to Apache traditions and culture. For instance, a folder was represented by a special pouch that Apache used to carry things when they traveled; turning on the computer would bring the sun, but turning it off would bring the moon and stars. Myths, religion, art, and philosophy of the culture will interface with the use of technology.

- Explicit learning strategy: In the classroom, besides using sheltered English methods, teachers need to look at the differences in learning depending on culture. For instance, Armenian and Korean students prefer to work individually while Latino, Hmong, and Vietnamese students prefer to learn in cooperative groups (Park, 2002).

- Explicit technology strategy: Regardless of the learning preference, the same author reported that all English language learners learn better if a combination of visual objects; kinesthetic activities, including tactile learning; and auditory activities is used as part of instruction; an interactive multimedia Web site or presentation would be an excellent way of using technology for this group of students.

- Explicit technology strategy: Administrators and teachers must know that there are two types of technology use in the classroom: traditional and authentic (Holum & Gahala, 2001). In the traditional type, technology is used to do old things with new tools. That is, technology is used to complete a crossword puzzle, read a linear document, reinforce skills, or perform any other activity that does not require technology. Examples of this technology include some integrated learning systems, computer-assisted instruction, and computer-based tutoring systems (Boethel & Dimock, 1999). The authentic type, on the other hand, gives the user control over the functions of the technology itself and uses technology to complete complex tasks, such as investigation reports where the student may use a word processor to write the text, format it, edit it, add hyperlinks to Web sites, and add pictures. It is pertinent to reiterate that both uses of technology have their niche in the classroom and that the best teacher is the one who is eclectic and knows when to apply the best use of technology (pp. 173–174).

- Explicit technology strategy: The work of Kirkhart and Lau (2007) shows that most children with disabilities who receive adequate support (including technology) and education eventually become independent and productive members of society (p. 175).

- An **explicit learning and technology strategy** is a combined well-defined activity using both technology tools and learning theory: At the most basic level, awareness, training efforts should involve a broad audience of school personnel including general education teachers, related service personnel, instructional assistants, and administrators. The emphasis of training efforts at this level is on creating a broad-based awareness of the benefits of AT [assistive technology] devices, creating an understanding of the legal requirements for providing AT devices and services, developing awareness-level knowledge of the range of possibilities across AT device and service types, and helping the trainees identify AT resources they can call upon in the future when they work with students who use AT devices (pp. 179–180).

- Explicit technology strategy: School systems sometimes do not have the resources to hire these types of specialists, choosing to subcontract instead. If employed by the school district, these persons with high-level knowledge and skills may be used by districts as their "assistive technology specialist" or serve as school systems as a consultant for instructional staff with their most difficult cases. Persons with this highest level of knowledge and skills can help districts address the remaining 15%–20% of their complex AT needs (p. 180).

Chapter 10

Reksten (2000) provides several practices and strategies for administrators as they begin thinking about how they can protect their schools in an easy and efficient manner. She suggests that principals

- Explicit technology strategy: continuously manage the technological environment at school;

- Explicit technology strategy: prepare the staff through professional development activities for the challenges and potential threats that exist when students use the Internet;

- Explicit technology strategy: support teachers who are willing to use the Internet correctly with time and resources;

- Explicit technology strategy: Collaborate with all stakeholders to acknowledge the appropriate way to use the Internet and the school's technology;

- Explicit technology strategy: be open-minded about the possibilities for the future of the educational process that the Internet can provide;

- Explicit technology strategy: learn about the various types of technologies that are offered and utilized on the campus; and

- Explicit technology strategy: accept the fact that technology and the use of the Internet do not have to be separate or independent from the other instructional disciplines offered at the school (p. 193).

From the very first day of school, teachers and students should learn that while the Internet will open several doors and has the potential to exponentially increase their learning, there are several safety issues and concerns directly connected to the use of the Internet. Criddle (2008) identifies at least three definite actions that principals can employ to prepare their students and staff as they become responsible users of campus technologies:

- Explicit technology strategy: The entire population of the school should be constantly aware of the appropriate use of computers, software, and available technology. This information should correlate with district standards regarding the use of the Internet.

- Explicit technology strategy: Impress upon the entire student population and staff members that they should always protect themselves, respect the rights of others, and be responsible enough to follow existing rules and guidelines when using the Internet.

- Explicit technology strategy: Address every infraction of the school's Internet use policy when and if any misuse of the Internet or the school's technology occurs (pp. 194–195).

The Nemours Foundation in its 2008 KidsHealth report on Internet safety provides several online protection tools that may prevent the misuse of technology. They encourage the school to

- Explicit technology strategy: provide a means of control for access to unwanted sites;
- Explicit technology strategy: teach students to recognize online predators;
- Explicit technology strategy: incorporate Internet service providers to stand guard when adults cannot be present; and
- Explicit technology strategy: continually protect the identity of students when using the Internet at school (p. 196).

Picciano (2002) addresses the importance of security when dealing with the issue of technology. He contends that technological leaders acquaint themselves with the following concepts:

- Explicit technology strategy: The protection of the school's software regarding the management of school records is vital to ensure students' records remain confidential.
- Explicit technology strategy: Students' records must be protected at all costs and only used for educational purposes.
- Explicit technology strategy: Policies must be in place to detail how computers are used and the degree of access.
- Explicit technology strategy: The purchase of antivirus software prevents extensive damage to the existing computer system in place.
- Explicit technology strategy: Procedures at the school should mirror district procedure for protecting all the components of technology afforded to students and teachers (p. 196).

The principal is the key to developing security guidelines that protect students at all times, especially when they use the Internet. Administrators can use the following tasks to help them protect their schools:

- Explicit technology strategy: Become familiar with the technology support system provided by the district.

- Explicit technology strategy: Secure students' confidential information by using an alternative means (a backup system) to save it.

- Explicit technology strategy: Know and enforce the acceptable use policy.

- Explicit technology strategy: Employ filtering software.

- Explicit technology strategy: Constantly reinforce procedure for using computers and the Internet.

- Explicit technology strategy: Establish and enforce disciplinary policies for any infractions that occur.

- Explicit technology strategy: Strategically place computers on the campus to avoid possible theft and ensure those rooms are always kept locked and secured (p. 197).

Knowing this, administrators face security issues regarding technology that create an ever-present need to protect their schools from current or future attempts to ruin or sabotage existing software, hardware, or students' records. Kearsley (1990) offers several potential considerations for school leaders:

- Explicit technology strategy: Piracy of existing software programs

- Explicit technology strategy: Maintenance of private and personal student records

- Explicit technology strategy: Prevention of incoming viruses

- Explicit technology strategy: Protection of the school site from theft

- Explicit technology strategy: Prohibiting access to illegal Web sites (pp. 197–198)

Moore-Howard and Davies (2009) believe that this "getting tough" approach with severe punishments (e.g., using automated plagiarism-detection devices such as Turnitin.com) as an attempt to legislate the wired world is an approach that does not work. The authors offer the following as a guide to preventing cyberplagiarism:

1. Explicit learning strategy: Discuss intellectual property and what it means to "own" a piece of writing.

2. Explicit technology strategy: Discuss how to evaluate both online and print-based sources (for example, comparing the quality of a Web site created by an amateur with the reliability of a peer-reviewed scholarly article).

3. Explicit learning strategy: Guide students through the hard work of engaging with and understanding their sources, so students don't conclude that writing a technically perfect bibliography is good enough.

4. Explicit learning strategy: Acknowledge that teaching students how to write from sources involves more than telling students that copying is a crime and handing them a pile of source citation cards. (Moore-Howard & Davies, 2009, p. 65) (p. 200)

Part IV: Leadership Digital Assessments and Evaluation

Chapter 11

You should be looking for evidence of active engagement by your online teachers.

- Explicit learning strategy: Is there evidence that teachers are logging in to read students' postings? Are they welcoming students by perhaps mentioning something they have in common in response to a student's self-introduction post (e.g., having visited that geographic area, a hobby that they share) or otherwise actively engaging with students in the icebreaker activity (p. 216)?

We are all familiar with the stereotype of the online classroom as "just a cold, impersonal correspondence school." Coupled with this is the sense of abandonment an online student may feel when he or she has a question or when something is confusing or doesn't work as it should. This student may truly feel lost in cyberspace, as if he or she is dealing with only an inanimate computer screen rather than a real live human being (p. 217).

- Explicit learning strategy: According to Dereshiwsky's (2008) continual engagement best-practice concept, students who receive prompt, helpful responses to posted questions are more likely to feel connected (p. 217).

- Explicit learning strategy: Continued teacher engagement in announcement and question-and-answer postings remains important as the instructional session continues (p. 217).

- Explicit learning strategy: As with the question-and-answer posting area, *timeliness* in responding to student assessment submissions of quizzes, tests, and assignments is key (p. 220).

In your role as evaluator of K–12 courses, you also want to assess what teachers are doing to ensure safe learning environments for their students. A discussion of online classrooms therefore must include mention of cyberbullying.

- Explicit technology strategy: [Teachers should] advise students to keep passwords and real last names confidential. They can also show students how to block messages from sources who have harassed them. Students should be advised to delete suspect e-mail messages. In addition, teachers should be alert to signs of students who appear to be in emotional distress or quieter than usual, as this may be a sign that they have been the targets of cyberbullying. Targets should be advised to confide in trusted adults about the problem (p. 223).

- Explicit technology strategy: [Teachers should teach students] to Google themselves to look for potentially harassing or abusive postings about them on the Internet. . . .

- Explicit learning strategy: If [students] are angry or upset, [teachers should recommend students instead] seek a healthier outlet for their anger (e.g., exercise, deep breathing).

- Explicit learning strategy: What should teachers do when a student confides that he or she has been the target of such cyberbullying? . . . [They should] take the report seriously. Students should never be told that it's their fault or that they are overreacting to the situation. . . .

- Explicit learning strategy: A clear, consistent school policy is key [to controlling cyberbullying] (p. 223).

Chapter 12

NETS for Administrators (International Society for Technology in Education, 2009) Standard 4, Systemic Improvement, emphasizes the importance of educational leaders to "continuously improve the organization through effective use of information and technology resources."

- Explicit technology strategy: One method for ensuring improvement is to "establish metrics, collect and analyze data, interpret results, and share findings to improve staff performance and student learning." To monitor and evidence continuous improvement requires data, qualitative and/or quantitative. However, in order for an assessment system to be successful, it must be manageable and feasible to implement. At a class, school, or district level, technology should be leveraged to help make assessing instructional strategies and student performance on project-based and other authentic activities both manageable and feasible (p. 230).

- Explicit learning strategy: The underlying premise for building a rubric is to improve student learning. By clarifying objectives via a rubric, teachers are providing students with a "road map" to where they are going in relation to academic standards or learning objectives. This is good practice for all students but is especially helpful for English language learners or other learners who are struggling with comprehending class materials and instructions.

- Explicit learning strategy: However, new instructional strategies often need to be taught, so it is important to provide rubrics to students consistently over the course of an academic year so they become more aware of the type of information the rubric is communicating and how to best use the assignment rubric as a tool for meeting expectations and self-evaluating their own work (p. 241).

Final Word on Codes, Standards, and Adult Learning

Program evaluation processes and integration strategies when informed by the administrator's code of ethics and the various standards (from ISLLC 2008 to NETS-S [2007], NETS-T [2008], and NETS-A [2009]) can be both daunting and exhilarating. Basic human dignity and respect for others are at the heart of the school leader's ability to promote change and exploration while evaluating progress of students.

Surowiecki (2005) wrote that "the solutions to cooperation and coordination problems are real in the sense that they work. They are not imposed from above, but emerge from the crowd" (p. 271). Common good intent develops from community learning experiences.

Figure 13.2 displays the technology strategies that can be used for each of the four adult learning approaches discussed in Chapter 5 (p. 102): *Hear It* focuses on the learner who needs to read and write the concepts in order to learn the content. *See It* offers a visual for the learner, such as writing in chat rooms. *Say It* refers to learners who must talk about the concept and are frequently those who ask a lot of questions. This strategy is good for peer-to-peer online work and group work done in online learning communities. *Do It* is the hands-on application that allows for trial and error. These strategies have been described throughout the chapters in this book.

Hall (2009) finds that "tools provide the capacity for linking specialists through highly collaborative communities and these communities are of a greater diversity that shares knowledge and expertise to accomplish the work task at hand" (p. 10).

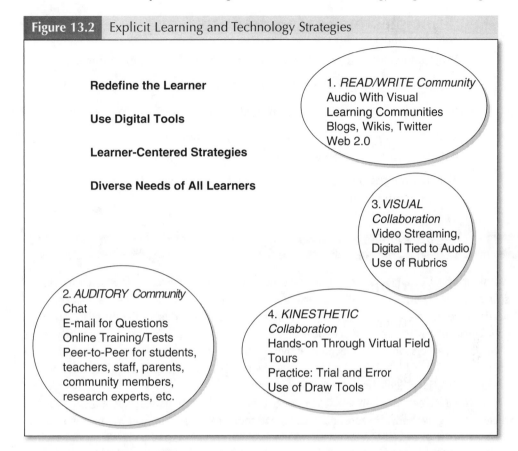

Figure 13.2 Explicit Learning and Technology Strategies

Redefine the Learner

Use Digital Tools

Learner-Centered Strategies

Diverse Needs of All Learners

1. *READ/WRITE Community*
Audio With Visual
Learning Communities
Blogs, Wikis, Twitter
Web 2.0

3. *VISUAL Collaboration*
Video Streaming,
Digital Tied to Audio
Use of Rubrics

2. *AUDITORY Community*
Chat
E-mail for Questions
Online Training/Tests
Peer-to-Peer for students,
teachers, staff, parents,
community members,
research experts, etc.

4. *KINESTHETIC Collaboration*
Hands-on Through Virtual Field
Tours
Practice: Trial and Error
Use of Draw Tools

Conclusions

Thomas L. Friedman (2009) wrote, "We live in a technological age where every study shows that the more knowledge you have as a worker and the more knowledge workers you have as an economy, the faster your incomes will rise. Therefore, the centerpiece of our stimulus, the core driving principle, should be to stimulate everything that makes us smarter and attracts more smart people". (p. A31)

Adults, by nature, will learn best when in a mentoring, collaborating working community. In this environment the educational leader acknowledges that he or she is a learner as well. Figure 5.2 (Chapter 5) describes how adults can be taught using methods that reach all learners. Figure 13.2 has the educational leader understand that if the learning strategies are changed, all adult learners *can be* engaged in technology practices . . . and *must be* engaged for effectiveness of teaching practices and strategies and ensuring the students in our schools are receiving the highest-quality learning practices possible. A good leader knows this. A great leader does it!

Key Principles for Leaders to Know

- Program evaluation processes are critical to curricular innovations.

- Technology strategies are essential learning guides to the school leader.

- Serendipitous data should be explored.

- Training programs are needed with enrichment activities at various levels—nonusers through those able to integrate, expand, and refine.

- The learning/technology strategies that make sense for your building or district should be used.

CASE STUDY 13.1 | Technology Planning for Program Evaluation

As the principal of a medium-sized middle school, you are reviewing data on mathematics scores that show a high degree of diverse learners (English language learners and special-needs students) are not achieving well on standardized tests. Your difficulty articulating your curriculum with the high school is also part of the problem. You want to strategize with your teachers on their teaching activities and know that some are recalcitrant in changing their teaching methods. The blame-the-student game is even suggested by several loud, emotional long-timers. You have several young new teachers who are tech savvy and have convinced you behind closed doors that the recalcitrant teachers are wrong in their teaching methods. If scores do not improve soon at your school, you will be removed.

Discussion: Discuss in groups your goals to improve the success of your students and to plan a program evaluation that will use data to convince your teachers to change their methods and strategies to include greater technology use.

Activity: Using the program evaluation model in this chapter, develop a plan for your students' improvement. Use Figure 13.2 to identify your teachers' optimal learning styles and tie them to technology practices in which they should receive staff development.

Web Resource

The **Northwest Educational Technology Consortium** (NETC; http://www.netc.org/planning/eval/) describes program evaluation as the use of research.

References

Anderson, R. E., & Dexter, S. (2005, February). School technology leadership: An empirical investigation of prevalence and effect. *Educational Administration Quarterly, 41*(1), 49–82.

Boethel, M., & Dimock, K. V. (1999). *Knowledge with technology: A review of literature.* Retrieved February July 5, 2009, from http://www.sedl.org/pubs/catalog/items/tec27.html

Carlson, W. B. (2007). Diversity and progress: How might we picture technology across global cultures? *Comparative Technology Transfer and Society, 5,* 128–155.

Council of Chief State School Officers (CCSSO). (2008, June 3). *Educational leadership policy standards: ISLLC 2008* [Press release]. Washington, DC: Author.

Criddle, L. C. (2008, September). *Back to school and Internet safety.* CyperPatrol: Protecting people online. Retrieved February 26, 2009, from http://blog.cyberpatrol.com/?p=22

Cronbach, L., & Snow, R. (1977). *Aptitudes and instructional methods: A handbook for research on interactions.* New York: Irvington.

Dereshiwsky, M. I. (2008, February). *Continual engagement: Why it's important to effective online instruction.* Presented at the Learning Resource Network Annual Conference, Savannah, Georgia.

Friedman, T. L. (2009, February 11). The open-door bailout. *The New York Times,* p. A31.

Gardner, H. (1983). *Frames of mind: The theory of multiple intelligences.* New York: Basic Books.

Gardner, H. (1999a). *The disciplined mind: Beyond facts and standardized tests: The K–12 education that every child deserves.* New York: Simon & Schuster.

Gardner, H. (1999b). *Intelligence reframed: Multiple intelligences for the 21st century.* New York: Basic Books.

Gardner, H. (2006). *The development and education of the mind: The selected works of Howard Gardner.* London, United Kingdom: Routledge.

Hall, D. (2009, February). Web 2.0 or tidal wave 2.0? *Learning & Leading with Technology, 36*(5), 10.

Holum, A., & Gahala, J. (2001). *Critical issue: Using technology to enhance literacy instruction.* Naperville, IL: North Central Regional Educational Laboratory. Retrieved February 3, 2009, from http://www.ncrel.org/sdrs/areas/issues/content/cntareas/reading/li300.htm

International Society for Technology in Education (ISTE). (2007). *National educational technology standards for students* (2nd ed.). Washington, DC: Author.

International Society for Technology in Education (ISTE). (2008). *National educational technology standards for teachers* (2nd ed.). Washington, DC: Author.

International Society for Technology in Education (ISTE). (2009). *National educational technology standards for administrators.* Washington, DC: Author. Retrieved July 5, 2009, from http://www.iste.org/Content/NavigationMenu/NETS/ForAdministrators/2009Standards/NETS _for_Administrators_2009.htm

Kaufman, R., & Thomas, S. (1980). *Evaluation without fear.* New York: New Viewpoints.

Kearsley. G. (1990). *Computers for educational administrators: Leadership in the information age.* Norwood, NJ: Ablex.

Kirkhart, A., and Lau, J. (with W. Lazarus and L. Lipper). (2007, March). *Helping our children succeed: What's broadband got to do with it?* Retrieved August 28, 2009, from http://www .childrenspartnership.org/AM/Template.cfm?Section=Technology&Template=/CM/HTML Display.cfm&ContentID=9734

Lave, J. (1988). *Cognition in practice: Mind, mathematics and culture in everyday life (Learning in doing).* Cambridge, MA: Cambridge University Press.

Moore-Howard, R., & Davies, L. (2009). Plagiarism in the Internet age. *Educational Leadership, 66*(6), 64–67.

Nemours Foundation. (2008). *KidsHealth: Internet safety.* Retrieved February 23, 2009, from http:// kidshealth.org/PageManager.jsp?dn=KidsHealth&lic=1&ps=107&cat_id=150&article_ set=22145

Northwest Educational Technology Consortium (NETC). (2005). Northwest educational technology consortium: Program evaluation. Retrieved February 2, 2009, from http://www.netc.org/planning/eval/

Park, C. C. (2002). Crosscultural differences in learning styles of secondary English learners. *Bilingual Research Journal, 26*(2), 213–229.

Picciano, A. G. (2002). *Educational leadership for planning technology* (3rd ed.). Upper Saddle River, NJ: Merrill Prentice Hall.

Reksten, L. E. (2000). *Using technology to increase student learning.* Thousand Oaks, CA: Corwin.

Spivack, R. N., & Sienkiewicz, R. (2008, March). *Technology program evaluation: Methodologies from the advanced technology program.* Washington, DC: National Science Foundation.

Surowiecki, J. (2005). *The wisdom of crowds.* New York: Anchor Books.

Williamson, J., & Redish, T. (2009). *ISTE's technology facilitation and leadership standards: What every K–12 leader should know and be able to do.* Eugene, OR: International Society for Technology in Education.

GLOSSARY

Academic information system—an information system devoted to curriculum and learning data

Academic technology—technology applications and tools focused on the acts of teaching and learning

Acceptable use policy—a set of guidelines and practices that govern a student's use of the Internet and technology and that, with parental permission, allow a student access to computers

Achievement gap—the disparity in educational measures such as standardized tests, dropout rates, and graduation rates between racial and ethnic majority and minority students, between rich and poor students, between students with access to technology and those without it, and so on

Adult learners—adults in a learning environment

Adult learning and pedagogy—teaching strategies for how adults learn

Adult learning theories—theories about how adults learn

Applications service provider—a firm providing Internet-based applications

Assessment—evaluating teaching performance for its effectiveness; synonymous with *evaluation*

Assessment system—the manageable and feasible process by which metrics are established, data are collected and analyzed, and results are interpreted for students, teachers, and staff

Authentic—describes performance-based activities

Bandwidth—the speed of data transfer usually measured in bits per second

Behavioral leadership—behaviors based on structure and consideration

Behaviorism or learning as cognitive constructivism—learners construct knowledge based on previous knowledge

Certified Online Instructor (COI)—certificate of qualification for an online teacher offered by the Learning Resources Network (LERN); based on completion of several courses on how to teach online, passing a review of one's online teaching, and passing a comprehensive exam covering online teaching and learning

Classroom-based assessments—assessments explicitly aligned to academic standards; second part of the assessment system process

Code of Ethics for Educational Leaders—the American Association of School Administrators' guidelines for the professional conduct of educational leaders

Cognitive constructivism—learners construct knowledge based on previous knowledge

Collective intelligence—aggregate intelligence that develops through community learning via social networking and connecting within a learning community

Community learning—learning within a community by the engagement of the members (the community as a whole is greater than the sum of its members); community understanding, knowledge, or learning that goes/grows beyond individual members

Community of practice—an organizational structure of administrators, teachers, and, if possible, students and parents working collaboratively to understand school-wide needs and develop goals, plans, and activities

Computer-based crimes—crimes involving unauthorized use of the Internet or related technologies

Contingency leadership—matching a leader's style with various situations

Control chart—a chart showing whether an activity is proceeding within acceptable bounds

Course management system (CMS)—software that includes most or many of the learning tools for online learning and online communication (i.e., e-mail, discussion boards, chats, grading systems, student grouping systems); see also *learning management system (LMS)*

Curriculum mapping—the first part of the assessment system process

Cyberbullying—harassing or threatening other students using such technology as instant message, e-mail, or posting in public areas such as Facebook or MySpace

Cyberplagiarism—downloading or copying material from an Internet source without providing proper acknowledgement

Dashboard—a condensed summary of key indicators

Data warehouse—a repository of an organization's electronically recorded data

Decentralized configuration—technology management that is implemented at a unit or department level

Decision making—engaging in the selection of various choices for action

Decision support system—an information system with data and the analytical capability required for informed decisions

Demonstration—an active learning strategy that models standards and objectives

Digital learning—using various forms of technology for instructional purposes

Discussion forum—posting area inside an online course where students and teacher share ideas on an open-ended topic of focus

Disruptive innovation—an innovation that, by its implementation, disrupts the status quo

Ecological fallacy—the assumption that a relationship at one level of analysis holds at another level of analysis

Electronic portfolios—electronic tools that serve as a repository of student work

Elemental level—a unit that is at the most disaggregated level

Enterprise configuration—a highly centralized model of technology management

Entrepreneurial leadership—translating ideas into action

Evaluation—assessing teaching performance for its effectiveness; synonymous with *assessment*

Every student database—a database with data on every student in a state

Explicit learning and technology strategy—a combined well-defined activity using both technology tools and learning theory

Explicit learning strategy—a well-defined and replicable activity used to guide future activities

Explicit learning theory strategy—a well-defined activity using explicit learning theory

Explicit technology strategy—a well-defined multimedia tool and replicable activity used to guide future activities

Feasible—describes the idea that an assessment system must be realistic and manageable

Filtering system—a system used by a school, district, or university to provide protection from inappropriate Internet sources, usually referred to as a "firewall"

Formative—describes the process to evaluate progress and mastery of content and principles throughout a lesson; tends to be informal in nature

Humanism—learning occurs at the personal level

Hyperlink—clickable Web page address inserted into online course reading material that takes students to supplementary learning materials on the Internet related to their main reading if they click on it

Individuals with Disabilities Education Act (IDEA)—federal legislation mandating a free and appropriate public education for all eligible children with disabilities

Inferred characteristics—unobservable traits one infers from a person's behavior, including responses on tests; also known as *unobservable characteristics*

Information and communication technologies (ICTs)—Internet-using electronic devices, usually computers, that connect people and machines

Instructional gaps—content standards that are not addressed; identified through curriculum mapping

Instructional strategies—well-defined and replicable activities used to guide those of the future

Integrative thinking—the predisposition and capacity to consider diametrically opposing ideas and then produce a solution superior to either of the opposing ideas

Internet-based application—application software available over the Internet

ISLLC 2008—Interstate School Leaders Licensure Consortium standards for principal and superintendent candidates

ISTE—International Society for Technology in Education

Leadership—exercising influence usually while interacting with others for mutual goal attainment

Learning—active use of content and/or technologies to develop deeper understanding and further application

Learning community—a community where the purpose of membership is for individual learning through the engagement with other community members

Learning management system—an information system that provides content and assessment to the learner

Manageable—able to be organized and implemented

Management—setting objectives and engaging in activities to meet those objectives

Mentoring—the most complete human skill to acquire

Modules—a unit of content in an online course equivalent to a cluster of chapters in a textbook

Motivation—degree with which the learner approaches learning

Net generation—people born after 1980—suggesting that these students fundamentally differ from previous generations in the way they process information, communicate, and learn

NETS-A—National Educational Technology Standards for Administrators 2009

NETS-S—National Educational Technology Standards for Students 2007

NETS-T—National Educational Technology Standards for Teachers 2008

NETS-TF—National Educational Technology Standards for Technology Facilitators 2001

NETS-TL—National Educational Technology Standards for Technology Leaders 2001

Observable characteristics—directly observable traits of individuals

Online analytical processing (OLAP)—real-time analysis of data

Online classroom—a place on the Internet where students and teachers log in to learn together and which contains links to learning modules, discussion forums, announcement posting areas, a question-and-answer posting area, quizzes, tests, and other online learning resources related to a given class

Online course—subject matter offered for teaching and learning over the Internet in an online classroom

Online learning—studying a topic area by interacting with teacher and students in an online classroom

Opposable mind—ability to hold conflicting ideas in constructive tension

Outlier—an observation outside the expected range on a control chart

Path-goal leadership—what motivates members of an organization to perform well

Personal learning environment—customizable online or virtual learning environment where learners determine tools, layout, and options; provides for personal rather than institutional learning decisions

Posting—composing and displaying a message that can be viewed by some or all parties in an online course (other students and/or the teacher); can also refer to submitting a course assignment in an online classroom

Practice—engaging in professional activity

Professional development—educators working with administrators, colleagues, and experts to better classroom practice; activities designed to provide knowledge and skills to users of technology

Program evaluation—the assessment of objectives followed by decisions based on data

Project-based—describes a discreet assignment

Quiz or survey tools—assessment-based tools

Reflection—a premeditated analysis of personal and community practice up to a specific point

Related service providers—any of a number of professionals who support the education of children with disabilities (e.g., physical therapy, speech pathology, audiology, occupational therapy, counseling)

Relational database—a collection of databases linked for data analysis

Repository—data storage center

Rubric generation software—computer-based assessment software

Schools Interoperability Framework (SIF) Association—provides standards to ensure education applications software products communicate with one another

Situational leadership—a different form of leadership for each different situation

Social constructivism—theory that learning occurs first on a social level and later on an individual level; supports coconstruction of knowledge, which is a more student-centered approach to learning

Spreadsheets—tools used for management, collection, and reporting of assessments; simple-to-use software applications that allow for sorting of data by columns, calculations, and reporting of aggregate assessment results from scoring guides

Standards-based scoring guides or rubrics—tools for both the student and teacher that provide explicit grading expectations

Student information system (SIS)—an information system containing student data

Student learning—instructional practices focused on student-based acquisition

Student outcomes—the skills and knowledge acquired by learners

Student response pads—handheld devices used to record responses in student response systems

Student response systems—information collection, analysis, and presentation systems used in real time in classroom settings to assess student comprehension

Summative—describes the process to help teachers evaluate comprehensive, integrated knowledge of students typically at the conclusion of a lesson or unit of study; such assessments are often documented

Teaching using technology—teaching practices that use technology

Technology—application of hardware intended to be used with or through a personal computer (Windows or Mac OS); electronic device that can aid in accomplishing a specific task, such as learning a concept or researching a term

Technology integration—the use of technology in a learning environment to enhance understanding of curricular content

Technology leader—an administrator who possesses the knowledge and skills to address the technology needs that enhance student and staff learning

Technology planning and implementation—preparing for activities to meet objectives of a goal and the subsequent monitoring of those activities to ensure they are used

Techsperts—individuals who are very knowledgeable regarding hardware, software, and related applications

Transformational leadership—attention paid to the needs and desires of an organization's members to achieve their highest potential

Unobservable characteristics—synonym for inferred characteristics

Voice recognition—an assistive technology that converts spoken language into written text

Web 2.0—online technologies that support, encourage, and provide Web space for content published by the user rather than the Web site designer or developer

Index

AASA (American Association of School Administrators), 22, 23 (table)

Absenteeism, 68–69, 87(n2)

Academic information systems, 61–82
  applying design principles, 71–72
  classroom level, 77–78
  defined, 62, 277
  defining and measuring characteristics, 67–68
  district level, 73–77, 75 (table), 76 (figure), 76 (table)
  existing information systems, 72–79
  explicit learning strategy, 260–261
  identifying characteristics being measured, 66
  identifying entity being measured, 64–65
  reasons for measuring characteristics, 68–69
  relationships among characteristics, 69–70
  selecting, 79–81, 80 (table)
  setting standards to assess data, 70–71
  state level, 72–73
  system design, 63–72

Academic technology, 49–51, 277

Acceptable use policies, 192, 277

Accuracy, of assessment systems, 240

Achievement gap, 167, 171, 277

Administration of technology, 45–55
  administrative outcomes and needs, 52–54
  curricular outcomes and needs, 49–52
  evaluating educational technology decisions, 54–55
  explicit learning strategy, 260
  explicit technology strategy, 260
  technology leader attributes, 46–49

Adult learners, 91–102
  adult learning theories, 83–98, 93–94 (table)
  defined, 91, 277
  engaging, 98–102, 99 (figure)
  explicit learning and technology strategies, 272, 273 (figure)
  explicit learning strategy, 261
  mentoring, 99–101
  teaching and leading, 101–102, 102 (figure)

Adult learning and pedagogy, 91, 94 (table), 97–98, 99 (figure), 277

Adult learning theories, 83–98
  adult learning, 99 (figure)
  adult learning and pedagogy, 94 (table), 97–98
  behaviorism, 93 (table), 95
  cognitive constructivism, 93–94 (table), 95
  defined, 91, 277
  humanism, 94 (table), 96
  intelligence, 94 (table), 97
  motivation, 94 (table), 96
  social constructivism, 94 (table), 96
  timeline of theory development, 93–94 (table)

Affirming announcements, 218

American Association of School Administrators (AASA), 22, 23 (table)

American Recovery and Reinvestment Act (2009), 87(n6)

Andragogy, 94 (table), 97

Animation, 150

Announcements:
  affirming, 218
  posting area, 153–154, 154 (figure), 218

weekly wrap-up and preview, 220–221
wrap-up, 224
Applications service providers, 74, 277
Application stage, of rubric development, 239
APQC, 88(n16)
Architecture, in decision making, 12, 12 (figure)
Architecture of learning, 137
Arizona Student Accountability Information
System, 72–73
ASPIRE Assessment System, 77
Assessment, 231–248
curriculum mapping, 234–236
defined, 147, 277
developing district- or school-level systems,
234–244, 237 (table)
electronic portfolios, 245–246, 247 (table)
explicit learning strategies, 272
explicit technology strategy, 271
one-minute papers, 152
papers and case studies, 152–153
program evaluation effectiveness, 256
quiz/survey tools, 247, 247 (table)
scoring guides (rubrics), 238–240, 240
(table), 241–242 (table), 241 (table),
242–244, 244 (table)
spreadsheets, 248, 248 (table)
standards-based scoring guides, 244, 244 (table)
summative, 231, 282
ungraded self-quizzes, 151–152
Web-based open-book, open-notes tests, 152
See also Authentic assessment; Online
evaluation
Assessment systems, 232, 277
Assistive technology (AT):
IDEA regulations, 177–178
as integrated system, 179–180, 180 (figure)
models for usage, 179
supports for students, 180
training for school personnel, 181–182,
181 (figure)
training for students, 180
types, 178
Attendance codes, 67
Attitude Treatment Interaction, 94 (table), 97, 261
Audio, in online courses, 150
Audits, technology, 54–55, 256
Authentic assessment:
defined, 232, 277
described, 233–234, 237
implementation tools, 244–248,
247 (table), 248 (table)

Authentic technology use, 176, 266
Auto-grading of quizzes/tests, 222

Bain Assistive Technology System, 179
Bandura, A., 94 (table), 96
Bandwidth, 170, 277
Baraniuk, Richard, 13–15
Beginning level teachers, 37
Behavioral leadership, 7, 277
Behaviorism, 93, 93 (table), 95, 277
Bias, freedom from, 240
Bloom's taxonomy for educational
objectives, 94 (table), 95
Bodily/kinesthetic intelligence, 97
Brown, R., 94 (table), 96
Bruner, J. S., 93 (table), 95
Burns, James MacGregor, 9
Burrus, C. Sidney, 13–15

CAL (Characteristics of Adults as Learners),
94 (table), 98
Campus leaders, safety strategies for, 194–197
Case studies, 152–153
Causality, in decision making, 12, 12 (figure)
Cellular phones, as teaching tool, 13
Certified Online Instructor (COI), 148–151,
212, 221, 277
Change, managing, 46–47
Characteristics:
defining and measuring, 67–68
identifying, 66
inferred, 66, 279
observable, 66, 280
reasons for measuring, 68–69
relationships among, 69–70
unobservable, 66, 282
Characteristics of Adults as Learners (CAL), 94
(table), 98
Checklists:
end of online courses, 223 (table)
K–12 online products evaluation,
214–216 (table)
ongoing online courses, 220 (table)
online course prelaunch,
212–213 (table)
online course startup, 217 (table)
Children's Internet Protection Act (CIPA),
193–194
Children's Online Privacy Protection Act
(COPPA), 193
Civic participation, 170

Class notes, converting into online instructional materials, 157–158
Classroom-based assessments, 233, 278
Classroom-level academic information systems, 77–78
Classroom Performance System (CPS), 78
Clickers, 78
CMS (course management system), 132, 278
Code of Ethics for Educational Leaders, 22, 23 (table), 278
Cognitive constructivism, 93–94 (table), 95, 277, 278
Cognitive dimension, of Web 2.0 learning environments, 133–134
COI (Certified Online Instructor), 148–151, 212, 221, 277
Collaboration, 135–136, 263
Collective intelligence, 142, 263–264, 278
Communities of practice, 94 (table), 95, 111–112, 278
Community learning, 130, 278
Competition, 111
Computer-based crimes, 192, 278
Connectivity at home, 170
Connexions Project, 13–15, 201
Consistency, of assessment systems, 240
Contingency leadership, 8–9, 8 (figure), 278
Continual engagement, 216
Control charts, 70–71, 278
Control Theory, 94 (table), 96
COPPA (Children's Online Privacy Protection Act), 193
Copyright, 200–202
Council of Chief State School Officers, 21, 28
Course management system (CMS), 132, 278
Course retrospectives, 224
CPS (Classroom Performance System), 78
Craft knowledge, 26
Creative Commons copyright, 202
Crimes, computer-based, 192, 278
Cronbach, L., 94 (table), 97, 261
Cross, K. Patricia, 94 (table), 98
Culture, role in technology use, 175–176, 265
Curricular outcomes and needs, 49–52
    student perspective, 51–52
    teacher perspective, 49–51
Curriculum alignment, 234
Curriculum mapping, 234–236, 278
Curriculum standards, national, 36
Cyberbullying, 211, 224–225, 278
Cyberplagiarism, 202–203, 269–270, 278

Dashboards, 74, 278
Databases:
    every student, 72, 279
    relational, 71, 281
Data collection, 65, 235
Data-driven decision making (D3M), 81–82, 88(n21), 256
Data reporting guides, 237–238, 237 (table)
Data warehouses, 71, 75–76, 76 (table), 278
Davies, L., 202–203, 269–270
Decentralized configuration, 53, 278
Decision making:
    data-driven, 81–82, 88(n21), 256
    defined, 47, 278
    ethical, 48–49
    Martin's framework for, 11–12, 12 (figure)
Decision support systems, 79, 278
Demonstration, 233, 278
Deportment, 69
Designing technology, 120–121
Developing level teachers, 37
Dewey, J., 94 (table), 96
Digital divide, 167, 169–171
Digital learning, 190, 278
Directions, ability to follow, 241 (table)
Directive behavior, 7, 8 (figure)
Disabilities, students with, 177–182, 180 (figure), 181 (figure)
Discussion forums, 153, 154–155, 278
Disempowerment, 170
Disruptive innovation, 129, 132–133, 279
Distance learning:
    misperceptions about, 130–131
    Web 2.0 disruption of, 132–133
    See also Web 2.0 learning environments in distance learning
District-level academic information systems, 73–77, 75 (table), 76 (figure), 76 (table)
Diversity, 174–182
    role of culture in technology use, 175–176
    technology for students with disabilities, 177–182, 180 (figure), 181 (figure)
    technology in schools with high ethnic minority enrollment, 176–177
Draves, Bill, 157
Dropout rate, 66, 67
Dynamic assessment systems. See Learning management systems

E-based professional development, 48
Ecological fallacy, 65, 279

Economic divide, 171
EDEN (Education Data Exchange Network), 87(n4)
Educational Leadership Constituent Council (ELCC), 26–27
Educational Leadership Policy Standards: ISLLC 2008, 23–24, 24–25 (table), 26, 27–28, 27 (table)
Educational management systems. *See* Learning management systems
Educational success, 68–69
Education Data Exchange Network (EDEN), 87(n4)
"Education Schools in a Flat World" (Gallagher), 13
ELCC (Educational Leadership Constituent Council), 26–27
Electronic Learning Assessment Resources (ELAR), 79, 80 (table), 87(n10)
Electronic portfolios, 233, 245–246, 247 (table), 279
Elemental level, 64, 279
E-mail, 48
Empirical research, 26
Employee orientation, 7
Engagement:
    adult learners, 98–102, 99 (figure)
    continual, 216
    in online discussions, 221–222
English, Fenwick, 26–27
Enterprise configuration, 53, 279
Entrepreneurial leadership, 3–16
    conceptual framework, 10–15, 12 (figure)
    defined, 5–6, 279
    explicit technology strategy, 258
    historical context, 6–9
    importance of, 4–5
    opposable mind, 10–15, 12 (figure)
Erikson, Erik, 93 (table), 95
Ethical criteria, for evaluating technologies, 123
Ethical decision making, 48–49
Ethnic minority students, 176–177
Evaluation:
    defined, 231, 279
    educational technology decisions, 54–55
    goal-free, 257
    professional development, 121–122
    rubrics, 239–240
    technologies, 123–124
    See also Online evaluation

Every student databases, 72, 279
Excel pivot tables, 75–76, 76 (figure)
Existentialist intelligence, 97
Experiential learning, 94 (table), 96
Explicit learning and technology strategies, 266, 272, 273 (figure), 279
Explicit learning strategies:
    academic information systems, 260–261
    administration of technology, 260
    adult learners, 261
    assessment, 272
    defined, 258, 279
    online evaluation, 224, 225
    planning, designing, implementing, and evaluating technology, 262
    school, technology, and society, 265
    security, Internet security, copyright, and plagiarism, 269–270
    technology leadership standards, 258, 259
    Web 2.0 learning environments in distance learning, 262–263
Explicit learning theory strategies, 261, 279
Explicit technology strategies:
    administration of technology, 260
    assessment, 271
    defined, 258, 279
    entrepreneurial leadership, 258
    online evaluation, 224–225
    online learning space design, 264
    planning, designing, implementing, and evaluating technology, 262
    school, technology, and society, 264–266
    security, Internet security, copyright, and plagiarism, 267–269
    technology leadership standards, 258–260
    Web 2.0 learning environments in distance learning, 263–264

Fairness, of assessment systems, 239
Family Educational Rights and Privacy Act, 224
Favorite Book Presentation assignment instruction and rubric, 241–242 (table)
Feasible assessment systems, 232, 279
Feedback to students, 222–223
Fifth grade assignment instruction and rubric, 241–242 (table)
Filtering system, 190, 279
Flame wars, 222
Formal Operations (cognitive construction stage), 93 (table), 95

Formative assessment, 231, 279
Fragmentation, 111
Freire, P., 94 (table), 98
Freud, Sigmund, 93 (table)
Fullan, M., 46

Galileo (learning management system),
    77–78, 79, 80 (table), 82
Gallagher, Karen Symms, 12–13
Games, Web-based, 149–150
Gardner, H., 94 (table), 97, 261
Gilligan, Carol, 94 (table), 96
"Gimme Five!" (online math discussion topics), 153
Glasser, W., 94 (table), 96
Goal-free evaluation, 257
Goals, 254
Grades, final course, 224
Graduation rates, defining, 67
Graphics, 150
Grouping and Labeling stage, of rubric
    development, 239
Guilford, J. P., 94 (table), 97

Help desks, technology, 219
Human Activity Assistive Technology
    model, 179
Humanism, 94 (table), 96, 279
Hyperlinks, 148, 149, 279

Icebreaker activities, 217–218
ICTs (information and communication
    technologies), 169, 279
Implementing technology, 121–122
Individuals with Disabilities Education Act
    (IDEA), 177–178, 279
Inferred characteristics, 66, 279
Infinite Campus, 74–75, 76, 77–78
Information and communication technologies
    (ICTs), 169, 279
In-groups, 15
Instructional criteria, for evaluating
    technologies, 123
Instructional gaps, 235, 279
Instructional strategies, 232, 279
Instruction and practice systems. See Learning
    management systems
Integration dimension, of Web 2.0 learning
    environments, 135
Integrative thinking, 10, 11, 280
Intellect, structure of, 94 (table), 97

Intelligence:
    adult learning theories, 94 (table), 97
    collective, 142, 263–264, 278
    multiple, 94 (table), 97
Intentional reflection, 95
International Society for Technology in
    Education (ISTE):
    defined, 29, 280
    rubrics, 36–37
    standards, 4, 28–29, 29–34 (table),
        34–36, 172
    See also headings beginning with NETS
Internet-based applications, 61, 280
    See also Academic information systems
Interpersonal intelligence, 97
Interstate School Leaders Licensure Consortium
    policy standards, 23–24, 24–25 (table), 26,
        27–28, 27 (table)
Intrapersonal intelligence, 97
Inventing Better Schools (Schlechty), 15–16
ISLLC 2008, 23–24, 24–25 (table), 26, 27–28,
    27 (table), 280
ISTE. See International Society for Technology
    in Education (ISTE)

Knezek, Don, 28–29
Knowles, M. S., 94 (table), 97

Lave, J., 94 (table), 95
Leader-match theory, 8
Leadership:
    behavioral, 7, 277
    contingency, 8–9, 8 (figure), 278
    defined, 45, 280
    path-goal, 9, 281
    relationship-motivated, 8
    situational, 6, 7–8, 8 (figure), 281
    task-motivated, 8
    trait approach to, 6–7
    transactional, 9
    transformational, 6, 9, 282
    See also Entrepreneurial leadership
Learning:
    architecture of, 137
    community, 130, 278
    defined, 110, 280
    digital, 190, 278
    experiential, 94 (table), 96
    observational, 94 (table), 96
    online, 153, 280

student, 231, 281
See also Distance learning
Learning communities, 136, 280
Learning management systems, 61, 77–78, 280
See also Academic information systems
Learning Resources Network (LERN), 148
See also Certified Online Instructor (COI)
Levi, A. J., 238–239, 243
Levinson, D. J., 94 (table), 96
Listing stage, of rubric development, 239
Locus of control (LOC), 94 (table), 96
Logical/mathematical intelligence, 97

Manageable assessment systems, 232, 280
Management:
    defined, 45, 280
    technology for, 173–174
Martin, Roger, 10–12
Maslow, A. H., 94 (table), 96
Math online course resources, 149, 150, 153,
    154, 156–157
"Meet an Alien" (online math discussion
    topics), 153
Mentoring, 99–101, 280
Mission, 254
Mobility, student, 87(n5)
Modules, 148–149, 280
Moore-Howard, R., 202–203, 269–270
Motivation, 92, 94 (table), 96, 280
Multiple intelligences, 94 (table), 97
Musical/rhythmic intelligence, 97

National Center for Education Statistics, 67
National Council for Accreditation of Teacher
    Education (NCATE), 26–27, 237, 239
National Crime Prevention Council, 225
National curriculum standards, 36
National Educational Technology Standards for
    Administrators, 4
National Educational Technology Standards
    (NETS). *See headings beginning with NETS*
National Governors Association, 67
National Policy Board for Educational
    Administration (NPBEA), 23–24,
    24–25 (table)
National School Board Association, 123
National Staff Development Council, 115
Naturalist intelligence, 97
NCATE (National Council for Accreditation of
    Teacher Education), 26–27, 237, 239

Nemours Foundation, 193, 198, 268
NETC (Northwest Educational Technology
    Consortium), 257
Net generation, 131–133, 280
NETS-A (NETS for Administrators):
    as audit tool, 54–55
    defined, 29, 280
    described, 33–34 (table), 172
    systemic improvement, 232, 271
    value of, 38
NETS-S (NETS for Students), 29–30 (table), 280
NETS-TF (NETS for Technology Facilitation), 35
NETS-TL (NETS for Technology Leadership),
    35, 280
NETS-T (NETS for Teachers), 29, 31–32 (table),
    258–260, 280
Networking dimension, of Web 2.0 learning
    environments, 134–135
New York City elementary school student
    absenteeism, 87(n2)
No Child Left Behind Act, 231, 233
Northwest Educational Technology Consortium
    (NETC), 257
NPBEA (National Policy Board for Educational
    Administration), 23–24, 24–25 (table)

Objectives, 254–256
Observable characteristics, 66, 280
Observational learning, 94 (table), 96
Ohio State University, 7
One-minute papers, 152
Online analytical processing (OLAP), 75–76, 280
Online classrooms, 147, 280
Online courses, 147, 280
    See also Online evaluation; Online learning
    space design
Online evaluation, 151–153, 211–226
    cyberbullying, 224–225
    explicit learning strategies, 224, 225
    explicit technology strategies, 224–225
    initial classroom visits, 216–219, 217 (table)
    one-minute papers, 152
    ongoing classroom visits, 219–223, 220 (table)
    papers and case studies, 152–153
    setting up online courses, 212–213 (table),
        212–216, 214–216 (table)
    ungraded self-quizzes, 151–152
    Web-based open-book, open-notes tests, 152
    winding down course, 223–224, 223 (table)
    See also Assessment; Evaluation

Online learning, 153, 280
Online learning space design, 147–158
    adding creative personal touches, 155–156,
        156 (figure)
    announcement posting area, 153–154, 154
        (figure), 218
    assessments, 151–153
    converting class notes and other learning
        activities into online instructional
        materials, 157–158
    discussion posting areas, 153
    explicit technology strategies, 264
    packaging instructional content effectively,
        148–157
    question-and-answer discussion forum,
        154–155
    student issues and online learning, 159–160
    tips, 156–157
Online rubric generation tools, 244, 244 (table)
Open educational resources, 200–201
Operational competence, 180
Opposable mind, 10–15, 12 (figure), 281
Organizational criteria, for evaluating
    technologies, 123
Outcomes, student, 46, 281
Out-groups, 15
Outliers, 70, 281

Papers, 152–153
Path-goal leadership, 9, 281
Pearson Benchmark, 79, 80 (table)
Personal digital assistants, 174
Personal learning environments, 137–138, 281
Piaget, J., 93 (table), 95
Pivot tables, 75–76, 76 (figure)
Planning, 117–118, 139–140
Portfolios, electronic, 233, 245–246, 247
    (table), 279
Posting, 147, 281
PowerPoint files, 150–151
PowerSchool Premier, 77
Practice, 5, 281
Preparedness and protection, 197–199
Presentation skills, 52
Production orientation, 7
Production skills, 52
Professional development, 114–124, 116 (figure)
    assistive technology, 181–182, 181 (figure)
    defined, 47, 281
    designing, 120–121

e-based, 48
    evaluating technologies, 123–124
    implementing and evaluating, 121–122
    importance of, 48, 50
    learning the technologies, 118–119
    planning, 117–118
    school, technology, and society, 173
    second cycle, 122–123
    Web 2.0 learning environments in distance
        learning, 140
Proficient level teachers, 37
Program evaluation, 254–257, 255 (table)
    activities to complete objectives, 255
    decision making based on data, 256
    defined, 253, 281
    looping back through revision and
        reflection, research, and craft
        knowledge, 256–257
    methods to assess effectiveness of the
        objectives, 256
    mission and goals, 254
    objectives to implement goals, 254–255
Project-based assignments, 232, 281
Project management software, 174
PROPEL (cooperative research project), 236

Question-and-answer discussion forums, 154–155
Quiz/survey tools, 233, 247, 247 (table), 281
Quizzes, 151–152, 222–223

Reactiveness, 111
Reflecting stage, of rubric development, 238–239
Reflection, 95, 112, 281
Related service providers, 182, 281
Relational databases, 71, 281
Relationship-motivated leadership, 8
Repositories, 201, 281
Research skills, 51–52
Resolution, in decision making, 12, 12 (figure)
Rice University Connexions Project, 13–15, 201
Rogers, A., 94 (table), 96
Rubric generation software, 233, 281
Rubrics:
    benefits, 242–243
    defined, 238
    developing, 238–239
    evaluating, 239–240
    ISTE, 36–37
    online generation tools, 244, 244 (table)
    samples, 240 (table), 241–242 (table)

Safety, 191–197
  acceptable use policies, 192
  federal laws, 192–194
  principal and Internet safety, 194
  strategies for campus leaders, 194–197
SAIS (Student Accountability Information
    System), 72–73
Salience, in decision making, 12, 12 (figure)
Schlechty, Philip, 15–16
School CIO, 81
Schools:
  ethnic minority enrollments, 176–177
  security issues, 199–200
  technology integration, 112–113
  transforming, 110–114
Schools Interoperability Framework (SIF)
    Association, 80–81, 281
Scoring guides. *See* Rubrics
Scriven Goal-Free Evaluation, 257
Seattle Public Schools, 225
Security issues, 197–200
Self-quizzes, ungraded, 151–152
SIF (Schools Interoperability Framework)
    Association, 80–81, 281
Situational leadership, 6, 7–8, 8 (figure), 281
Skills:
  presentation, 52
  production, 52
  research, 51–52
  21st-century, 167–169
Skinner, B. F., 93 (table), 95
Smyth County, Virginia, School Board,
    193–194
Snow, R., 94 (table), 97, 261
Social constructivism, 94 (table), 96, 281
Social dimension, of Web 2.0 learning
    environments, 134
Social inclusion, 170
Social networking tools, 174
Software implementation, 51
Spreadsheets, 248, 248 (table), 281
Standards:
  data assessment, 70–71
  defined, 21
  ISLLC 2008, 23–24, 24–25 (table), 26,
    27–28, 27 (table)
  ISTE, 28–29, 29–34 (table), 34–36
  national curriculum, 36
  See also Technology leadership standards;
    specific standards

Standards-based scoring guides, 234, 244,
    244 (table), 281
State-level academic information systems, 72–73
Stevens, D. D., 238–239, 243
Strategic competence, 180
Student Accountability Information System
    (SAIS), 72–73
Student information systems:
  defined, 61, 281
  district-level, 73–77, 75 (table), 76 (figure),
    76 (table)
  federal government money for states to
    improve, 87(n6)
  Schools Interoperability Framework (SIF)
    Association certification, 80–81
  state-level, 73
  systems and vendors, 75 (table)
  technology for management, 174
  See also Academic information systems
Student learning, 231, 281
Student outcomes, 46, 281
Student response pads, 78, 281
Student response systems, 78, 282
Students:
  assistive technology training for, 180
  coaching to be successful online, 149
  curricular outcomes and needs, 51–52
  ethnic minority, 176–177
  mobility, 87(n5)
  supporting teachers in learning of
    technologies, 119
Success, educational, 68–69
Summative assessment, 231, 282
Supportive behavior, 7, 8 (figure)
Survey tools, 233, 247, 247 (table), 281
Suskie, L., 239–240
Suspension, alternatives to, 88(n21)

Task-motivated leadership, 8
Teachers:
  beginning level, 37
  curricular outcomes and needs, 49–51
  developing level, 37
  proficient level, 37
  responses to cyberbullying, 224–225
  responses to posted questions and answers,
    219, 221
  responses to student initial postings, 217–218
  transformative level, 37
  use of technology, 176–177

Teachers' Tools for the 21st Century
    (Smerdon et al.), 176–177
Teaching using technology, 50, 282
Technical criteria, for evaluating
    technologies, 123
Technology:
    defined, 109, 282
    designing, 120–121
    impact of, 190–191
    implementing, 121–122
    for management, 173–174
    planning, 117–118
    in schools with high ethnic minority
        enrollment, 176–177
    for students with disabilities, 177–182, 180
        (figure), 181 (figure)
    teaching using, 50, 282
Technology audits, 54–55, 256
Technology help desks, 219
Technology integration, 257–272, 273 (figure)
    defined, 109, 282
    leadership digital assessments and
        evaluation, 270–272
    leadership policy and innovative practice,
        258–261
    leadership (social, cultural, and legal),
        264–270
    leadership teaching and learning, 261–264
    school transformation, 112–113
Technology leaders, 46–49, 190, 282
Technology leadership standards, 21–38
    AASA Code of Ethics, 22, 23 (table)
    explicit learning strategies, 258, 259
    explicit technology strategies, 258–260
    ISLLC 2008, 23–24, 24–25 (table), 26,
        27–28, 27 (table)
    ISTE standards, 28–29, 29–34
        (table), 34–36
    leader's tool kit, 36–38
    research about standards, 26–28, 27 (table)
    See also specific standards

Technology planning and implementation,
    49, 282
Techsperts, 47–48, 282
Tests, 152, 222–223
Timeliness, in providing feedback to students,
    222–223
Traditional technology use, 175–176, 266
Trait approach to leadership, 6–7
Transactional leadership, 9
Transformational leadership, 6, 9, 282
Transformative level teachers, 37
21st-century skills, 167–169

University of Michigan, 7
Unobservable characteristics, 66, 282

Verbal/linguistic intelligence, 97
Visual/spatial intelligence, 97
Voice recognition, 178, 282
Vygotsky, L. S., 94 (table), 96

Watson, J., 93 (table), 95
Web 2.0, 132, 174, 282
Web 2.0 learning environments in distance
    learning, 129–142
    constructs for, 133–136
    critical issues, 140–141
    district structure and processes, 136–138
    explicit learning strategies, 262–263
    explicit technology strategies, 263–264
    misperceptions about distance learning,
        130–131
    net generation, 131–133
    professional development, 140
    strength of Web 2.0 tools, 138–140
Weekly wrap-up and preview announcements,
    220–221
Wegner, E., 94 (table), 95
Wrap-up announcements, 224

Zone of Proximal Development, 94 (table), 96

About the Editor

Rosemary Papa, EdD, was director of the Center for Teaching and Learning (2000 to 2007) at a large urban public comprehensive university in California. She was responsible for the delivery of faculty development services across all academic disciplines, which included the use of multimedia tools. Under her direction, six *Teaching Using Technology Summer Institutes* were offered with over 600 full-time faculty participating and over 35,000 students being served in high-tech classrooms. She also delivered train-the-trainers workshops to various state agencies and businesses (e.g., California Environmental Water Resources). Internationally, she has delivered workshops in adult pedagogy and use of technology at Peking University in Beijing for over 80 universities throughout China and worked with Franco-speaking universities along the Gold Coast of Africa. For the past 2 years she cochaired the revision of the Interstate School Leaders Licensure Consortium standards for school administrators, which includes technology standards that are part of every administrative certification program in the nation. In the fall of 2007 she was invited to become the Northern Arizona University (NAU) College of Education first endowed chair in learning-centered leadership. In this role, Papa is active at the national, state, and university level promoting NAU and working with faculty members across the College of Education on their research. This includes technology and multimedia. Recent books include *Restoring Human Agency to Educational Administration* (coauthored); SAGE major works, *Encyclopedia of Educational Leadership and Administration, Volumes 1–4* (U.S. editor); *So You Want to Be a Higher Education Administrator? Avoid Crossing to the Dark Side or What They Don't Teach in Summer Leadership Institutes* (coauthored); *Leadership on the Frontlines: Changes in Preparation and Practice* (editor); *At the Tipping Point: Navigating the Course for the Preparation of Educational Administrators* (associate editor); *Leadership on Purpose: Promising Practices With African American and Hispanic Students* (coauthored); and over 80 peer-reviewed journal articles. Papa's focused areas of teaching are educational policy, ethical decision making, adult learning, and uses of technology in teaching.

ABOUT THE CONTRIBUTORS

Shadow W. J. Armfield, EdD, earned his doctorate in curriculum and instruction with a focus in technology in education from Northern Arizona University (NAU). He is currently an assistant professor in the Educational Technology Program at NAU. His research agenda focuses on the use of technologies by teachers and students in the K–12 classroom and the preparation of preservice educators for the integration of technology into the K–12 classroom. Past publications include "Case Study Research" in *Research Essentials: An Introduction to Designs and Practices* (2009), *A Descriptive Case Study of Teaching and Learning in an Innovative Middle School Program* (2007), and *Meeting the Needs of Students, Administration, and NCATE: Redesigning an Undergraduate Educational Technology Course to Meet Changing Needs* (2008).

J. Michael Blocher, PhD, is an associate professor at Northern Arizona University, where he teaches online courses in the Master of Education in Educational Technology degree program. His current research agenda includes the use of social networking tools to enhance online learner group interaction. His publications have focused on group interaction and collaborative activities in online learning environments.

Ric Brown, EdD, has spent over 30 years in higher education as a professor and administrator. Starting in 2001, he was the chief academic officer at California State University, Sacramento, retiring in 2006 as provost and vice president for academic affairs. During those years, one of his major responsibilities was overseeing all technology operations for the university. He was especially active in revamping the academic technology infrastructure and personnel to better serve faculty.

Cynthia Conn, PhD, is assistant chair of the Department of Educational Specialties and a lecturer for the Educational Technology Program at Northern Arizona University. Her administrative responsibilities include overseeing assessment of degree programs both in the Department of Educational Leadership and for the Educational Technology Program. Additionally, she teaches online courses related to instructional design for the Master of Education in Educational Technology degree program. Her research focuses on assessment methods in higher education.

Theodore Creighton, EdD, is presently a professor in the Department of Educational Leadership and Policy Studies at Virginia Tech. Prior to joining the faculty at Virginia Tech, he served as director of the Center for Research and Doctoral Studies in Educational Leadership at Sam Houston State University. His background includes teaching at all grade levels in Washington, DC; Cleveland, Ohio; and Los Angeles, California. He holds a bachelor's degree in teacher education from Indiana University of Pennsylvania; a master's degree in educational administration from California State University, Long Beach; and a doctorate from California State University, Fresno/University of California, Davis. He is widely published in the area of school leadership with recent publications *The Principal as Technology Leader, Leading From Below the Surface: A Non-traditional Approach to School Leadership,* and *Schools and Data: The Educator's Guide for Using Data to Improve Decision Making.*

Mary I. Dereshiwsky, PhD, develops and teaches educational research courses for online delivery at Northern Arizona University's (NAU's) College of Education where she is a professor of educational leadership. She holds a bachelor's degree from Southern Connecticut State University, a master's degree from the University of New Haven, and a doctorate from the University of Massachusetts Amherst. She has served as a statistical analyst for the Arizona Career Ladder teacher incentive and development pilot project; the Winslow, Arizona, "Beat Diabetes" community intervention; the Chandler (Arizona) Unified School District's after-school pilot program; and the NAU/Arizona Trust Academy (a partnership with attorneys and school administrators). She serves as chair of the international Faculty Club, a consortium of Web-based higher education instructors, and she holds the designation of Certified Online Instructor awarded by the Learning Resources Network.

Lawrence Gallagher, EdD, is an associate professor of special education at Northern Arizona University. Dr. Gallagher is currently serving as the chair of the Department of Educational Specialties. He teaches courses in special education with an emphasis area in severe/profound disabilities. Dr. Gallagher earned his doctoral degree in special education from the Johns Hopkins University. His research interests include positive behavior support, assistive technology, leadership in special education, and instructional methods for students with severe disabilities.

Stephen Lawton, PhD, is a professor of educational administration and supervision at Arizona State University, where he conducts policy research related to educational quality, cost, and effectiveness. His current research includes charter school effectiveness, higher-education accreditation practices, school district receivership legislation, academic information systems, and the fiscal implications of English language learner policies in Arizona. He has chaired departments of educational leadership at the University of Toronto and Central Michigan University and published books and articles on school finance, teacher unions, urban economics and education, school dropouts, and administrator selection and evaluation. He has developed and teaches online courses on school finance and currently serves on the editorial board of the Association of School Business Officials

International. He recently completed a term as the first president of the Arizona Professors of Educational Administration.

Jessica Papa is currently a communication studies graduate student at Texas State University, San Marcos. She earned a bachelor's of science degree in graphic design from California State University, Sacramento, and uses her visual communication knowledge in her current research interests regarding gender, adult learning, and communication.

Laura Sujo-Montes, PhD, is an associate professor of educational technology at Northern Arizona University where she teaches undergraduate and online graduate courses. She earned a doctoral degree in curriculum and instruction with emphasis in learning technologies and a master's degree in TESOL (Teaching English to Speakers of Other Languages) at New Mexico State University. Her research interests focus on investigations about online learning environments, professional development, and culturally and linguistically diverse students.

Janet Tareilo is an assistant professor at Stephen F. Austin State University in the Department of Secondary Education and Educational Leadership. After receiving her undergraduate degree in elementary education from Stephen F. Austin, she taught in the Lufkin (Texas) Independent School District for 7 years. Returning to Stephen F. Austin, she earned her master's degree in educational leadership and served as an elementary principal for 16 years. In December 2004, she received a doctorate in educational administration from Sam Houston State University. Dr. Tareilo's contributions to higher education include research endeavors in the areas of social justice, improving principal preparation programs, and the impact of the campus principal as an instructional leader. Additionally, she has presented at several national conferences such as National Association of Secondary School Principals, National Council of Professors of Educational Administration, and Texas Association of School Administrators. Through her role as a team leader with Project DEVELOP and her recruitment efforts, Dr. Tareilo continues to work with many school communities to foster the leadership development of aspiring campus administrators.

Chih-Hsiung Tu, PhD, is an associate professor of educational technology at Northern Arizona University and an educational/instructional technology consultant with extensive experience in distance education, e-learning, technology training in teacher education, online learning communities, learning organizations, and knowledge management. His research interests include distance education, sociocognitive learning, sociocultural learning, online learning communities, learning organizations, and knowledge management. He has edited and published one book; published many articles and book chapters; and presented book proposals, conference proceedings, and other materials.